The Rising Song of African American Women

the rising song of

AfricanAmericanWomen

Barbara Omolade

ROUTLEDGE
New York and London

Published in 1994 by
Routledge
29 West 35th Street
New York, NY 10001

Published in Great Britain by
Routledge
11 New Fetter Lane
London EC4P 4EE

Copyright © 1994 by Routledge

Printed in the United States of America on acid-free paper.

Library of Congress Cataloging-in-Publication Data

Omolade, Barbara.
    The rising song of African American women / Barbara Omolade.
    p.   cm.
    ISBN 0-415-90760-8 : -- ISBN 0-415-90761-6 (pbk.)
    1.   Afro-American women.   I. Title.
E185.0456 1994
305.48'896073--dc20   94-4752

                                                    CIP

LET THE WORDS OF MY MOUTH
AND THE MEDITATION OF MY HEART,
BE ACCEPTABLE IN THY SIGHT,
O LORD, MY STRENGTH, AND MY REDEEMER
Psalm 19:14

CONTENTS

PREFACE

I AM A PRODUCT of an intellectual tradition which until twenty-five years ago did not exist within the academy. Like patchwork in a quilt, it is a tradition gathered from meaningful bits and pieces. My tradition has no name, because it is embraces more than womanism, Blackness, or Africana studies, although those terms will do for now. I consider myself a griot historian and sociologist who primarily writes for, speaks to, and organizes with African American women and anyone else who finds meaning and significance in our lives.

My tradition lifts up the lives and work of John Coltrane, W. E. B. Du Bois, Audre Lorde, Ella Baker and other Black geniuses as its ideal. It moves and weaves through music, and political work, writings and songs. It can be demonstrated in well prepared food at a church supper, a soul stirring speech at a political rally and a finely written volume. I come from the old school of Black life. You might call me a race woman who has compassion for all who suffer and an intellectual bound by the obligation to serve and minister. I am a worker and family woman who frankly looks down on folks who are not willing to be part of the necessary struggles of everyday life, or who think themselves too educated to learn from those around them.

My parents and grandparents were literate farmers from Virginia and North Carolina who became factory workers, and, in my father's case, an ambulance driver, in the north. I am a first generation northerner and the first in my family to receive a college degree, although my only sibling, a sister received one five years after me. We both became committed teachers, perhaps because education was so important in our family.

My father was a thoughtful race man who challenged and argued with me, although he was without organization or a movement. Because my mother didn't ask me to do household chores, I had a lot of time to think, daydream, and read. I read most of the time, and considered Anne Frank and Helen Keller my personal heroines.

My church, like most Black churches, was an intellectual, spiritual, and social experience. The Bible was read as a text to be expounded and interpreted. The oratory skills of the Black preacher served, and still serve, as a profound intellectual model for me, as does the inspirational tradition of singing, collectively and individually, that was such an important part of the church experience.

Every child in Sunday School had to participate in the Easter, Christmas, and May Day programs as well as other special events for which we memorized lines and performed parts. Again, our voice and presence in front of an audience was required. I remember a retarded boy, my own age, who was in our Bible classes and had a regular part in these performances. All he could say and memorize for these programs was "Jesus loves me," for which he received the same applause as everyone else. This profound act taught me, even as a young child, to be tolerant of everyone, humble about my own talent, and respectful of performance.

Periodically, there was a youth Sunday in which teenagers in the church conducted service and a visiting young minister preached the sermon. I usually read the Bible verse. College students were asked to stand up and be introduced to the congregation. These events, year after year, developed and reinforced my "voice."

In 1954, I was selected by my all Black elementary school to attend and integrate the white junior high school only four blocks away, under the tracks of the Broadway "el" train from Bed-Stuy into Bushwick. I excelled in both junior and high school and was equally skilled in math, writing, and the social sciences. I was also popular and comfortable despite being in an overwhelmingly white school, primarily attended by Italian and German students who were the children of recent immigrants.

I was on the academic track in high school, one of a small group of "nerds" who ran student government, the newspaper, and excelled in school work. At my recent high school reunion I realized that this group was predominantly female. Our mutual support for one another validated our skills and work long before feminism or the women's movement. As a Black woman I was different, but in many ways very similar to my white female school mates. We were a community of learners and school activists who spent more time talking about our schoolwork and ideas than boys and dating.

However, there was no such community or support system in the commuter college I attended. There were so few Black students I might as well have been the only one. In high school my white teachers encouraged me, but in college I was exposed to blatant racism. I accepted the C grades that should have been A's and accepted being misplaced in remedial courses. Feeling silenced and marginalized, I burrowed in. Since I was neither a quitter nor a complainer, I endured these tests of fire. As a representative of my family, my race, and my self, I knew I had to graduate from college.

It was the days of the beatnik and I relished listening to "communists," radical thinkers, and folk music in the cafe. I lived in the margins of many contradictions: a Black female history major—in a white male discipline; a worker while other students were not. I lived in what my text books described as a ghetto. College bored and disappointed me because it dulled my mind and made me doubt myself. I was not merely learning my subjects, I was attempting to be a subject, and my presence in the classroom as a learner directly contradicted my absence from the scholarship.

All over the country, the Black world was thrusting its girls and boys into the white world to represent the race. Intellectual inquiry became both our weapon and a political act requiring great courage because there were absolutely no role models or books and nothing to sustain us except the training and encouragement we received from families our communities.

Everything changed in 1962, half way through college, when the civil rights movement imposed itself on our television screens. Its presence was felt in every sermon and in every place where we gathered. As a daughter of Black southerners, I grew up reading "white only" signs on our trips south, and saw my father's silent rage at Jim Crow, so I understood the urgency of the movement.

At college, the movement empowered me to speak. In every course, I focused my research on Black people. There were virtually no books and Black studies was a decade away. I carved out my own place because I had a hunger to know. By the time I became a senior I was a working in the New York office of the Student Nonviolent Coordinating Committee (SNCC). College seemed irrelevant in light of the revolution that was going on around me. By the time of my graduation, I had outgrown the concerns of formal education.

The movement taught me how to think. It made me an intellectual. I learned about social construction, political science, radical politics. I studied the perspectives and world views of people in the movement as well as the praxis in which we were engaged. Like Kwame Ture has said, "we learned more in the movement from the local people than from all the college professors we sat under." Local people in the south, like Fannie Lou Hamer, taught us how to read—not books but the situation we were in. They understood the necessity for studying the terrains of hierarchy and power and hypocrisy and authenticity. The people with whom we served taught me how to survive, when to bow and to whom, and who and when to resist. Their knowledge was gathered orally, and transmitted by word of mouth. Their interrogations were done late at night, in the fields, among those who could be trusted. They spent a great deal of time angling, and as my grandmother said, "studying." They saw themselves as part of a communal process. I learned and internalized all these things as I participated in the movement, grateful I had been "thrown off" my regular life course long enough to learn how to think.

It was Ella Baker who taught me how to be a different kind of Black woman—one who could and should take politics seriously and use her mind to analyze, strategize and move. After the movement waned, I travelled first to California and hippydom and then to Israel and England, which strengthened my inner resources and reinforced my work ethic.

By the age of twenty-five I had learned a great deal: the discipline of learning from my parents, the skills and expression of my voice from church and high school education, the tenacity required of privileged marginality in college, and the transformative power of learning authentically about one's social location and condition.

It took considerably longer—in fact, the next twenty-five years—to learn how to deal with the complexity of being female, especially the heterosexual woman's sexual and sexist tensions with men. I plunged myself into African culture, nationalism, Black music, and marriage. I struggled to maintain an intellectual life in the margins of mothering and mating. I was nursing my third child in five years, living on welfare in the lower east side of New York City, with no particular dream except survival, when I read Gerda Lerner's book, *Black Women in White America*. This event immediately transformed my consciousness. Soon after, I decided to get a masters degree from Goddard College's external degree program, and studied African and slave mothering.

My first job after welfare was in a battered women's shelter where I learned to read about feminism using the tools I had acquired during the civil rights movement: dialogue and contention, conferences and campaigns. During the late 1970's I was hired to teach a course on Black women to Black women college students which marked my return to the academy and thrust me in the middle of intellectual work. When I began teaching in college, I had a rich and complex intellectual background which had absolutely nothing to do with academia and everything to do with my involvement in political movements. I had also been a participant observer in my own life.

From 1976–1982, I was employed by two predominantly white feminist organizations,the Women's Action Alliance and Women's Survival Space, and during my spare time, I volunteered with two Brooklyn based organizations, The Black United Front and The Sisterhood of Black Single Mothers. Like many Black women I was more a doer than a speaker. I patterned myself after veteran civil rights activist, Ella Baker who worked behind the scenes of many civil rights organizations. She often said she had no need to be in the forefront or lead. However, many organizations and groups began asking me to speak about feminism and Black women, because I was one of the few Black women working in the largely white woman's movement, researching and teaching about Black women, and was also active in the Black community.

Although my voice was tentative and small, I knew I didn't want to speak like male political leaders who held audiences captive with their impromptu rantings and rhetoric. I most admired those Black male scholar activists who spoke from written papers which presented thoughtful analysis based upon scholarship as well as passion.

My speech writing was also influenced by Michelle Wallace. In 1979, we were in a study group at the time of the publication of her *Black Macho and the Myth of the Superwoman*. I felt her portrayals of women in the civil rights movement did not accurately reflect my experiences. I was profoundly shaken by her response to my critique, which implied that the act of writing gave the writer the power to interpret and preserve the events of the past. After that encounter, I decided to put every speech I made in writing in order to document my own experiences.

I made speeches whenever I was asked. I spoke to all-white women's workshops on feminism and Black women. I addressed rallies opposing apartheid and colonialism. White and Black women professors invited me to participate in scholarly conferences on Black women. I spoke before large Black organizations and smaller Black women's groups. Most of the themes of my presentations are in this book. My attempt to capture the intimacy and emotional intensity of these speaking engagements have shaped the way I write.

From my studies, I have learned that Black women's most pronounced form of intellectual—or thinking—work has been through singing. Whether it was blues or gospels, chanting or praise songs, Black women have sung whenever and wherever they could in order to express their ideas, philosophies and experiences. In the past most Black women were denied formal education, speaking platforms or pulpits, so they sang their verbal messages. Black women writers such as Toni Morrison and Maya Angelou have captured the lyrical cadences of Black women's voice in their work. But I lament the ways that formal scholarship crimp and cramp the voices of Black women scholars when attempting to speak to or write about Black women.

Essays in *The Rising Song* weave together scholarship, Black political oratory against injustice, and personal testimony. For me, writing and speaking have become two sides of one process. They document my own and other Black women's experiences which reveal a long denied and muted intellectual heritage.

ACKNOWLEDGMENTS

I WANT TO BEGIN by giving all the glory and honor to God and to Jesus Christ. I can recall no significant person in my history who has not claimed faith and belief in God as a crucial part of his or her walk and work. Like all Black Christian women I acknowledge that I've come this far by faith.

Writing this book has taught me that no one ever creates anything alone. In the most profound way possible, each of us is the product of those we meet and love. *The Rising Song* reflects my own ideas and thoughts but in no way did I create it alone.

I am grateful for the inspiration and lessons from my four wonderful children. Kip has taught me that artists stay true to their craft and continue to work at it every day. From Eskimo I learned about the elements of personal courage: street wisdom, prudence, sensitivity, and a sense of humor. From Krishna I learned that brains and ball playing do go together. Ngina taught me that the love of God is the true way to a better life. I also thank the entire Omolade-Glover families, and, especially, Brenda.

I give thanks for my mother's faith and for my father's gentle patriarchy. My aunts, Henrietta Webb, Marjorie Taylor, and Celestine White encouraged and supported me and my children. The power and strength of these three working women deserve their own book. I acknowledge my energetic and wonderful birth sister, Beatrice Jones, whose kindness and love predates any kind of womanist sisterhood.

My family of origin reared and sustained me, but a new kind of family of Black women midwifed an intellectual and emotional birth. My sisters Arlene Parker, Safiya Bandele, Deborah Edwards, Daphne Busby, and

Sandy Watson have given me unconditional, steadfast love. They saw my talent and nourished its growth, and by their pushing me ahead I blossomed and flowered as a woman. The Sisterhood of Black Single Mothers and the Medgar Evers College Center for Women's Development became the places for me to grow roots and wings. Barbara Smith, publisher of the Kitchen Table Press, personally supported my book *It's a Family Affair.*

The Black women who have laid their hands and love on me during these last two decades have helped me more than I can ever acknowledge. Thanks to the students at the College of New Rochelle, the Empire State College Center for Labor Studies, and, especially, the City College Center for Worker Education, who have taught me the most about the lives of Black women.

Thanks to Tillie Blackbear, whose ring I still wear, Andaye de la Cruz, a Woman Warrior, and to all my my Latin, Asian, and Native American sisters. Special and often contentious relationships with white feminists, especially Randy Meadoff, Dorothy Helly, and Florence Tager have been and remain powerful influences in my work.

I thank my pastors and my church, who are nurturing me through another birth and have inspired me to lift up my voice in prayer and song each day.

I am grateful to the Black men, friends and brothers who have taught me a great deal about politics, books, and music.

Lastly, I am also very grateful for the loving support of Cecelia Cancellaro of Routledge Press.

INTRODUCTION

THE FIRST RISING SONG was a thirteen-week lecture series on Black women's history I organized during the spring of 1981 for the Sisterhood of Black Single Mothers. It attempted to bring the scholarship about Black women being developed by Black women scholars and intellectuals to the Black community. In those days Black women's scholarship, and audiences for it, were slowly coming together.

Poised somewhere between activism and scholarship, I used speeches and writings to capture and develop all that I learned about Black women and their/our relationships to everything around us. This book, *The Rising Song*, is a volume of previously published and original essays which combine historical voices, spiritual consciousness, and liberation politics. I am deliberately setting aside traditional scholarly boundaries and language because they tend to restrict rather than illuminate knowledge about Black women. The many levels of Black women's oppression and power require a scholarly approach with flexibility and breadth. I use historical facts, sociological data, participant observations, and newspaper accounts to create a scholarly narrative of Black women's conditions.

Public speaking has encouraged me to disregard the structures and limitations of narrow intellectual discourse and base my writings upon the way Black classical music is constructed. Musical compositions in this tradition contain and reinforce relationships between virtuoso (the singer) and community (the chorus) in a call and response dynamic. They also interchange structured melodies with innovation. In *The Rising Song*, I am creating a three-part social science composition which captures the Black woman novelist's focus on language and personal narrative, the gospel singer's concern with innovation and expression, and the social scientists' concern with understanding the objective and generalized world.

The essays in Part One: Historical Context, Contemporary Meanings, describe how experiences of sexuality, family, and labor during slavery persist in the psyche and daily lives of contemporary Black women. The first part of "Lay Down this World" was presented at a Black Woman's History Conference held on April 23, 1983 at Essex County Community College in Newark, New Jersey. There were nearly 500 participants. Willa Blackshear was the Chairwoman of the steering committee of the 15 Black women's organizations that sponsored the conference.

It was the largest gathering of Black women I'd ever addressed and my first keynote speech. Its title and theme was from Sweet Honey in the Rock's *Good Times* album which kept inspiring me that spring. I wanted to give the dedicated and hard-working professional women in the audience a historical context, and a challenge for using their positions and talents to "lay down this world" and struggle to transform the society as their foremothers had done with less education or resources.

"Hearts of Darkness" developed from another kind of women's conference. In 1982, I was asked to join the planning committee of the Barnard College Scholar and Feminist Conference IX: Towards a Politics of Sexuality. When I walked into the first meeting, I heard a room of white feminists debating and discussing sex in a serious and emotional language and cadence I had never heard before. Titles of articles were flung around, projects and works of various women were talked about, and the intricacy of allowing each woman's perspective to be heard was discussed. They were intellectually deciphering and deconstructing the myths and assumptions of sexuality while planning a conference to continue the debate. I went home and wrote my first notes for examining the construction of sexuality developed from Black women's experiences. I presented them at a workshop at the conference and was encouraged to developed them into an article for the book, *The Powers of Desire: The Politics of Sexuality*.

The essay "Gender in Black" examines sexuality from within the Black community. The themes emerged from countless workshop presentations on Black male and female relationships. The workshops were reminiscent of the call and response dynamic of traditional Black songs and speeches. I would write my remarks, present them, entertain questions and comments, and rethink and rework my ideas while incorporating our discussions and debates. Discussions with Black audiences about male-female relationships and male sexism revealed so much individual pain and anguish they became collective shouts and screams in which, ironically, the voices of both Black men and women meshed and merged into each other.

The essays, "The Unbroken Circle: A Historical Study of Black Single Mothers and Their Families" and "It's A Family Affair: the Real Lives of Black Single Mothers" are two sides of the same discussion: one historical and the other contemporary. Here my public voice joins my personal experience to create a discourse about Black single mothers in which we are meaningful and significant rather than just another "social problem."

Part Two: Invisible To the Naked Eye: Black Women and The Academy uses multiple perspectives to expose and study Black women's relationship to learning, teaching, and knowledge production. The essays in this section explore Black women's passive and active roles as students, teachers, and intellectuals, while challenging Black women educators to do more to radically transform schools and the academy.

"The Silence and the Song" focuses on how academic culture silences Black women and prevents them from singing their own intellectual song. "Origins: The Roots of the Black Feminist Intellectual Tradition" explores the social and historical context for the development of a Black women's intelligentsia. The essay "A Black Feminist Pedagogy" focuses on issues of empathy, privilege, and power concerning a Black woman teaching Black women.

The contradictory meanings of Black women's intellectual life is illustrated in the title essay of this section, "Invisible to the Naked Eye: A Case Study of Black Women Students at the Center for Worker Education" a case study of Black women college students at the City College, Center for Worker Education where I work. "The Lion's Rock Speech" was delivered in 1991 at a meeting of the Lion's Rock Network of Black Women at the City University of New York (CUNY). It challenges Black women college administrators to confront the relationship between institutional power and knowledge production in the university.

Though our voices as Black women have been enlarged by our participation in the academy, we remain invisible in terms of institutionalized power. The academy contains an archaic bureaucracy, an ivory tower elitism, and dated knowledge bases which smothered and manacled every Black women's authentic song. Not only is scholarship by and about Black women minimized and excluded, we have yet to make a fundamental impact on the academy's culture and mores. Hence, I view both the academy and the community as sites of political struggle for power and control. In the academy, it is a struggle over who produces and reproduces knowledge, where the very thoughts and expressions of all Black women are contested terrain. The essays in this section document the complex dimensions of that terrain.

My own praxis or political work as a Black feminist has been influenced by having organized university-wide women's support groups as well as having supported efforts of Black students, faculty, and staff at Medgar Evers College to better meet the needs of its constituents. Part Three: Praxis and Struggle explores the limits and possibilities of a Black feminist praxis and addresses the questions: What do Black feminists do? What is the relationship between Black feminism and political work?

In "Ella's Daughters," I trace the political praxis of the Black women I have worked with in central Brooklyn during the 1980s to the legacy of the political philosophy of civil rights activist Ella Baker. Though she did not identify herself as a Black feminist, she did establish a model for Black women who organize against oppression. The Black feminist praxis derived from Ella Baker's work involves the organizing and mobilizing by Black women to transform their own lives. Black feminism is sometimes referred to as womanism because both are concerned with struggles against sexism and racism by Black women who are themselves part of the Black community's efforts to achieve equity and liberty.

In the essays, "Black Codes and Racial Drama: The Central Park Jogger Case," and "Black Men, Black Women and Tawana Brawley: The Shared Condition," I explore the tensions between feminist (implying white women), Black feminist/womanist, and nationalist (indicating Black male) interests as a way of delineating a Black feminist perspective on race.

I am as critical of Black womanists as I am of any group of self-proclaimed progressive intellectuals who continue to avoid consistent political organizing which could significantly ameliorate the deplorable conditions of the men and women around us. Many intellectuals never write about or analyze those conditions.

However, I was challenged to begin to "speak for the planet" after hearing scientist Carl Sagan urge us to consider ourselves citizens of the cosmos. The essay, "We Speak for the Planet" is a Black woman's view of global politics and militarism posed alongside efforts toward peace. Written nearly a decade ago, many of this essay's issues have been overshadowed by more ominous developments such as Black women's uncritical integration into the armed services, the rise of ethnic warfare, and the economic and social dislocation of young people.

My global perspectives in 1994 are a lamentation—a cry in the dark—about the trouble I see in the world. I am convinced that the silence of American intellectuals is in part responsible for daily violence and destitution. After surveying some of the deadly trends and incidents taking place around the world and linking them to violence and destruction within the African American community, I again challenge the Black feminist and nationalist intelligentsias to do more than engage in intellectual sparring and ethnic validation.

Black women's relationships to the history of race and gender, to knowledge production and education, and to community organizing and political struggle, places them at the intersections where personal and collective transformation and change can be realized. Songs have always been the primary way Black women have expressed their thoughts and dreams. Through song, their intellect, philosophies, and analysis of the world are reflected. *The Rising Song* with its many sections and parts, hopefully brings them together in a unified composition of harmony and completeness. The essays hope to capture the dynamism and lyricism of dialogue and the spoken word. They attempt to speak on several levels simultaneously: as conversation and story, documentation and scholarship, lament and challenge. They are a defense, an appeal, and hopefully a celebration not only of what Black women are and what they've done, but also what they must do.

ANNOTATED BIBLIOGRAPHY

Amott, Teresa and Matthaei, Julie. *Race, Gender, and Work: A Multicultural Economic History of Women in the United States.* Boston: South End, 1991. A primer describing the historical experiences of all women workers: American Indians, Chicanas, Puerto Ricans, European Americans, African Americans, and Asian Americans.

Braxton, Joanne M. and Andree Nicola McLaughlin. *Wild Women in the Whirlwind: Afra-American Culture and the Contemporary Literary Renaissance.* New Brunswick: Rutgers University Press, 1990. One of the most significant collections of Black feminist writings. It includes a selected bibliography of "English-Language Works by Black Women of the Americas."

Cantarow, Ellen. *Moving the Mountain: Women Working for Social Change.* New York: The Feminist Press, 1980. A volume of oral history of three political activists, Florence Luscomb, Ella Baker, and Jessie Lopez De La Cruz. The book is part of the Women's Lives, Women's Work series especially designed to bring material on women to high school students. It is the most useful source of information about Ella Baker in her own words.

Chase-Riboud, Barbara. *Sally Hemings.* New York: Avon Books. A fictionalized account of an important Black woman in American history. Sally Hemings was the slave "wife" of Thomas Jefferson, who fathered her children. Chase-Riboud did a great deal of research to emphasize the female and racial complexities of Black women's enslavement.

Collins, Patricia Hill. *Black Feminist Thought: Knowledge, Consciousness, and the Politics of Empowerment.* New York: Routledge, 1990. A classic work bringing together scholarship from Black feminist intellectual perspectives and sociological research on Black women's lives.

Davis, Angela. "Reflections on the Black Woman's Role in the Community of Slaves." *The Black Scholar: Journal of Black Studies and Research* 12, no. 6, November/December 1981: 2–16. One of the most influential articles about Black women. It challenges the myth of a Black women's matriarchy during slavery. Davis underscores the oppressive nature of Black women's work, their pivotal role in the slave family and community and their sexual exploitation. According to Davis, Black women were critical to the survival of Black people and essential for the development of opposition and resistance to slavery.

Du Bois, W. E. B. *Philadelphia Negro: A Social Study.* New York: Schocken Books, 1967. First published in 1899. The first sociological work to study African Americans by the most important Black intellectual of the twentieth century. Du Bois singlehandedly interviewed thousands of Black residents and provided information about the connections between family, housing, and work.

Dumas, Rhetaugh Graves. "Dilemmas of Black Females in Leadership." In *The Black Woman.* Edited by La Frances Rodgers-Rose. Beverly Hills, CA: Sage, 1989. An article that explodes the myth behind the successful Black woman professional and exposes the subtle forms of racial and gender biases which relegate her to new kinds of mammy roles.

Evans, Sara. *Personal Politics: The Roots of Women's Liberation in the Civil Rights Movement and the New Left.* New York: Vintage, 1980. Documents how the women's movement grew out of the social movements in the Black community. It refutes widely held notions that second wave feminism was solely a result of consciousness raising among college-educated white women.

Henri, Florette. *Black Migration North: 1900–1920.* New York: Anchor, 1975. A historical study detailing the conditions of Black migrants, especially the lives of Black women and children in New York City.

Higginbotham, A. Leon. *In the Matter of Color—Race and the American Legal Process: The Colonial Period.* Oxford: Oxford University Press, 1978. Documents how race was intertwined with the establishment of social order and the legal status of Black men and women from the inception of the United States.

Lerner, Gerda, editor. *Black Women in White America: A Documentary History.* New York: Vintage, 1973. The best introduction to Black women's historical experiences in the United States. The documents cover sexuality, work, family, and community organizing.

Lorde, Audre. *Sister Outsider.* New York: The Crossing Press, 1984. Though recognized as an important Black lesbian poet, Lorde's essays offer critical insights about the Black female psyche. Included is the essay, "The Uses of the Erotic: The Erotic as Power" which offers a radical exploration of the political and social role of female sexuality.

McLaughlin, Andree Nicola. "The International Nature of the Southern African Women's Struggle," Edited by Lewis Shelby. *Network: A Pan-African Women's Forum* 1, no. 1, Winter 1988: 49–56. The proceedings from a conference on Women in Southern Africa: Struggle Within Struggle, held on November

13–14, 1987 in Harare, Zimbabwe. In her presentation, McLaughlin, one of the most significant Black feminist social theorists, provides her analysis and vision of two competing global systems: one promoting violence and exploitation, and the other promoting peace and liberation.

McNeil, Genna Rae. *Groundwork: Charles Hamilton Houston and the Struggle for Civil Rights.* Philadelphia: University of Pennsylvania Press, 1983. A biography of Charles Hamilton Houston who established the Howard University Law School, where Supreme Court Justice Thurgood Marshall trained. By using his skills as a law professor, Houston created Black civil rights law and provided a model of how Black intellectuals can serve the needs of their people.

Morrison, Toni. *Beloved.* New York: Alfred Knopf, 1987. In this award-winning novel, Morrison probes the meaning and motives of a Black mother who commits infanticide to prevent her daughter from being returned to slavery. The story is a mythic narrative of the depth of Black women's pain and rage, as well as their determination to find freedom, love, and redemption.

Snitow, Ann, Christine Stansell, and Sharon Thompson. *Powers of Desire: The Politics of Sexuality.* New York: Monthly Review Press, 1983. A collection of essays by feminists discussing the social construction and meanings of sexuality.

Sokoloff, Natalie. *Black Women and White Women in the Professions.* New York: Routledge, 1992. This feminist sociologist analyzes women's advances in the professions and indicates the commonality and differences between Black and white women professionals.

Strickland, William. "The Road Since Brown: The Americanization of the Race," *The Black Scholar: Journal of Black Studies and Research.* September–October, 1979: 2–8. This essay is the finest description of the impact of integration and the civil rights movement upon the Black community. Strickland provides moving testimony of Black people's "prevailing unity" under segregation and their loss of community after its end.

Terborg-Penn, Rosalyn, Sharon Harley, and Andrea Benton Rushing, editors. *Women in Africa and the African Diaspora.* Washington, D.C.: Howard University Press, 1987. This volume contains papers from the Association of Black Women Historians' conference on Women in the African Diaspora: An Interdisciplinary Perspective, which was convened at Howard University on June 12–14, 1983. Its first part, Theoretical Approaches and Research Methods, includes articles by Filomina Chioma Steady and Niara Sudarkasa who locate their analyses of African feminism within a worldwide perspective.

The Human Rights Watch World Report 1994. New York: Human Rights Watch Publications, 1994. The most recent update of human rights abuses around the world, reinforcing the deplorable state of ethnic warfare and social dislocation in the aftermath of the collapse of the Soviet Union and the global economic restructuring.

Wallace, Michele. "Variations on Negation and the Heresy of Black Feminist Creativity." *Invisibility Blues: From Pop to Theory.* London and New York: Verso, 1990. Wallace provides a critical analysis of Black women's high visibility but lack of voice in the media and the academy, as well as in intellectual discourse and critical theory.

Williams, Patricia. *The Alchemy of Race and Rights.* Cambridge, MA: Harvard University Press, 1991. In these essays, Williams, a Black female attorney and social theorist, provides a lawyer's eye for detailed analysis and complex passions about Black women as symbol and subject in the law and in American society.

PART I

HISTORICAL CONTEXT, CONTEMPORARY MEANINGS

1

HEARTS OF DARKNESS

THE SEXUAL HISTORY of the United States began at the historical moment when European men met African women in the "heart of darkness"[1]—Mother Africa. They faced each other as conqueror and conquered: African women captives were considered the sexual property of the European conquerors.[2]

The African sexuality confronted by European men was an integral part of a sensuality that permeated music, dance, and religion. West African women often performed dances such as the "crotch dance, an improvised folk drama enacted by women at the height of the birth celebration, in which women strike their crotches firmly with both their hands."[3] However tactile, pleasurable, and comfortable these daily creative art forms, they were not necessarily indicative of sexual promiscuity. Rather, African cultures taught men and women to use their bodies in fluid, rhythmic ways, within a sexual code of behavior that frequently countenanced murdering women who committed adultery and often practiced female clitoridectomy.[4] The African woman who faced the European man was a wife, a mother, a daughter, a sister, nestled in tribal societies and protected by fathers, husbands, and brothers who upheld the sanctity and primacy of marriage and motherhood for women.

Nevertheless, in the hip-shaking, bare-breasted women with sweating bodies who danced to drums played by intense black men, in the market women and nursing mothers wrapped in African cloth, in the scantily clad farming women, the European man saw a being who embodied all that was evil and profane to his sensibilities. He perceived the African's sensual ways according to his own cultural definitions of sex, nudity, and blackness as base, foul, and bestial. He did not attempt to understand how Africans defined their own behavior.[5] He made assumptions and invented knowledge about their behavior as he created the conditions for this "knowledge" to become the reality. He viewed the African expression of sensuality through public rites, rituals, and dances as evidence of the absence of any sexual codes of behavior, an idea that both fascinated and repelled him and also provided him with a needed rationale for the economic exploitation of African men and women.

As historian Richard Hofstadter explains:

> Naked and libidinous: for the white man's preoccupation with the Negro sexuality was there at the very beginning, an outcome not only of his own guilt at sexual exploitation—his easy access to the black woman was immediately blamed on *her* lasciviousness—but also of his envious suspicion that some extraordinary potency and ecstatic experience were associated with primitive lust.[6]

Within the strange "commingling of desire and hate,"[7] white men would continue to penetrate and plunder Mother Africa for five centuries while creating a world view centered around the myth of race and racism that upheld white supremacy and the total domination of black people.

The sexual history of the United States became fused with contradiction and duality, with myth and distortion, with the white man's hate and desire for the black woman, with competition and jealousy between white and black women for white men, with love and struggle between black men and black women. American sexual history reflects the development of patriarchal control stretched to its maximum extent by European men operating within a racial caste system supported by state power in which white maleness becomes the only definition of being. Simultaneously, the extremes of American patriarchy, particularly under slavery, pushed black women outside traditional patriarchal protection, thereby transforming all previous definitions of womanhood, particularly the idea that woman requires male protection because of her innate weakness and inferiority.[8] Black women were oppressed and exploited labor and as such were forced to redefine themselves as women outside of and antagonistic to the racial patriarch who denied their being. Most black women refused to accept the traditional notions of subordination of woman to man. The black woman resisted racial patriarchy by escaping, stealing, killing, outsmarting, and bargaining with her white master while she had sex with him, had babies by him, ministered to his needs, growing "to know all there was to know about him."[9] At the same time, most black women accepted traditional notions of patriarchy from black men because they viewed the Afro-Christian tradition of woman as mother and wife as personally desirable and politically necessary for black people's survival.

The racial patriarchy of the white man enabled him to enact his culture's separation between the goodness, purity, innocence, and frailty of woman, and the sinful, evil strength, and carnal knowledge of woman by having sex with white women who came to embody the former and black women who came to embody the latter.[10] The white man's division of the sexual attributes of women based on race meant that he alone could claim to be sexually free: he was free to be sexually active within a society that upheld the chastity and modesty of white women as the "repositories of white civilization."[11] He was free to be irresponsible about the consequences of his sexual behavior with black women within a culture that placed a great value on the family as a sacred institution protecting women, their progeny and his property. He was free to use violence to eliminate his competition with black men for black or white women, thus breaking the customary allegiance among all patriarchs. He was also free to maintain his public hatred of racial mixing while privately expressing his desire for black women's bodies. Ultimately, white men were politically empowered to dominate all women and all black men and women; this was their sexual freedom.

From the beginning, the founding fathers assumed the patriarchal right to regulate and define the sexual behavior of their servants and slaves according to a fusion of Protestantism, English Common Law, and personal whim. During the early colonial period the distinctions between indentured servant and slave were blurred and relative: most workers, black and white, male and female, worked without direct payment or without control over their labor. These laborers shared enough common experiences to jointly attack their masters and to have sex with each other.[12] The master's racial attitudes of antipathy toward black people and his fears of a unified antagonistic force of all workers, including Indian women and men, demanded that the category "white" be expanded to give political power and freedom to all white men (theoretically and potentially, if not at that actual historical time) and patriarchal protection and white privilege to all white women. Thus, during the later colonial period, black men and white women who had sex, married, and/or had children were punished and persecuted as American society denied them the right to choose each other as mates.[13] The category "white" would also mean that the people designated "black" could be held in perpetual slavery.[14] Therefore, laws were passed and practices instituted to regulate the sexual and social behavior of white and black, servants and slaves. The legal and actual distinction between slave and servant was widened with "slavery reflecting more temporary relationship of service."[15] In other words, in spite of the common experiences of black and white workers in colonial America, indentured servants were whitened as slaves became black.

Though black people were less than 5 percent of the population in the later part of the seventeenth century, a 1662 Virginia statute stipulated that "all offspring follow the condition of the mother in the event of a white man getting a Negro with child."[16] A 1664 statute prohibited all unions between the races.[17] In 1665, the first English slave code in New York provided that slavery was for life.[18] Colonial law and custom reflected the parameters that would continue to govern American sexual behavior: regardless of who impregnated black women, any offspring would be slave. As Hofstadter puts it, this "guaranteed in a society where interracial sex usually involved the access of white men to black women, that without other provisions to the contrary, the mulatto population would be slave."[19] Well before the institution of slavery was firmly established in the antebellum South during the nineteenth century, these laws and others prohibiting black political participation, ownership of land, and the right to carry arms[20] were aimed at creating a black population in perpetual servitude.

Slavery and slaveholders dominated American political and economic life for about two hundred years. As Carl Degler describes it:

> The labor of slaves provided the wherewithal to maintain lawyers and actors, cotton factors and publishers, musicians in Charleston, senators in Washington, and gamblers on the Mississippi river boats. Slave holders were agricultural entrepreneurs in a capitalistic society: their central importance as a class resided not in their numbers, which were admittedly small, but in their ability to accumulate surplus for investment.[21]

Degler's phrase "ability to accumulate surplus for investment" tends to obscure all traces of the inhumanity of slavery: black women's bodies were just a primary means of accumulating the surplus: "My mother was young—just 15 or 16 years old. She had 14 chillen and you know that meant a lots of wealth."[22] New slave owners with one or two slaves attempting to "construct an initial labor force" and establish an economic base in order to realize profits broke up slave communities or African clans by obtaining individual slaves through purchase, gift, or marriage. The fecundity of black women was key to the slave owner's goal. Gutman documents that as one planter said, "An owner's labor force doubled through natural increase every 15 years."[23] A slave, looking back, agrees:

> They would buy a fine girl and a fine man and just put them together like cattle; they would not stop to marry them. If she was a good breeder, they were proud of her. I was stout and they were saving me for a breeding woman, but by the time I was big enough I was free. I had an aunt in Mississippi and she had about 20 children by her marster.[24]

"Natural increase" meant that the black woman was encouraged and sometimes forced to have sex frequently in order to have babies, whether by black men or white men, in stable or unstable relationships.

But as early as 1639, black women resisted forced sex:

> [O]ne source ... tells of a Negro woman being held as a slave on Noddles Island in Boston harbor. Her master sought to mate her with another Negro, but, the chronicler reported, she kicked her prospective lover out of bed, saying that such behavior was "beyond her slavery."[25]

But though it was beyond *her* concept of enslavement, it was not beyond her master's, for every part of the black woman was used by him. To him she was a fragmented commodity whose feelings and choices were rarely considered: her head and her heart were separated from her back and her hands and divided from her womb and vagina. Her back and muscle were pressed into field labor where she was forced to work with men and work like men. Her hands were demanded to nurse and nurture the white man and his family as domestic servant whether she was technically enslaved or legally free. Her vagina, used for his sexual pleasure, was the gateway to the womb, which was his place of capital investment—the capital investment being the sex act and the resulting child the accumulated surplus, worth money on the slave market.

The totalitarian system of slavery extended itself into the very place that was inviolable and sacred to both African and European societies—the sanctity of the woman's body and motherhood within the institution of marriage. Although all women were slaves under patriarchy, the particular enslavement of black women was also an attack on all black people. All sexual intercourse between a white man and a black woman irrespective of her conscious consent became rape, because the social arrangement assumed the black woman to be without any human right to control her own body.[26] And the body could not be separated from its color.

Racial oppression tends to flow from the external to the internal: from political institutions, social structures, the economic system and military conquest, into the psyche and consciousness and culture of the oppressed and the oppressor. In contrast, sexual oppression tends to direct itself directly to the internal, the feeling and emotional center, the private and intimate self, existing within the external context of power and social control. Black women fused both racial and sexual oppressions in their beings and movements in both black and white worlds.

Black women moved through the white man's world: through his space, his land, his fields, his streets, and his woodpiles.

> The Negro woman carried herself like a queen, tall and stately in spite of her position as a slave. The overseer, the plantation owner's son sent her to the house on some errand. It was necessary to pass through a wooded pasture to reach the house and the overseer intercepted her in the woods and forced her to put her head between the rails in an old stake and rider fence, and there in that position, my great, great grandfather was conceived.[27]

In the white man's world, black women would have a place: "I know at least 50 places in my small town where white men are positively raising two families—a white family in the 'Big House' in front, and a colored family in a 'Little House' in the backyard."[28] In the white man's world, black women were separated from black men: "When I left the camp my wife had had two children by some one of the white bosses, and she was living in fairly good shape in a little house off to herself."[29] They became the teachers of sex to white boys: "Testimony seems to be quite widespread to the fact that many if not most southern boys begin their sexual experiences with Negro girls."[30]

White men tortured and punished black women who refused them: For fending off the advances of an overseer on a Virginia plantation, Minnie Falkes' mother was suspended from a barn rafter and beaten with a horsewhip "nekkid" til blood run down her back to her heels.[31] Madison Jefferson adds:

> Women who refused to submit themselves to the brutal desires of their owners, are repeatedly whipt to subdue their virtuous repugnance, and

in most instances this hellish practice is but too successful—when it fails, the women are frequently sold off to the south.[32]

The black woman worked in the white man's home, both before and after formal emancipation. She knew her master/lover as a man; she was intimate with his humanity; she fed him and she slept with him; she ministered to his needs.[33] One slave remarked, "Now mind you all of the colored women didn't have to have white men, some did it because they wanted to and some were forced. They had a horror of going to Mississippi and they would do anything to keep from it."[34]

Black women and white women were sisters under the oppression of white men in whose houses they both lived as servants. In the antebellum South, Mary Chesnut wrote, "There is no slave after all like a wife."[35] A white woman married to the planter/patriarch endured, suffered, and submitted to him in all things. White women, though viewed as pure and delicate ladies by southern myth, had to serve their husband/masters as did the female servants and slaves; managing the household, entertaining the guests, overseeing the feeding and clothing of both slaves and relatives.[36]

Both white and black women were physically weakened and often died from birthing too many of the master's children. White men often had several wives in succession because many died in childbirth. While white wives visited relatives for long periods of time to have space between pregnancies,[37] exercising a much-needed control over childbearing, black women all too often filled the gap for both recreational and procreational sex. Ann Firor Scott writes of one South Carolinian who thought, "The availability of slave women for sex avoided the horrors of prostitution. He pointed out that men could satisfy their sexual needs while increasing their slave property."[38] To be a white woman in the antebellum South meant accepting the double standard: brothers, fathers, and mates could enjoy sex with her sisters in bondage, black women. White women however, were prevented from enjoying sex because they were viewed as "pure women incapable of erotic feeling."[39]

Many southern white women privately disliked the double standard and the horrors of the sexual life it implied: "Under slavery we lived surrounded by prostitutes like patriarchs of old, our men live in one house with their wives and concubines."[40] An ex-slave woman agreed:

> Just the other day we were talking about white people when they had slaves. You know when a man would marry, his father would give a woman for a cook and she would have children right in the house by

him and his wife would have children too. Sometimes the cook's children favored him so much that the wife would be mean to them and make him sell them.[41]

Yet for all the private outrage of white women at the "injustice and shame" to all womanhood of the sexual activities of white men, black women stood alone without the support of their sisters. Most white women sadistically and viciously punished the black woman and her children for the transgressions of their white men. One study states:

> To punish black women for minor offenses, mistresses were likely to attack with any weapon available—a fork, butcher knife, knitting needle, pan of boiling water. Some of the most barbaric forms of punishment resulting in the mutilation and permanent scaring of female servants were devised by white mistresses in the heat of passion.[42]

White women used the social relationship of supervisor of black women's domestic labor to act out their racial superiority, their emotional frustrations, and their sexual jealousies. Black women slaves and domestic servants were useful buffers between white men and white women, pulling them together, resolving their conflicts, maintaining continuity and structure for the white family whose physical and emotional needs they fulfilled.[43]

When the daughter and son of the white man and the black woman faced the father, they reflected the fruits of his passion as well as the duplicity of his life. Their light skin or light eyes, their straight hair or nose reflected himself to himself and yet he still refused to acknowledge paternity. The exceptional white father/master/lover who cared would often free his black children and wife, hustle them out of town, educating and supporting them from afar, helping them rise within black society while hoping for silence and anonymity. But in spite of traditional patriarchal concerns for fatherhood, most white fathers did nothing for their colored children. Most colored children shared the experience of this ex-slave: "My grandfather was an Irishman and he was a foreman, but he had to whip his children and grandchildren just like the others."[44] Those few slaveholders who loved and respected their slave wives were limited by societal criticism and the law from formally marrying them.[45]

Though she had no privacy, away from the view of all, could the black woman have ever desired and loved her master/lover? Could she have separated the hands that whipped her body from the hands that gripped her body in lovemaking? After all, the master/lover was only a man who desired the slave woman and had the power to take her as a woman. Patriarchal society would define the perfect man as the perfect master, and it was the submissiveness of the slave woman that made her the perfect slave and the perfect woman. After all, a man's power over a woman was like the master's power over a slave. It came from "innate superiority."[46] But the intimate place of desire and fulfillment of the submissive and perfected woman was in violent conflict with the rage and humiliation and forced labor of being a slave woman forced to lie in the arms of the enslaver, the enemy ultimately responsible for her humiliation and her suffering. Yet the woman could not be separated from the color. One black woman remembers:

> One mark in particular stands out in my memory, one she bore just above her right eye. As well as she liked to regale me with stories of her scars, this one she never discussed with me. Whenever I would ask a question concerning it, she would simply shake her head and say "White men are as low as dogs, child. Stay from them." It was only after her death, and since I became a woman that I was told by my own mother that she received that scar at the hands of her master's youngest son, a boy of about 18 years, at the time she conceived their child, my grandmother, Ellen.[47]

Though mulattoes were "common as blackberries,"[48] most black women resisted white men's sexual advances and resented being a convenient scapegoat for the white women's sexual suppression. Black women were often unwilling participants in the sexual lives of white men and women. In spite of close contact, many did not necessarily admire or identify with white families. They often longed to go home to the black world to care for their own men and children.

As she crossed the tracks to the black world she could breathe a little easier, soften and slow up her steps. She could smile at her neighbors and kin along the road or warn them away with her stern and tired face. They understood that her day had been rough. The care of her children, her men, and her sisters would occupy her time now. She would find private space in cleaning her house, tending her garden, fixing her room with doilies and trinkets. She would sew sister's dress, braid her baby girl's hair, and fix that hat for Sunday's church meeting. In this world there was space for her to pull herself together. The space was contained and narrow but it did give her easement from the white man's world and his desire for her body.

Against the white man's animal panting and arbitrary carnal desires that stalked their daughters, the old ones' harsh words and demands of modesty emphasized with a slap or a hard look forced the girls to hide and conserve the precious darkness between their legs. The old ones would frequently frustrate and confuse their daughters' sexual desires, for though their rage originated from the sexual abuses of white men, they extended taboos against all sexual expression.

African cultural values taught deference and respect to the elderly, who set parameters for sexual, romantic, and marital relationships within tribal rituals and rites. Within slave and rural black communities, away from the interferences of white men, the deference continued.[49] Young black men courted and romanced young women with African-like ritual and respect, always under the watchful eyes of the old ones.

> When this courting process proceeded naturally and freely, the couple might eventually have a child, or if the girl had already had her first baby (often by a different man) they might marry and settle into a long-lasting monogamous union.[50]

The old ones in the new world were consulted for their approval and consent to marital plans or pregnancies by their daughters and sons. Sometimes, mothers and grandmothers (fathers and grandfathers also) were unmoved by romance or youthful passion and clamped down on their daughters' sexual desires for any but the most stable mates with the firmness of an iron chastity belt.

Though black women were mothers, midwives, and farmers, with daughters growing up close to them, frequently in crowded homes with many siblings and relatives, most young black women learned little explicit information about sex.[51] Thus, in spite of and because of the historical sexual abuse of black women, both black men and black women lived sexually conservative lives characterized by modesty and discretion. In fact, most black women were reluctant to openly discuss specific sexual abuses against their person by white men, even within their own families.[52]

The black man moved toward the black woman, clothing her raped and abused body with the mantle of respectable womanhood, giving protection and sometimes claiming ownership of her. Many black men agreed with white men that "wives should submit themselves to their husbands in all things."[53] As the dominant institution within the black community, the black church reinforced and supported the traditional patriarchal view of men claiming wardship over women.

Protecting black women was the most significant measure of black manhood and the central aspect of black male patriarchy. Black men felt outrage and shame at their frequent inability to protect black women, not merely from the whippings and hard work, but also from the master/lover's touch. During and after slavery, black men spoke out angrily against the harsh treatment of black women, many vowing never again to allow black women to be sexually abused and economically exploited.[54] Their methods often became rigidly patriarchal; however, they did in many instances keep black women from becoming the open prey of the white man. W. E. B. Du Bois summed up the feelings of many black men:

> . . . but one thing I shall never forgive, neither in this world nor in the world to come: it's [the white South's] wanton and continued and persistent insulting of the black womanhood which it sought and seeks to prostitute its lust.[55]

After the Civil War, black men and black women married each other in droves, giving their unions legitimacy and validating their right to choose and love each other.[56] Many felt that the slave master could no longer come between black men and black women for the law connected them. Yet in their successful attempts to recapture political and economic power, white men claimed a glorified past of total domination over black people, continuing to enter the "heart of darkness" as their right.

Although during Reconstruction terror and hunger forced black men and black women into peonage and sharecropping, the black community resisted the new chains of white male domination. Women vowed to stand by their men, never to return to the fields, to the kitchens, or to the beds of white men. As the white community attacked and extended its dominion, black women carved out new ways to survive as well as uphold their marriages and the implied sanctity of their bodies.

Black men struggled to farm their own land in order to provide for their families, keeping wives and daughters away from white men's farms and arms. Many asserted as one ex-slave did to his white father/master who doubted his ability to provide for his family, "I am going to feed and clothe them and I can do it on bare rock."[57] Black women withdrew from farm labor for the white man, and, when they had to work, insisted on day work rather than sleep-in domestic work.[58] Black women also sewed, dressed hair, washed clothes, and cooked meals in their own homes for wages, in order to keep out of white men's homes.

In the context of the black community of resistance, "heterosexual privilege usually became the only privilege black women had. For without racial or sexual privilege, marriage and motherhood becomes the last resort."[59] The very traditional experiences of motherhood and sex within marriage were not necessarily viewed as oppressive to black women, for they were the literal and symbolic weapons she could utilize to assure the biological and social reproduction of black people. Marriage and motherhood were humanizing experiences that gave her life meaning, purpose, and choice. These experiences were denied within the racist milieu where her humanity was questioned and her human rights and privileges to love and be loved were denied.

The African values retained within the black community in combination with its learned Christian values reinforced sexual loyalty and monogamy for black women. Although white society described her as an insatiable animal with no feelings of love and commitment, in one way or another, and with a variety of consequences, black women have been monogamous, serially monogamous, and sexually loyal partners to black men (and sometimes white men also).

Black men held a wide range of views about black women, from those that reinforced female subordination to those that reinforced equal social relations between the sexes. Many black men, moving away from traditional patriarchal views, supported and encouraged independence in their wives, and more often in their daughters.[60] Black women were supported by black men in building black elementary schools and community institutions and in encouraging their daughters to become educated as teachers to escape the "abominations" of the white man. As teachers, black women could be kept within the black community away from the sexual advances of white men and under the watchful protecting eyes of male principals and ministers. Teaching required of black women an even more rigorous adherence to a sex code enjoining chastity and model womanhood than that guiding other black women.[61]

Sex codes upholding the values of monogamy and sexual loyalty were part of the extended kinship networks that provided valuable emotional, physical, and economic support for black women. Kin accepted children sired by white men into the family. There was no such thing as "illegitimacy," for each child was considered part of the community, where its mother might be stigmatized, but rarely ostracized. Women abandoned by their husbands were viewed with sympathy. To a great extent, black women forced into sexual relations with white men were still considered suitable mates by black men. There was the widespread practice of black men parenting children not sired by them, even when a child's father was white. Nearly every black family had a white absentee father or grandfather and a wide range of skin colors. Only those women who continued to live outside the sexual code, which condemned adultery and promiscuity with white or black men, were viewed as sinful.[62] Both during and after slavery, black women and men have had a complex history of struggling together to maintain stable, monogamous families, transmuting the destructive forces from without, cooperating and supporting each other from within.

The historical oppression of black women and men should have created social equality between them, but even after the end of slavery when the white patriarch receded, maleness and femaleness continued to be defined by patriarchal structures, with black men declaring wardship over black women. In the black community, the norm of manhood was patriarchal power; the norm of womanhood was adherence to it, though both black men and women selected which aspects of these norms they would emphasize.

Many black women became enraged at the thought of being owned and taken by any man, even if he had black skin. The whippings, the work, the penetration by the whipper and the white master/lover left them with rage and rebellion against the traditional roles of wife and mother. They would resist as Rose Williams resisted when

> Forced to live with a man named Rufus because the master wanted them "to bring forth portly chillen" [she] warned the slave to stay away from her "fore I busts yous brains out and stomp on dem." She finally relented when threatened with a whipping, but she never married explaining, "after what I done for de massa I's never wants no truck with any man—de lawd forgive dis cullud woman, but he have to 'scuse me and look for some other to 'plenish de earth."[63]

Black women within the rural black community often defied the restrictions on their womanhood and sexuality by living alone (near family and kin) and working their own farms, running their own lives without men as mates and protectors, frequently sojourning for truth and God. Many of these women learned these independent ways from their fathers and brothers. Women often lived with women as both emotional and sexual companions. Women in urban black communities had several male lovers and companions but did not submit to them in traditional ways because they maintained an independent life as community workers, political and social activists, and workers within the paid labor force.

At the beginning of the twentieth century both rural and urban black women followed the role models of black female artists, singers, dancers, and actresses who expressed and reinforced the sensuality of African traditions by shaking and shimmying on stages and in clubs and road-houses. Black women leaving the restrictions of the rural south agreed with Bessie Smith:

> I'm a young woman and ain't done runnin' roun . . .
> Some people call me a hobo, some call me a bum.
> Nobody knows my name, nobody knows what I've done.
> See that long, lonesome road? Lord you know it's gotta end.
> And I'm a good woman and I can get plenty men.[64]

These black women lived lives of explicit sexuality and erotic excitement with both men and women. As they broke away from the traditional paternal restraints within the black community, they were castigated for seeming to reflect the truth of the white man's views of black women as whorish and loose. But these "wild women"[65] did not care, modeling for southern rural black women a city life full of flashy clothes, fast cars, and access to sophisticated men.

However, most black women did not have access to the mobility of a freer sexual life, even within marriage, until the 1960s, when large-scale urbanization, a shift from domestic to clerical jobs, and the break-up of the traditional kinship networks of the rural South took place. Even then, black women's sexuality was still contained within a white male patriarchy that continued to view her as already sexually liberated.

A black woman could not be completely controlled and defined by her own men, for she had already learned to manage and resist the advances of white men, earning and internalizing a reputation for toughness and strength, for resiliency and resolve, that enhanced the myth of her as both matriarch and wild woman. Her political resistance increased her potential to become a woman of power, capable of defining herself and rising to protect herself and her children, frequently throwing the mantle of protection over black men as well.

Slavery and womanhood remained interconnected long after the formal bondage of black people was over. Being a black woman with a black man could still mean slavery. And the woman could not be separated from the color. Being a black woman without a black man could also still mean slavery. And the color could not be separated from the woman.

These contradictions have been fully explored by only a few black women, for black women and black men continue to be engaged in a community of struggle to create a space in which to live and to survive:

> Black women speaking with many voices and expressing many individual opinions, have been nearly unanimous in their insistence that their own emancipation cannot be separated from the emancipation of their men. Their liberation depends on the liberation of the race and the improvement of life in the black community.[66]

Sex between black women and black men, between black men and black men, between black women and black women, is meshed within complex cultural, political, and economic circumstances. All black sexuality is underlined by a basic theme: where, when, and under what circumstances could/would black men and black women connect with one another intimately and privately when all aspects of their lives were considered the dominion of the public, white master/lover's power?

If the sexual act between white men and black women was a ritual reenactment of domination, the oppression failed to completely dampen the sexual expression of black women within the black community, which often became a ritual enactment of affirmation of her freedom and happiness within intense emotional connections with her men, her sisters, her children, her gods, and more often with herself. In spite of centuries of personal and political rape, black women could still say, "i found god in myself/and i loved her/i loved her fiercely."[67]

History, traditionally written as a record of public events, has obscured and omitted the relationship between public events and private acts. Therefore, sex has always been in the closet of American history, hidden away from and kept outside the public realm of political and economic events. White men used their power in the public sphere to construct a private sphere that would meet their needs and their desire for black women, which if publicly admitted would have undermined the false construct of race they needed to maintain public power. Therefore, the history of black women in America reflects the juncture where the private and public spheres and personal and political oppression meet.

The master/lover ruled over the world; he divided it up and called everyone out of their name. During the day, he would call her "wench," "negress," "Sable Venus," "dusky Sal," and "Auntie." He described and wrote about her endurance, ate her biscuits, and suckled her breasts. At night he would chant false endearments and would feel engulfed within her darkness. He would accuse her of raping herself, naming his lesser brothers as the fathers of his and her children. He would record every battle, keep every letter, document each law, building monuments to himself, but he would never tell the true story, the complete story of how he used to rape to make the profit, of how he used the bodies of women to satisfy his needs. He would never tell how he built a society with the aid of dark-skinned women, instead telling the world he did it alone.

He would cover the tracks between his house and hers, he would deny the semen-stained sheets she was forced to wash. History would become all that men did during the day, but nothing of what they did during the night. He would forge her children. He would deny his love or lust for her. He would deny his failure to obey his own laws. He refused to listen to the logical extension of his argument for the massacres, the slave raids, the genocide, the lynch mobs, the Ku Klux Klan. He could not live up to his own fears and arguments against mongrelization of the race, the separation of black from white. He built an exterior world that reflected his fragmented insides.

But the woman learned to face him, the rapist who hated and loved her with such passion. She learned to use her darkness to create light. She would make the divided, white and black, external and internal world into wholeness. She would "lean on Jesus," reaching out to help and for help, and would gather around her children and kin to help them make the world whole and livable. She would mother all the children—black and white—and serve both men—conqueror and conquered—knowing "all there was to know," for she could not separate the color from the woman.

Only a few daring men, mostly black ones, would recognize that only she understood what it had taken for white men to dominate the world and what it would mean, finally, to be free. But some black women who voiced what they knew did not survive:

> A slave woman ain't allowed to respect herself, if she would. I had a pretty sister, she was whiter than I am, for she took more after her father. When she was 16 years old, her master sent for her. When he sent for her again, she cried and didn't want to go. She told mother her troubles, and she tried to encourage her to be decent and hold up her head above such things if she could. Her master was so mad, to think she had complained to her mother, that he sold her right off to Louisiana, and we hear afterward that she died there of hard usage.[68]

But others sold down river survived and remembered their mothers and fathers, remembered the white master/lover, the black master/lover, and the black brother/lover. They, in their turn, gave their daughters and sons the gifts of determination and freedom, the will to love and the strength to have faith. Some would accept these gifts, some would reject them. History, however, would obliterate the entire story, occasionally giving it only a false footnote. But deep within the daughters' hearts and minds it would be remembered and this memory would become the historical record everything had to be measured by.

2

THE UNBROKEN CIRCLE

A HISTORICAL STUDY OF BLACK SINGLE MOTHERS AND THEIR FAMILIES

INTRODUCTION

FAMILIES AND HOUSEHOLDS managed solely by Black women have been an integral part of American society since the days of the British colonization of North America and, as such, have been at the nexus of race, gender and class within the United States. Because racism permeates and transcends all social relationships, economic and political arrangements such as slavery, segregation, and desegregation have not operated in the public arena alone, but have seeped into the private arenas of sexuality, marriage and family, and into the personal lives of Blacks and whites, men and women.

The history of Black single mothers and their families is part of the history of American family life. Three principles have shaped the development of American families:

> First, there was the puritanical tradition, which condemned fornication with the threat of fire and brimstone. Second, there was a highly developed sense of racial purity frequently codified in laws against misce-

> genation. And third, there was a strong moral commitment to a patri-
> archal family. (Patterson, 1982, p. 261)

Black families have been shaped by sexual conservatism, a patriarchal family life and a strong sense of racial pride. However, Black single-mother families have existed outside the patriarchal family, and often reflect the reality of sexual intercourse outside marriage. In their earliest states, such families reflected interracial sex (that is, white male sexual exploitation of Black women slaves.) In fact, both Black and white family life was undermined by the actions and guilt of ruling elite white men who violated their own social codes by having sex with Black slave women. In addition, this elite group ignored the desires of Black women and men to have marriages and families of their own.

Black single-motherhood first evolved as the manifestation of the slave woman's legal and cultural social death. Her capacity for the social and biological reproduction of slavery assured maximum profits and social control for the racial patriarch or ruling elite. However, Black single-motherhood was also a viable family type which Black men and women adopted in response to a system which did not recognize their right to a legal marriage and family. Within the slave community, single-mother families coexisted with outlawed two-parent families. After emancipation, during Reconstruction and during the segregation era, Black single-motherhood continued to provide a survival strategy for Black families still relegated to second class citizenship and social marginality by racism, apartheid, pogrom and poverty. During the desegregation era of the last thirty years, Black people have achieved legal recognition as citizens and have forced the dismantling of segregation and apartheid. But new forms of racism have emerged, characterized by racially-based economic injustice, contentious gender and class relationships within the Black community and use of the media to amplify the social sciences which camouflage, promote and shape public policies that continue racism and strengthen white nationalism. Today, Black single-motherhood is both chosen by and imposed on Black women attempting to address social and economic changes.

In each era, Black single-motherhood has been interwoven both with Black estranged and nonresidential fatherhood and the emasculated patriarchal status and power which has accompanied the social death of Black men. The sexism of the ruling elite is not only directed at women; it is also aimed at stunting the development of Black manhood, whether it takes a patriarchal or non-sexist form.

This essay examines Black single-mother families and their historical development during three eras: slavery, segregation and desegregation. It focuses on the beginnings and contemporary condition and experiences of these families. The concept "social death," which is the theoretical framework for the study, comes from Orlando Patterson's cross-cultural study, *Slavery and Social-Death*. The study includes a Black feminist perspective and expands Patterson's concept "social death" beyond the institution of slavery into the second class and marginal position of Black people within racist society. In addition, the study examined another theoretical framework, the dialectics of oppression, and found that the debased condition and position of the oppressed always led to their conscious resistance and desire for freedom. Black resistance to social death took the form of creating viable families, whether patriarchal or female-headed, and of developing extended kinship networks along with political and protest strategies.

To consider Black women as historical human beings, all that we have been taught about the assumptions and givens of historical development, societal progress and personal and political power must be unlearned. These notions have been given to us through the prism and eyes of white men, whose wealth, privilege and power has been based upon the subjugation and domination of men and women whose skin is darker. To understand the story of those darker-skinned men and women we must become both expansive and thorough, visionary and scientific, Africanized and feminist. The traditional framework upon which we have based our person and our politics, our commitment to law and society, our experiences and learning about the family and home must change if we include the history and experience of Black single mothers.

SLAVERY AND WOMEN

> All fixed, fast-frozen relations, with their train of ancient and venerable prejudices, and opinions, are swept away, all new-formed ones become antiquated before they can ossify. All that is solid melts into air, all that is holy is profaned, and men at last are forced to face . . . the real conditions of their lives and their relations with their fellow men [sic]. (Berman, 1982, p. 21; quoting Marx 1848)

In describing the vision of the modern environment and the impact of the profound transformational capacities of capitalism, Marx unwittingly also described the transition of Africans from free men and women into captured and chattelized slaves. In a larger sense he also described the essence of their relationship to a society which designated them mules of the new world economy and used racism to banish them to the realm of the socially dead.

Social death shadowed every African captive chattelized into lifelong servitude in the Americas. The now familiar story of holocaust and uprooting was underscored by color, cultural and language differences between African and European people. To be socially dead was more than being separated from the music and tastes of one's motherland. It was to exist perpetually outside the circle where people decided things, allocated resources, made laws, communicated with God, wrote histories of the past and made plans for the future. The socially dead could neither choose, nor dream; they could only watch others choose and dream.

Yet as everything traditional and familiar was fleeting and transitory for the African captives, they clung to that which remained both solid and intangible: love, spirit, freedom, and of course, family. The bare relationship of exploitation and hatred between Black and white men, and the social distance between their worlds and histories were contrasted by the connection and commitment between and among Black men, women and children.

As Patterson's study of slavery demonstrates, "the definition of slave, however recruited, is a socially dead person" (Patterson, 1982, p. 5). Slave women were subject to a particular kind of social death. "In all slaveholding societies slave couples could be and were forcibly separated and the consensual "wives" of slaves were obliged to submit sexually to their masters; slaves had no custodial claims or powers over their children and children inherited no claims or obligations to their parents" (Patterson, p. 6).

Without marriage or human right, the female slave is a sexual vessel as well as chattel. There is no patriarchy to protect her unless the master assumes the role of protector, that is, if she is his concubine and has his children. Her men have no power or status; they are socially dead and thus are unable to come to her aid, unable to father the children they sire. There are no laws to protect her because she has no place in the law.

Furthermore, as subordinate members of patriarchal societies, especially those with slaves and class hierarchy, women become socially relevant solely because of their connections to men. The patriarchy is a worldwide system in which men are the heads of their households and families and women become socialized and organized into subordinate positions. Patriarchy is a system which requires control of women's fertility and sexuality in monogamous or polygamous marriages and is based upon a sexual division of labor regulated by male chauvinism.

In terms of worldwide historical considerations, the patriarchy at one time was perhaps a humane attempt at an arrangement in which women and children had protection and stability. The patriarchy has persisted, in part, because women gain from their relationships with men: as daughters, wives, mothers or sisters. In African societies, women had social recognition as members of the society. They had social and political rights and responsibilities. They had the right to join women's societies, which often shared birth control and sexual information. Women's bonding was a recognized part of the society. The men were also in a social relationship to women in which male domination had limits and responsibilities.

The advent of slavery changed these basic relationships because the traditional patriarch, the Black man, lost his status and economic and political power, which included wardship and protection of his women. Both Black man and woman fell under the domination of the racial patriarch, the white man. This fall was disastrous because all women, even those under bondage and racism, benefit from being connected to the patriarchy of their own men, no matter how weak or emasculated the status.

Under racism and bondage, Black women lose recognition and status as "women." The only "women" are those whose men have ultimate control and domination over people of color. Thus, it becomes understood and axiomatic—to be white and female is to be "woman" and to be white and male is to be "man." Black men and women are neither man nor woman; they are nonbeings, e.g. chattel, niggers, underclass.

In the years immediately following the Jamestown settlement, white and Black men and women commingled as slaves and servants. Many Blacks, whites and Native Americans were pressed together as unfree laborers with varying statuses. Not all whites were free and not all Blacks were slaves.

> Moreover, those Blacks who were imported before about 1660 were held in various degrees of servitude, most for limited periods and a few for life. (Nash, 1974, p. 149)

The first legislative enactment making reference to Blacks was a statute in 1639 which stated that:

> All persons except Negroes are to be provided with arms and ammunition or be fined at the pleasure of governor and council. (Higgenbotham, 1978, p. 32)

In 1665, the first English slave code in New York provided that slavery was for life. By the 1680s when the first major slave codes were issued in Virginia, and Blacks were denied the right to assemble, move freely, or defend themselves, Black skin began to mean perpetual servitude and stigma. The freedom of "free" Blacks was also limited and proscribed.

During this period, the status of unmarried women servants and slaves, and their children, was also the focus of special legislation. Black and white women were usually outnumbered by their male counterparts. Interracial sexual relationships, common-law and legal marriages existed along with monogamous marriages among Black servants, slaves and free people. However, the status of the children of bound women, especially of interracial parentage, most concerned the ruling elite.

In 1662 the Virginia legislature penalized the unmarried mother indentured servant by requiring an additional two years of service, regardless of her race. However, by the 1690s the treatment of Black and white "unwed" mothers differed. Eventually, Black women slaves or servants were not punished for bearing children fathered by white men, while white women servants were punished for bearing children fathered by Black men. "A woman servant who had an illegitimate [sic] child by a black or mulatto was fined 15 pounds and if unable to pay was sold for 5 years after her time of service expired" (Higginbotham, 1978, p. 45). If the unmarried mother was a free white woman she was also "subject to a 15 pound fine or 5 years of service." In 1664 all marriages between the races were prohibited and interracial couples were banished in 1691 statutes. By 1792, whites were penalized by imprisonment if they married a Black person. But interracial relationships between white men and Black women servants and slaves were commonplace and existed outside the laws.

In fact, English traditional precedent was broken in the 1662 statute which required that "children got by an Englishman upon a Negro woman shall be bound or free according to the condition of the mother." English common law and worldwide patriarchal customs always required that the status of the child follow his father. In order to prevent a free or quasi-free mulatto class from developing, which could undermine slavery, and to assure the maximum profits of a slave labor force, which could so easily reproduce itself, the racial patriarch treated Black women and children as distinct entities. He legally isolated them from Black men and regarded them differently from white women servants.

Because the right of slaves to marry each other or to marry whites was outlawed, Black women were also denied any form of patriarchal protection. Furthermore, sexual activity between white men and slave women could not be considered rape, because these women had no legal voice or choice not to submit. By forcing Black children to follow their mother's status and condition, slave masters could deny any responsibility for paternity, thereby enslaving their own children. In addition, Black men were prevented from assuming any responsibility for the children they sired. By requiring slavery to become the lifelong condition of Black men and women, the position of Black women would almost always be unmarried, raped, enslaved, and/or childbearing.

SLAVE FAMILY LIFE:
IT WAS NEVER OUR WISH TO BE SEPARATED

From the beginning, slaves, the socially dead, captive African, men and fathers, women and mothers, took in all that the slave master and his hypocritical system put on them: whippings, torture and unrelenting toil. Yet they turned it around to work for themselves and their progeny: language, religion, law, and family became Afro-American tools and weapons which slaves used to hone their humanity. In spite of restrictions on marriage and family, from the beginning slaves constructed both. When they could, they wrote and received love letters from distant "husbands" and "wives." When they could, they traveled long distances to see their families. Children knew their fathers or heard about them from their mothers.

In rejecting and ignoring the negative notions associated with Black single-motherhood, especially the separation of marriage from family, Black women assumed the role of family head. In the absence of spouses and mates, the Black single mother assumed that she and her children were a family. She protected, nurtured and fought for a new kind of family, one which emerged outside the patriarchy of her man, yet remained within the oppressive sphere of the racial patriarch. Her family developed within a slave community which provided sustenance, love and resistance from the horrors of slavery. The slave community also socialized, protected and reproduced human beings who were born into families and who expected to have families of their own.

Large slave families met the financial interests of slave masters, some of whom could boast that "a plantation of 50 or 60 persons had been established from the descendants of a single female, her children formed both two-parent and single-parent families." The birth register from the Good Hope Plantation in South Carolina, studied by historian Herbert Gutman, revealed important information about the slave family. The register was "an unusual historical document because it listed fathers' as well as mothers' names and because it covered a lengthy period of time, from 1760 until 1857. From the first to the last recorded slave birth, 175 men, women and children made up the Good Hope slave community. Of these 28 families, all but 5 of them contained a mother, father and their children" (Gutman, pp. 46–47). Two-parent households usually occurred on large plantations and coexisted with single-parent families.

The birth records also revealed another quite common practice among slaves: prenuptial intercourse and pregnancy. Many young women had children before settling into long-term marriages, a practice common to many pre-industrial societies, but one which would cause considerable alarm and confusion much later, in the 1980s. In some cases a woman had children by one man in her teens, but settled into a long-term marriage with another man and had the rest of her children by him. Prenuptial intercourse, bridal pregnancy and teenage motherhood were frequent aspects of slave family life. Most young, unmarried slave mothers lived with their families of origin when they could.

However, in spite of Good Hope and other plantations which supported long term and stable two- and one-parent households, family separations were an all too common occurrence which increased the number of single-mother families. Fear of separation was constantly hanging over families. Stable marriages and committed relationships were used by slave masters to keep their slaves obedient. Lewis Clarke, an ex-slave, explained, "if a woman slave had a husband and children, and somebody asked her if she would like her freedom? Would she tell 'em yes? If she did, she'd be down the river to Louisiana in no time, and her husband and children never know what become of her" (Blassingame, 1977, p. 153).

Some slave men left their women and children behind, thus creating Black female heads of families. Henry Bibb, in a letter to his former owner, attributed his flight from home and family to his treatment.

> To be compelled to stand by and see you whip and slash my wife without mercy when I could afford her no protection, not even by offering myself to suffer the lash in her place, was more than I felt it to be the duty of a slave husband to endure, while the way was open to Canada. (Blassingame, p. 49)

His wife and children undoubtedly continued to endure the whip and hard work without him.

George Pleasant, a hard-working father and husband wrote, "If I live to see Nexct [sic] year I shall have my own time from master by giving him 100 and twenty dollars a year . . . I hope with gods [sic] helpe [sic] that I may be abble [sic] to rejoys [sic] with you on the earth" (Blassingame, p. 19). Fathers and husbands worked to purchase themselves from their masters and then to redeem their wives and children from the same servitude. Because they were legally prevented from remaining in slave-holding areas, such free husbands and fathers were separated from their wives and children for long periods of time. They often tried to raise the money with the help of northern abolitionists, though sometimes women and children were separated and sold before the money could be raised.

Black women sadly remained separated from the men they loved. One such wife writes, "I have no news to write you, only the children are all well. I want to see you very much, but am looking forward to the promest [sic] time of your coming. Oh, Dear Dangerfield, com [sic] this fall without fail, mony [sic] or no mony [sic]. I want to see you so much" (Blassingame, p. 117). Many single mothers never saw their husbands and mates again, though they frequently sought to find them after slavery ended. Other Black single mothers were widows such as Phoebe on the Good Hope plantation who "was still living with five of her nine children. Jack had been the father of the first four; Tom the father of the rest" (Gutman, p. 47).

By the eve of the emancipation, the slave community had become a powerful and distinct social construction which had persevered and protected the slave. The slave community, perhaps begun with the sexual exploitation of a single young slave woman, was often a network of blood and fictive kin which supported resistance to the slave system.

Ironically, Black single mothers, as unprotected "non-women" who lived alone, became human beings in their own right and were thus "annulled as woman, that is, as woman in her historical stance of wardship under the entire male hierarchy" (Davis, 1981, p. 7). Black slave women could "freely" participate with other members of the community in resisting slavery. They could attempt to protect their own children, a role usually reserved solely for the patriarch. For instance, Moses Grandy, an ex-slave, remembered his mother hiding his brothers and sisters in the woods to save them from being sold and fighting back when her young child was about to be sold (Frazier, 1939, p. 42). When slavery ended, Black mothers who were unmarried, widowed or separated from their mates had become a distinct family which complimented and often fostered two-parent households. These families and extended families in turn made it possible for Black single-mother families to survive. Help with childcare and childbearing, emotional support for lonely women, sharing of food and shelter, as well as protection from torture and hard work characterized the mutual support which had developed in slave communities.

These communities persisted in spite of the legal and economic contours of slavery and national politics. The expansion and shift of the slave economy from the upper to the lower South during the early nineteenth century forcibly separated slave families over long and unsurmountable distances.

> About one in ten (slave) men and women born between 1835 and 1845 had experienced a forcible separation by 1864, a percentage sufficiently high to indicate that in the pre-Civil War decades the peculiar institution retained its grimmest quality, the breakup of marriages and the damage thereby inflicted on husbands and wives, parents and children. (Gutman, p. 146)

Black single-mother families made it possible for slaves to spread family and kinship cultural values in the same way as two-parent families. New fictive kinship relationships among slaves on plantations far from their families of origin helped slaves survive the trauma of separation. Afro-American culture was also spread by slaves who moved into the lower South, thus fostering creation of Blacks as a homogeneous people, not merely diffused slave groupings.

During slavery, the slave and the slave master were in constant struggle: the slave master attempted to restrict the slave, while slaves pressed to expand their rights and opportunities for a free life, which especially included the right to a family within their own communities. They struggled for marriage and families in spite of the pronouncements of a North Carolina Supreme Court Justice, who, writing in 1853, expressed a common opinion:

> Our law requires no solemnity or form in regard to the marriage of slaves, and whether they "take up" with each other by express permission of their owner, or from a mere impulse of nature, in obedience to the command "multiply and replenish the earth" cannot, in the contemplation of the law, make any sort of difference. (Gutman, p. 146)

Justice Taney's decision in the Dred Scott case was more to the point and reiterated the social death of slaves, regardless of their efforts to resist:

We think they are not, and that they are not included, and were not intended to be included, under the word "citizens" in the Constitution, and can, therefore, claim none of the rights and privileges which that instrument provides for and secures to citizens of the United States. . . . [T]hat neither the class of persons who had been imported as slaves, nor their descendants, whether they had become free or not, were then acknowledged as part of the people. (Commager, 1958, pp. 340–41)

BLACK FAMILIES AFTER SLAVERY: THE LAND AND LOVE UNREALIZED

Slaves fought against the law and the economics of slavery, and included themselves as "people" and "citizens." They worked with abolitionists and free brethren and sisters to topple the slave system. Neither war, amendments nor proclamations alone ended slavery. The political mobilizations of abolitionists, the campaigns of Harriet Tubman, John Brown, and other conductors on the underground railroad, the changing national economy, and Black labor's withdrawal from the southern plantations during the war combined to end slavery. The slave family and community which sustained and nurtured the slaves and their progeny helped to prepare the slave for freedom.

After slavery ended, large numbers of the newly-freed people legalized long-term slave unions by marrying. They desired to legalize their families and begin a new self- and community-defined legitimacy. The dislocation and devastation of the war and continued attacks by former masters caused the ex-slaves hardship, but they persevered in creating self-sustaining farm communities based on the labor of family and kin. The slaves hoped Black women would at last be able to care for their husbands and children without having to work outside their own homes and farms.

Many women did settle into marriages in which men headed their families and households, upholding both African and American patriarchal values about monogamy, sexual modesty, and divisions of labor based on gender. However, there were significant numbers of Black female-headed households and Black single mothers. Young Black single mothers remained within the households of their parents, and female-headed households tended to belong to widows or older women who had been separated from their husbands and spouses for long periods.

Values about the negative aspects of childbearing outside marriage were in part fostered by the churches and schools established in Black communities. Many ex-slaves wanted to put the horror of sexual abuse against slave women behind them and establish families headed by married couples. Harry McMillan, a former slave said, "They are thought low of by their companions unless they get a husband before the child is born and if they cannot the shame grows until they do get a husband" (Gutman, pp. 444–45). Conversely, the journalist Nordhoff said, "It was held no shame for a girl to bear a child under any circumstances" (Gutman, p. 66). Special words described the status of children born prior to or outside of settled unions, namely "stolen" or "outside" children.

Outright promiscuity was condemned in all Black communities, even though prenuptial intercourse, teenage marriage and pregnancy continued in most. When children were conceived outside of common-law or legal marriages, the mothers and children were stigmatized but rarely ostracized or banished. Women could overcome stigmatization by becoming faithful Christians and church-goers, and faithful and hard working wives. Thus, social stigma against "illegitimacy" coexisted with the social reality of Black single mothers and their families.

Internal community concerns over values and morals as they pertained to single mothers were overshadowed, however, by the political and economic realities of late nineteenth-century Black southern life. The promise of Black enfranchisement, economic self-sufficiency and social equality were eroded by pogroms, lynchings and racial violence. These horrors affected many of the very Black men who strove to build their family life on the economic base of private farm ownership. Prosperous, even modest, black farmers became dangerous Black men in the eyes of the white power structure, especially, though not exclusively, in the Black-belt South.

The migrants to Kansas who left the south to improve and protect themselves from pogrom often left in family groups. When ex-slaves did not, Black single-mother families were created: "I have no family along with me; I have a wife and two children down south; I brought my parents with me" (Gutman, 1976, p. 434). James Brown, on the other hand, brought his wife, three orphans, his mother-in-law and five of her six children with him. She had no husband (Gutman, 1976, p. 435). Women whose husbands were lynched or run out by night riders had to rely upon themselves and kin to help support their families in the rural southern Black communities. A letter from Joseph Starks asking the Kansas governor for advice about migration provides a glimpse of those troubled times for Black men and women alike.

> We want to come out, and have no money hardly. We have to be in secret or be shot, and [are] not allowed to meet. . . . We have about fifty widows in our band that are workmen and farmers also. The white men

here take our wives and daughters and do [with] them as they please, and we are shot if we say anything about. . . . We are sure to have to leave or be killed. (Gutman, 1976, p. 437)

By the 1880s, "[w]omen at least forty years old headed a large percentage of father-absent households and subfamilies; many of these had been conventional two-parent households in which the husband had died." (Gutman, 1976, pp. 444, 489) (or perhaps had been killed or run out of town). Gutman studied four urban and four rural areas and found that 28% of the households and subfamilies in urban areas were headed by women, and, in rural areas, 16% were headed by women. Single women and mothers often moved to urban areas in search of wage-earning work to sustain themselves and their families.

Furthermore, as Black families continued to slip more and more into the mire of peonage and poverty all family members were needed to work for wages or shares. Economic pressures prevailed over marital custom. In order for families to survive most Black women went back to work in the fields and kitchens of white men under slave-like, economically and sexually exploitative conditions. But the ideology and hope of the Black patriarchy remained, assisted by Calvinistic religious principles spread by Black churches, Black schools and the emerging Black ruling elite. Many extolled the virtues of marital rather than common-law unions, monogamous rather than serial monogamous relationships, and childbearing after marriage rather than birth outside of marriage. Those who abided by the virtues of monogamous marriage were accorded status and respect. Men who worked to take care of their families and women who were loyal to their men were regarded as the ideal and preferred family. As long as the options for Black women were only patriarchal marriage or severe economic struggle alone, women as well as men strove for the ideal of monogamous marriage, in spite of the forces which hampered them from obtaining it.

The cheap dependable labor of Black women as domestics and busy-season farm hands also motivated local white politicians, police and merchants to prevent, in some cases by statute, Black women from staying home to work on their family farms. Thus, soon after the end of the Civil War, whether married or single, Black women had become wage-earning workers to support the depressed wages of Black men. Black girls were socialized to become mothers, wives, and workers, often workers first. By the early twentieth century it became evident that rigid sex role divisions would never be realized for large numbers of Black families. Black family members were constantly called upon to adjust and shift to forces stronger than their will, desire, culture, and ideology. Family breakups were not merely the mark of chattel slavery, they were the mark of wage slavery and peonage as well.

Black people had become quite adept at making their families and households into havens from oppression. However, they were often havens where male dominance and power relationships also prevailed. Black women were the "slave of a slave" within their marriages. Poor Black men, though oppressed and dominated themselves and dependent upon their women's wages, could also be abusive and brutal toward their wives and children. Black women often looked the other way while their men fathered children by other women. Undoubtedly some Black women also suppressed their own lesbian desires and ignored their husband's homosexual relationships. Abortions, viewed as un-Christian and sinful, were nevertheless performed "underground." Women were often vague about the fathers, birthdates and relationships of some children in the family. Young Black women working in the cities sent many of their "outside children" back home to the rural South or Caribbean to be raised by their kin.

The period of legal segregation lasted nearly a century, from the 1896 "separate but equal" decision of Plessy v. Ferguson until the 1954 decision in Brown v. The Board of Education, which overturned the 1896 doctrine. During that time, Black people suffered the quasi-free status of all manumitted slaves. Though not designed to include people of color and white women, the American commitment to legal democracy became a powerful weapon in the struggle to end racial segregation in the United States. But this commitment was offset by American color prejudice and racism. Both the commitment and the aversion amplified the movement and the struggles of Black people.

The racism, peonage and pogrom in the South caused Black people to move into urban areas so that by mid-century the majority of Black people had become urban dwellers. The exodus had become even more poignant because of the low status and wages of Black workers. Black women merely exchanged southern for northern domestic servitude, with some increase in wages and some personal mobility. Black men moved from rural farm work and menial labor to northern menial labor and the lowest level of industrialized work, lower than white women or immigrants, both in terms of wages and job security.

The movement of Blacks into urban areas was accompanied by more than poverty and lower caste status, however; a Black cultural renaissance, the strengthening of Black education and religious institutions and the expression of profound political and ideological concerns also emerged. The century began with white social scientists questioning Blacks' humanity; twenty years later whites were dancing to Black music, reading books by Black authors and slowly developing a personal and cultural fascination with Black individuals and expressions, while still maintaining a racist society and protecting white interests.

By the 1920s questions about class solidarity were raised by Black workers in every sector of workers' organizations, from the work place to the unions to the Communist Party. Marcus Garvey assembled the largest group of Blacks ever in one organization to preach Black pride, self-development and racial separation. Meanwhile, other Black leaders, such as A. Philip Randolph and W. E. B. Du Bois, continued to press for civil rights, in spite of lynching and coon shows or class and nationalist movements. But the protests and the writings, and the emergence of a distinct Black culture and sense of peoplehood, often masked the underlying similarities in values, especially family values, shared by most Blacks and whites. Puritanical values about sexuality were backed by references to the Bible. Regular church attendance was an integral part of the Black as well as white experience. Certainly both Blacks and whites at least professed the same basic Protestant religious and spiritual value system, and though Black theologians assert a more liberatory tradition, this difference does not negate the common religious heritage and roots shared by the two groups.

Similarly, Black people lived in family groupings, fell in love, married, and raised children. In fact, Black people extended their family concerns for the future of their own children into an intensive and extensive social movement for welfare, education and other health benefits for children. Both the white and Black communities adhered to rather strict notions of proper sexual conduct. Prostitution in the Black community was confined to areas, or "houses." Young people were warned against associating with "those" women and listening to their music (jazz, blues), though daring men and women frequently did. Also, customers of prostitutes were frequently white men as well as black men. Homosexuality was taboo and not viewed as a valued social practice in the Black community, though gay men and lesbians were treated individually and often viewed with pity and sympathy, rather than hatred.

But single-motherhood occupied a different place in the Black community than in the white community. It seems that unless they were widowed, white single mothers were viewed as prostitutes and were brutally ostracized. But Black single mothers, if they worked hard to provide for their families, were generally accepted into working class communities everywhere, though less accepted in Black middle-class communities.

Analyses of the Black family, generally reflecting both Black patriarchal and white racial standards, have been common in the twentieth century. Nearly all studies and discussions have focused on the Black family's economic survival and cultural mechanisms. Most have failed to discuss the sexist position and oppression of women within the family and community as powerful rationales for marital breakup. Nor have they included the strengths and choices of Black women as actors in creating and sustaining Black single-mother families.

SOCIAL MOVEMENTS AND NEW RACISM

During the segregation period, most Black families did adapt to the norm of two-parent married families with strong male heads but were still neither equal to whites nor free from oppression. In fact all Black family members regardless of family type were attempting to survive the continued terror and subjugation of apartheid in the South and the vicious "ghettoization of Black life" in the North. During the years immediately after World War II, the dismantling of segregation was uppermost in the minds of Black family and community members, especially those who wanted a better life for Black children. Few stopped to demand that those children come only from two-parent homes.

The movement for civil rights was an all-embracing Black community effort to change the practices of society that had long denied Black people equal access and opportunity. Its original goals were to end legal segregation, provide movement and access to public facilities regardless of race, and promote integrated schools and equal employment. The goals were moderate and fell within the existing parameters of the legal system.

The influences of the civil rights movement quickly spread to many other aspects of the society. White women who had participated in the movement unearthed their own history of protest and current personal grievances. This reaction created second wave feminism and a women's movement which attacked women's oppression within the patriarchal family as well as second class citizenry within the large society. The women's movement pushed for flexible gender roles, shared power relationships and respect for diverse families (Evans, 1979). Feminists further pointed out that the traditional white nuclear family, the standard against which Black families were being measured, was not an ideal to be emulated because a woman's place within that idealized family was one of an abused and dominated appendage to her husband and his property.

Both the civil rights and women's movements demanded jobs to accompany social equality as the economy was simultaneously being transformed from an industrial to a service employment base. The service-based economy increased the employment of women within this economy. By 1970, for the first time in 250 years of wage work, Black women were no longer employed predominantly as domestic workers or farm laborers. Thirty-two percent were employed as white collar workers and 21% were working in sales and clerical jobs. These social and economic changes accelerated Black women's "de-mammification". "De-mammification" was also accompanied by changes in Black men's and women's consciousness, perceptions and feelings, as Black women moved from the mammy role in private households into clerical and secretarial roles in public corporations and bureaucracies. For many women the consistent meager wage gave them the wherewithal they needed to dissolve unwanted marriages and relationships. Black single-motherhood during the post-segregation era made a radical shift: Black women no longer considered themselves primarily tied to their legal or common law husbands.

The social movements of the 1960s and the "de-mammification" of Black women changed the personal, familial and societal norms, but it did not transform the economy or the political power in the nation. By the 1970s, another social movement gained momentum. Predominately white male, middle class and middle American, it embraced and promoted the traditional values of Puritanism, patriarchy and racial purity of the founding fathers and pushed American nationalism to new heights of militarism and chauvinism. The conservative movement equated the American way of life with two-parent, hard-working Christian families. By the election of President Ronald Reagan in 1980, it had gained national authority.

The conservative social movement exacerbated the new racism of the desegregation era. The Black community, which had become a visible stimulus for interpreting social problems and promoting public policies to meet them, became less and less powerful. The civil rights movement had effectively responded to and ended the racism of segregation, lynch mobs and overt hatred. But the new racism was more systematic, subtle and rational. In fact, charges of racism were viewed as inaccurate and obsolete. The proponents of the new racism saw economics and motivation, and not color or culture, as the principal reasons for Black inequity. "They don't want to work" was the response to charges of racial discrimination and lack of jobs. "No more handouts" was the answer to demands for increased government spending to help the oppressed. "They have themselves to blame" was the reply to demands for government actions on homelessness and destitution. (For one of the best recent examples of these policy ideas see Murray, 1984.)

Under the new racism, ideology replaced sociology and rhetoric replaced attention to economic reality in examining Black people's condition and position. Black single mothers, especially poor teenagers, had become the symbol of all that was wrong with Black people and women and their movements.

CONCLUSION

Poverty is the contemporary form of continuing the social death of Black people that has always been the design of a racist society. To be Black and poor is the current version of being Black and a slave. But being poor, stripped of all its ideological and moralistic veneer, only means that one does not have the resources to meet one's needs. Just as slavery was not a system that could make human beings chattel, poverty is not a condition which makes the poor inhuman.

Current social policy perpetuates the deliberate creation of a strata of people—Black men, women and children—who live outside the society of men and women who decide things, allocate resources, make laws, communicate with God, write histories of the past and make plans for the future. The new racism promotes the fabrication of an underclass (or is it a permanent caste system) that masks the displacement of the Black working class, of those denied economic enfranchisement within the society.

In the long history of Black people in this land, we have tried everything: marches, petitions, speeches, nonviolent and violent campaigns. Still social death separates us from the power and wealth we deserve. We might have to try all those things and more, for we remain at the mercy of those who want us to have neither power nor wealth. We've gone around to come around, back to the beginning, where all we have to fall back on are the men and women who love us and nurture and protect us: our families.

3
LAY DOWN THIS WORLD

"De nigger woman is de mule uh de world so fur as Ah can see."
—Zora Neale Hurston, *Their Eyes Were Watching God*

She was pushed into the new world. She was destroyed and created. She was wrenched from the old world. She was murdered and birthed. She was one and she was many. She was a wheel in the middle of a wheel. She was chained and coffled. She was led. She was raped. She lived in a box on a ship—a concentration camp named Jesus, named Justice, named Integrity. The box contained her dreams. It contained her blood. It contained her body. She was raped by cockney sailors. She lived the holocaust for four hundred years before the holocaust. She survived the holocaust. She was pushed into the new world. She was a warrior. Her weapons were her body, her mind, her visions, her dreams. Her head was creased by a two pound weight thrown at an escaping slave. She too escaped. She bared her breast to the world demanding they redefine womanhood to include her. She would mother all the children: the children of the white man, the children of the black man, the children of the red man. She would slash her children's throat in order to free them. She would murder her master. She poisoned her mistress. She burned their house. She was forced to build the world that enslaved her children. She would create the world that would free her children. She would create us her daughters and we would become wheels in the middle of wheels.

She worked. She was a mule.

I

Whether slave or free, Black women became synonymous with the toil of a beast of burden. As the nation evolved from colonial to agrarian/plantation to industrial to post-industrial societies, Black people moved from chattel slavery to segregation to "post-segregation's" segregation. The Black woman meanwhile moved from being African woman to "mule" to "mammy" to de-mammified worker only to become "colonized professional" and mammified in new ways. For the nearly four hundred years of her presence in the new world, the Black woman's work has been that of a domestic laborer. She has cleaned, cooked, and nursed, as both paid and unpaid worker, in the homes of white families. She has also created a domestic sector of households and communities in the Black community for herself and her people. Until the mid-twentieth century, farm labor was likely to accompany her paid and unpaid domestic work. The Black woman taught school, fought the Klan, wrote poetry, created stage shows, started businesses, but it was her face slapped on a pancake box as an always serving Aunt Jemima which became the enduring emblem of her laboring life.

At the end of the Civil War, Black men and women made valiant efforts to stabilize their families through traditional marital arrangements, with women and children remaining at home, working, on family farms. "Upon emancipation anywhere from one third to one half of African American women refused to work for the planters." (Amott and Matthaei, 159)

> For their part southern leaders could not reconcile themselves to the fact of emancipation; they believed that "free black labor" was a contradiction in terms, that blacks would never work of their own free will. An unpredictable labor situation therefore required any and all measures that would bind the freed people body and soul to the southern soil. (Jones, 45)

It was widely recognized that Black women's labor was integral to the predictable laboring needs of the planters of the agrarian South. However, the determination of the newly freed Black families to create independent and viable farms was often defeated by the depressed earnings available to them. Pogrom and mass murder caused Black men to lose the vote. With neither political nor military protection, Black people could not stave off economic exploitation. Poverty forced Black women to return to the fields and kitchens of the white man. "In southern cities at the turn of the century, Black women made up 90 percent of servants. Their wages were so

low that all but the poorest white families could afford some sort of help."
(Amott and Matthaei, 161)

In 1912, an anonymous "colored nurse in the south" described her
work:

> ... I frequently work from fourteen to sixteen hours a day. I am com-
> pelled ... to sleep in the house. I am allowed to go home to my chil-
> dren, the oldest of whom is a girl of 18 years, only once in two weeks,
> every other Sunday afternoon even then I'm not permitted to stay all
> night. I not only have to nurse a little white child, now eleven months
> old, but I have to act as a playmate ... to three other children in the
> home ... So it is not strange to see "Mammy" watering the lawn in
> front with the garden hose, sweeping the sidewalk, mopping the porch
> and halls, dusting around the house, helping the cook, or darning the
> stockings ... You might as well say that I'm on duty all the time—from
> sunrise to sunrise, every day of the week. I am the slave, body and soul,
> of this family. And what do I get for this work ... The pitiful sum of ten
> dollars a month! ... (Lerner, 227)

Her salary was not unusual. "Because they had virtually no other
employment opportunities, these women had to accept the most meager
wages—$4.00 to $8.00 per month for cooks and maids, $1.50 to $3.00 for
nurses (often girls who were children themselves)." (Jones, 128) But it
wasn't only the low wages and grueling nature of domestic work which
reminded Black women of slavery. The humiliation and the status of the
work connected it to their horrific past. Domestic work, racial violence,
peonage, and limited educational opportunity caused continued slavelike
social relations between blacks and whites, in spite of the efforts of Black
men and women to "uplift the race." Black school teachers, maids, and
farm laborers shared the same vision of the power of education to expand
opportunities for Black children. Supported in their efforts by Black men,
poor Black women, with great sacrifice and struggle, sent their children to
the schools and institutions founded by better-educated and more "middle-class" women. Black children were needed by the family as wage earners or unpaid farm and household workers. However, their mothers often
performed their chores in order for them to attend school. Poor women
also took in extra laundry and sold pies to help pay the salaries of the
teachers. Many rural schools were located in churches that poor Black
women had also helped build. "A 1904 article noted that African American women had raised $14 million for the education of Black children and
educated over 25,000 Black teachers." (Amott and Matthaei, 163)

Unlike many white immigrants, Black women often worked in order to spare their children exploitation in the labor force. In her study of the experiences of working wives between 1896 and 1911, Elizabeth Pleck noted that "in nearly all American cities in 1900, the rate of employment for black married women was anywhere from four to fifteen times higher than for immigrant wives." (Pleck, 490) Yet Black children were more likely to attend school than Italian immigrant youngsters who were expected to work. "If a black mother chose to keep her older children in school rather than sending them to work, she may have been compelled to earn the extra income for her family." (Pleck, 499).

Black people began to migrate north in large numbers in order to attain greater economic opportunity and a better social environment. Between 1910 and 1930, 1.2 million Black workers migrated north in families or as individuals. (Amott and Matthaei, 164) Nearly all of these migrating women became domestic servants.

World War I increased employment opportunities for Black women migrants as "unskilled laborers in the tobacco industry, garment trades, paper-box factories, munitions factories, meat packing plants, and tanneries in such cities as Philadelphia and Chicago . . ." However, these jobs were the most marginal with the least pay and were available to Black women only where labor shortages were most acute. Not surprisingly, many women were forced back to domestic work as soon as the war was over and industrial employers no longer needed them.

Interestingly, the rate and numbers of northern migrants so alarmed southern officials that they attempted to use the 1918 US Army "work or fight" rule to force black women to work as domestics in the homes of white families. Walter White of the NAACP reported several incidents where Black women who stayed home because their husbands' earnings were adequate were designated as "unemployed" and fined for not working. Black women who demanded better wages and working conditions were often fired and then faced with arrest and fines for not working! The Birmingham Municipal employment agency "issued an order stating that all Negro [sic] women . . . must either go to work or go to jail." (White, 726–727) But these efforts did not prevent the northern movement of Black female labor, nor its removal from the work force.

"Thousands of young Black women migrated North to work as domestic servants. Many were recruited by employment agencies, such as the Dixie Maid Service, which promised a bus ticket and a job for a fee, but often failed to deliver on the promise." (Amott and Matthaei, 168)

However, most often family members living in the north arranged for southern kin to come north to work for white families. Women sent for younger southern kin to help with their children while they worked as sleep-in or day laborers.

During the nineteenth century, private household work was the main wage earning work of most, especially new immigrant, women. "In 1870, one-half of all women wage earners in the United States had been domestic servants." (Katzman, 53)

> Nearly all white women then, worked until they were married, and gainful employment represented a stage in their life before marriage. Work was but a temporary station between adolescence or early adulthood and an independent family role as wife and mother. Nearly half of all black women, however, could expect to work most of their adult life. The proportion of black women gainfully employed did not drop significantly with age until after sixty five. In 1900 and 1920, more than 40 percent of all black women regardless of age worked. (Katzman, 81–82)

Black males' wages, unlike those of white males, were simply not consistent or high enough to fully support women and children. Racist practices kept Black males marginally employed. Continuing income patterns from the agrarian South, Black families in the North needed Black female wages to supplement Black male income in order to survive. In his 1899 survey of the Black community in Philadelphia, Du Bois concluded that "the low wages of men make it necessary for mothers to work." In 1911, Mary White Ovington observed that in New York, the Black woman "often begins 'self-sustaining work' at the age of fifteen and remains in the labor force after marriage because of her husband's inability to support his family (save in extreme penury) on his wages alone." As a result "between 1900 and 1930 the share of Black women employed in domestic service increased from 44 to 54 percent." (Amott and Matthaei: 168) In 1922, Elizabeth Ross Haynes described the continuation of slave-like conditions of domestic service in the north:

> To-day they are found in domestic service, nearly a million strong . . . with all the shortcomings of ordinary domestic service; namely, basement living quarters, poor working conditions, too long hours, no Sundays off, no standards of efficiency, and the servant brand . . . (Lerner, 256)

Paid domestic work assumed that a stigmatized group of women would provide privileged women with an "extra pair of hands around the house." It was ". . . where a girl [sic], usually a mature woman most often Black— (was) hired to come into a private home to do the most physically demanding chores in an isolated environment, under complete subordination by the employer, for low hourly wages." (Katzman, 382) Domestic work meant that Black women entered into highly personalized relationships, usually with a white woman mistress of the household as her direct supervisor. There was no standardization or objective criteria for work which required compliance with the personal tastes and whims of the master or mistress of the house. Black female household workers had to fit into the "family" in order to make a living in the highly emotionally charged—private—sphere of the white home. They were expected to rear children, cook meals, clean house, and fulfill their employers' ideas about household care and maintenance as if they were her own. Under this personalized dynamic, Black women were often expected to put aside their own families and obligations to work late hours, weekends, and holidays for the white families.

Knowing they had no legal or social recourse, white families could pay Black women less than white immigrant women servants. When they didn't want to pay in wages, white employers substituted food pans and used clothes.

Servitude reduced and diminished Black women and their labor to an invisible but essential presence in the white home, while preserving white racial and class superiority. Uniforms, formal greetings, continual availability, and other rituals of submission went along with caring for the bodily needs of the master and his family. Black women washed toilets, made beds, polished silver, washed clothes, scrubbed floors and, in general, maintained the daily care necessary for a household to work. Many diapered, nursed, and played with white children, providing vital nurturing while the children's fathers ruled over the public sphere, a sphere from which Black people were, ironically, excluded.

However, Black domestic labor was essential for the smooth and orderly maintenance of the white man's private sphere. Black women maintained continuity and structure for the white families they cared for and their work propped up the developing white middle classes in urban areas. White women furthered their education, careers, and community work outside the home, knowing that poorly paid Black women would be available to do the demeaning and dirty household work and to serve as substitute mothers for their children.

Although domestic work was assumed natural to Black women, many were trained for the domestic sciences in Black- run southern institutes and schools. There was indeed more than instinct to efficiently balancing the chores and tasks of the family, maintaining a pleasant but firm demeanor, and negotiating fair payment, while fending off the sexual advances of the master of the household.

Sexual harassment reinforced the demeaning character of the work. White men assumed, stereotypically, that Black women who were available for domestic work were also available to meet their employer's sexual needs. The sexual aspects of the work were a major reason married women preferred day work and Black families tried to keep their daughters educated, and away from service altogether.

> This man picked me up and said his wife was ill and then when I got there his wife wasn't there and he wanted to have an affair. It seems like I just had enough sense not to let myself get involved with anything like that and I started crying and he didn't force me and I was able to get out. When maids would get together, they'd talk of it. Some of them was very attractive and good-looking. They always had to fight off the woman's husband. (Lerner, 275)

Each Black woman had to negotiate the conditions of her work, establishing which duties she would and would not perform. Many resisted payment of their wages in food and used clothing, while others successfully fought off the sexual advances of male employers and openly objected to the hostility and insults of both male and female employers. In fact, moves away from sleep-in domestic work to day work represented efforts by Black women workers to contain the white family's demands on their time and labor while also earning a wage.

In spite of the severe limitations of organizing household servants into a collective bargaining unit, efforts were made to unionize Black maids.

> In 1920, there were ten locals of domestic workers in Southern cities affiliated with the Hotel and Restaurant Employees Union, AFL. In 1936, a Domestic Workers' Union started by seven women in Washington, D.C. had over a hundred members one year later and had succeeded in raising the prevailing wage from $3 to $10 a week ... The most ambitious organizing effort was that headed by Dora Jones, the black executive secretary of the Domestic Workers' Union, which was founded in 1934 and was affiliated with the Building Service Union, Local 149, in New York City. Five years later the organization had 350 members, 75 percent of them black women. (Lerner, 231–232)

The success of the domestics' efforts to organize relied upon individuals negotiating with their employers for contracts with duties, wages, and conditions specifically listed. Vacation pay, sick leave, social security payments, and other benefits were eventually added to these contracts. In spite of the efforts by Black women to get decent wages and working conditions, paid domestic work continues to be stigmatized and low paying.

II

The Black woman domestic worked double shifts in two different worlds. She washed delicate and precious china in hot water in the white woman's kitchen. She cleaned the white woman's household with the latest appliances and products she couldn't afford or use in her own apartment. And later she returned home to wash her own dishes in cold water from broken pipes. While her own children were needy and neglected, she cared for the white woman's children in the midst of comfort and security. She saw what the white man did for his family and what her husband was prevented from doing for his.

She watched and compared. She hoped and she planned. She decorated her apartment with the white woman's left-overs. She remade hand-me-down dresses into the latest styles. She saved for her own china dishes and fur coats. She sacrificed and doted, determined to give her children what the white children had. She stretched her meager wages with catering, sewing, rent parties, and lodgers.

During slavery Black women were instrumental in developing a domestic sphere for themselves and their families. Insisting on solidarity with Black men, they maintained kinship ties by caring for all slave children as their own, and treating fellow slaves as sisters and brothers. This helped them all "bear up under the lash." Through songs, prayers, and stories they fostered a culture reflecting African perspectives.

In the years after slavery, Black women continued kinship work which included food preparation, making clothes, furnishing and cleaning households, socializing children, healing, and caring for the elderly. Like most women, they were unpaid domestic workers in their own homes and communities. However, these homes were different, because they were havens where Black people could be treated humanely, away from the dehumanizing impact of white racism. The communities' elaborate kinship network of female relatives and friends and an almost partnership arrangement with Black men helped Black women provide maintenance and care to both white families and their own.

Black women also created community-based social networks and institutions in order to sustain their employment. "And in all the city ghettos, black women formed clubs for operating day nurseries, and kindergartens, for instructing and helping migrant mothers, and to train women in such skills as sewing in order to place them in jobs." The Colored Women's Conference of Chicago represented over half a dozen such clubs. (Henri, 128)

> . . . the Hope Day Nursery for Colored Children (was) founded in New York in 1902 by a group of Black mothers whose children were rejected by a white day nursery. (Henri, 126)

Another Black women's self-help effort was the development of the White Rose Industrial Association founded by Victoria Earle Matthews, a former slave. The Association "operated the White Rose Working Girls' Home, its purpose to 'check the evil unscrupulous employment agents who deceived the unsuspecting girls desiring to come North' . . . The White Rose Working Girls' Home tried to place them in decent jobs, and taught them domestic science and 'race history'." (Henri, 126) The "Matthews' organization became part of the New York League for the Protection of Colored Women" and grew into a national organization as a result of Frances Kellor's 1905 book, *Out of Work*, which highlighted the plight of Black female migrants. (Henri, 126)

These efforts were part of the larger role that all Black women played in organizing and systematizing community work to provide necessary social welfare services to Black people: care of the sick, dying, aged, and indigent.

Away from their white families, Black domestics joined other Black women and men in the myriad of Black political and social movements and organizations. Black women made the crucial link between the ideas of Black men and their implementation by funding and supporting their actions, programs, and deeds. Black maids were socialists and Marxists, Pan-Africanists and Garveyites, pacifists and supporters of anti-colonial struggles. While passing out leaflets and demonstrating against injustice, Black women dreamed of a return to Africa, armed struggle against white racists, and redistribution of the wealth.

Black women workers also gave crucial support to the Black church: raising money, organizing committees, and inspiring the clergy. However, in the north, religious life was as varied as it was uplifting. Domestics could follow Father Divine, Adam Clayton Powell, messianic Christians, Hebrewites, the Bahai, Muslims, or Akans.

In 1890, 65 percent of all Black women over fourteen years of age were illiterate, but by 1910 that number had decreased to 33 percent. (US Department of Commerce, Table 69, 92) By the time of the Harlem Renaissance, Black women were writing plays, poetry, novels, and history. Black women also became professional artists, building upon their folk arts of clothing making, crocheting, quilting, and cooking. Some also worked as musicians and singers.

Interestingly, nearly all artists, community workers, educators, and churchgoers were either directly connected to domestic work as former maids and servants or were supported by family members who were domestic workers. These layers of women's lives in the Black world, however, were kept hidden from white employers.

The Black maid resisted the entire system of segregation, rejecting the employer's attempts to demean and denigrate both her labor and her person. She didn't merely birth babies, she helped create educational institutions which shaped Black children into Black professionals. She raised her daughters to reject domestic life and become educated and self-determining women. She used her rage against the abuse at her job to encourage others to better the conditions of Black people. Unlike other visionaries who were mystical and prayerful about the future, Black domestics knew how to do the practical work, to organize collective resistance to segregation. Domestic workers were "the sturdy Black bridges which everyone crossed over" to create and maintain the infrastructure of the community.

When job opportunities for Black workers expanded during World War II, domestics were ready to leave private duty to work in the war industry. Jobs in defense plants were available, but racist attitudes of workers and bosses, as well as unions, denied them access. It was not easy; to get work, Black women first had to join Black men in demanding entry even into labor deficient industries.

In January 1941, A. Philip Randolph, the President of the Brotherhood of Sleeping Car Porters, called for Negroes [sic] to march on Washington, D.C., under the slogan "We loyal Negro-American citizens demand the right to work and to fight for our country." The March on Washington Movement was the first major Black protest movement since Garvey, and it "foreshadowed the civil rights struggle of the post war period." (Foner, 240) The march never materialized but organizers won an executive order from President Roosevelt banning "discrimination in the employment of workers in defense industries or government because of race, creed, color or national origin" and establishing of the Fair Employment Practices

Committee to "receive and investigate complaints of discrimination in violation of the order." (Franklin, 579)

While Black workers continued to move into industrial jobs after the war, the NAACP accelerated its legal assault against segregation. NAACP lawyers were successful in outlawing the white primary, removing curtain partitions separating Negro dining car patrons from whites, and expanding integrated educational opportunities for Black college students. During the 1940s a field secretary for the NAACP named Ella Jo Baker was organizing voter registration and community campaigns for street lights and paved roads in the deep South.

The paths of labor and legal resistance would converge in 1955 in Montgomery, Alabama when E. D. Nixon (a Pullman porter with the Brotherhood of Sleeping Car Porters) and Rosa Parks (an officer with the NAACP) along with teachers, veterans, and domestics, organized and sustained the Montgomery Bus Boycott, propelling Dr. Martin Luther King Jr. into national prominence and the country into a ten-year civil rights movement. The most dependable supporters of every movement campaign—sit-ins, freedom rides, and voter registration drives—were Black domestic and farm workers and their college-educated children.

Black women benefited from this movement in which they had played such a leading role. When the public sector expanded its clerical and service ranks and large corporations expanded their clerical base during the 1960s, Black women workers were ready to take advantage of the opportunities which had been made available by the Civil Rights Movement.

> In 1940, 70 percent of the black females in the nation worked in service occupations, mainly private households . . . As the migration of black women from the rural South flourished during the World War II period, the private household function was gradually supplanted by movement into lower-paying service and blue collar jobs . . . Black female workers in the service occupations became cooks and waitresses, and by the late 1950's, they were the foundation of the health care system. (Stafford, 40, 41)
>
> Between 1950 and 1970, Black female clerical employment grew by over half a million, increasing the share of Black women workers in these jobs from 5 percent to 21 percent. Professional employment almost doubled, to comprise over 11 percent of Black women's jobs in 1970 . . . by 1979, almost one-third of employed Black women worked for the federal, state, or local government . . . (by 1970) factories employed 19 percent of African American women workers. With these

new opportunities, African American women finally were able to leave the homes and kitchens of white women, and the share of Black women in private household work fell to 18 percent in 1970 and 5 percent in 1980. (Amott and Matthaei, 179)

As a result of a complex weaving of Black struggle to end segregation, an expanding service sector, and the determination of Black working women to move, the 1960 census would indicate that for the first time in American history, Black women were no longer primarily employed as domestic workers in the private households of white families. Black women became demammified.

III

She would learn to work nine to five and the night shift. She would paint her nails. She would speak the white man's tongue. She would straighten her hair. She would cover her breasts with brassieres. She would learn to manage the white man's offices. She continued to maintain his world.

In return, she placed her children in his school and let him enslave her children's minds. She would not remember her mother, her daughter would not be hers. She would disown her man.

She would live confined to a box. Whether too black or too white. She would hate her body. She was too large. Her hair was not straight enough. Her clothes didn't fit like the media images she gloated over.

She would hate men, but need men and not need men and want men. She was a slave to her husband. She was a slave without a husband.

She grew mad. She grew sad. In her rage she grew tumors in her womb and in her breast. She would end her life.

She was a wheel in the middle of a wheel. She spun wheels to earn wages. She was a slave with an education. She was a slave with a job. She was a slave with a welfare check. She was a slave with a car.

She didn't matter to herself, she was half empty and half full.

During the last thirty years, Black women workers have made a radical and remarkable transition from "mammy work"— to public sector service, clerical, administrative, and professional employment, yet "there are increasing efforts to resurrect the Black Mammy in today's ambitious Black women who aspire to move up the socioeconomic ladder or into political arenas." (Dumas, 206) Sokoloff uses the image of the half-full and half-empty glass to describe the advances and limitations, and the expansions and restrictions of Black and white women in the professions. Higgenbotham describes Black professional men and women as "colonized" because their employment depends upon the dependent relationship of the Black poor to public institutions which are supposed to serve their needs for education, healthcare, and government services. (Sokoloff, 123)

Irrespective of setting and job title, the mammy legacy continues to weave itself into the lives of nearly all Black women workers. Not surprisingly, Black women themselves have created "habits of survival" (Scott) in the contemporary workplace which were learned from nearly two centuries of domestic servitude for white families.

> Significantly the proverbial "mammy" cares for all the needs of others, particularly the most powerful. Her work is characterized by selfless service. Despite the fact that most households in the United States do not have Black maids or nannies working in them, racist and sexist assumptions that Black women are somehow "innately" more capable of caring for others continues to permeate cultural thinking about Black female roles. As a consequence, Black women in all walks of life, from corporate professionals and university professors to service workers, complain that colleagues, co-workers, supervisors, etc. ask them to assume multi-purpose caretaker roles, be their guidance counselors, nannies, therapists, priests; i.e., to be that all nurturing "breast"—to be the mammy. (hooks, 154)

Breaking with the private and isolated mode of domestic service which had previously characterized the work, since the 1970s the majority of Black women have become socialized labor in the classical sense, sharing common experiences with other workers in productive and service employment. Civil service competitive examinations and general education requirements helped to rationalize and standardize Black women's labor force participation and attempted to blunt and mute racial and ethnic differences at the workplace. Many Black women workers enjoy the decent wages and health benefits of unionized public sector work. Unemployment compensation, union welfare funds, and even the availability of public assistance have also meant that private duty work is no longer needed by most Black working women as an option during layoffs. In some sectors, Black women's new social relationships with other workers and the work process have fostered collective action and union activity to beat back inequality on the job.

Racial, ethnic, and gender sparring and competition undermine employment equity. Black women still have to fight for wages, assignments, promotions, and raises on jobs which were supposed to use meritocratic standards to advance workers. Often, in no-win situations, the Black woman finds herself competing with Black men and white women for middle management and supervisory positions under white men. When she obtains these positions, her former competitors are often reluctant to give her the expected respect and support.

> "Roughly half of all women, Black as well as White, are clustered in a narrow range of low-paying 'pink collar' jobs: secretary, receptionist, salesperson, ticketing agent. The men who typically do the hiring still consider looking good a prerequisite for such jobs." (Russell, Wilson, and Hall, 132)

As a result of their entry into public and socialized employment, Black women have had to undergo an employment "make over." Maids were required to wear uniforms and old clothes which reinforced their invisibility and the servant brand, but an essential expectation of office workers is that they "dress up." Because appearance has become such an integral aspect of the workplace experience, Black women have undergone significant psychological and cultural changes.

In spite of their low wages, Black women must expend time and money meeting the "hairstyle" and dress requirements of their jobs. Some companies and employers do not allow short naturals, cornrows, African wraps, or other non-straightened hair styles. Others base assignments and promotions on whether women have the appropriate "corporate image."

Southern patois, Black English, and slang are unacceptable in today's workplace. Standard English and mainstream cultural knowledge are employment requirements, not the liability they often posed for domestics workers who had to mute and hide their education and communication skills in a workplace which demanded servility. However, Black women at today's work sites have had to learn to switch instantaneously from informal to formal speech in conversations with the many different levels of workers and clients.

Harassment and prejudices based upon color differences further complicate the work experience of Black women. Associating incompetence and ignorance with dark skin, employers often prefer light-skinned women, especially in front office jobs. Dark-skinned women have had to "pay close attention to their wardrobes, their manners, and particularly their language" in order to succeed at work. (Russell, Wilson, and Hall, 131)

As a consequence of all these new workplace "requirements," Black working women have become a major consumer market—a target of the credit card, beauty, and clothing industries. In addition, Black working women have become a large part of the market for adult colleges and job training classes. A virtual industry of training programs has developed to meet their workplace needs. Much of the "job training" in these programs simply involves teaching Black working-class women about the more middle class culture of the bureaucratic work place.

IV

The "half-full glass" of the advances of Black women workers has been even more dramatic for those who have entered the professions during the last thirty years. Black women "experienced a tenfold increased presence in law, medicine, and other prestigious professions". (Sokoloff, 2) Most of these increases were in the lower levels of the high-status male professions of medicine, law, and university teaching, and in the "semi-professions," such as nursing, social work, and elementary and nursery school teaching, which tended to be heavily female. They were nevertheless notable because of where Black women professional workers had come from both statistically and socially. "Only 1.5 percent of all Black women (workers), but 11.6 percent of all white women (workers) were employed in the professions in 1910. By 1980 the proportion of black women (professionals) almost equaled that of white women (professionals): 15.3 percent of black women and 17.4 percent of white women were in the professions." (Sokoloff, 95)

The remarkable successes of Black women professionals were due in part to the efforts of their communities and families during the segregation era. Black women were socially and academically prepared for professional work. Black maids and their husbands taught their daughters the language, dress, etiquette, and deportment observed among the upper-class white families for whom they worked. Black community organizations provided Black girls with opportunities to learn public speaking, performance, and leadership skills.

During the 1950s and 1960s Black parents and community members encouraged their more gifted daughters and sons to integrate white colleges and universities in order to improve themselves and their race. Educated along with white males, a small but significant group of Black women and Black men were prepared and qualified for prestigious professional employment when it became available to them. In spite of its critics, affirmative action legislation merely provided long-deserved opportunity for already qualified Blacks to enter professional schools and universities. Thus, Black female professionals and administrative workers represent the success of community efforts at cultivating female talent and ability. Black parents did this while prodding the government to initiate civil rights and affirmative action policies to provide their children with economic opportunity. As a result of the increase (from 3.4 to 10.1 percent) of Black female and male professionals, the Black middle class tripled in size between 1950 and 1976. (Sokoloff, 2)

While entry into the professions represents a substantial gain for Black women (and men), "once in the door" they have not received the respect, wealth, and success these positions seemed to promise. Although highly visible, the few Black female professionals in private sector companies are often isolated, lack mentoring, and languish in entry and low level positions in spite of their education and qualifications. Most of those in the "male" professions (lawyers, doctors, college professors) work in public sector colleges, hospitals, and agencies serving the needs of poor people of color. The majority of Black women professionals are concentrated in "handmaiden" professions, predominantly female occupations such as "nursing, teaching (elementary, kindergarten, and nursery school, librarianship and social work)." (Sokoloff, 128)

Black professionals are expected to fix systems which are in crisis because of underfunding, infrastructure deterioration, and demoralization of unskilled staffs. As "colonized" professionals, Black women are increasingly hired to repair the damage done to families and entire communities by social inequality and downturns in the economy. The work of these modern "mammies" is the care of the personal needs of the destitute and the weak in public institutions. These women teach and care for the children of workers of color; nurse the elderly and poor in public hospitals, nursing homes, and shelters; and teach and counsel in public colleges. Many are supervisors in charge of other Black women, especially those women who provide clerical backup for institutions or state agencies serving needy populations. Though given institutional responsibility, Black professionals do not have enough actual power over budget, hiring, or organization to truly repair and transform public institutions.

Hence, in spite of seniority and expertise, Black women professionals have privilege and status only in relation to their domestic past and their impoverished "clients." This "half-empty" aspect of Black women's professional and administrative work is merely a new form of *mammification*:

the continuation of a racialized and gendered job market, which employs black women but only in a place determined by others. The depression and alienation experienced by many Black women professionals is a hidden result of their half-full/half-empty status. This "half emptiness" is the tragedy of contemporary Black women's work.

Seeing heavy set, hobbling Black domestic workers with shopping bags evoked sympathy and veneration from the Black community of the past, while today's nicely dressed Black women with attaché cases are seen as the undeserving privileged. Both the Black and white public believe that Black women professionals are affirmative action "two-fers" whose race and gender, not ability, have earned them positions over allegedly more qualified white males and females, as well as Black males.

Black women professionals do earn good wages and have status over unemployed, homeless, or imprisoned Black men. As a result, many feel these Black women are taking employment away from Black men and avoiding their duties as wives and mothers. In these days of scarce employment opportunities for Black men, there is little community sympathy for the stressful job experiences of well-paid, middle-class Black female professionals.

While mammies of the former era worked in physically isolated environments, they were able to clearly identify the problematic nature of the racist system developed by white "folks" whose name, pedigree, and ways they intimately knew. They used that knowledge and experience to help create organizations and communities in opposition to racism and the white social order. New mammies, especially those educated after the civil rights movement era, have a hard time pointing to the source of their alienation and depression or clearly identifying with a base and constituency within the Black community. Black professional women are often in high-visibility positions which require them to serve white superiors while quieting the natives ... keeping poorer Black women and more angry Black men in check, or containing immigrant populations. They are often taking care of the elderly and children. They are often torn between their connections to the culture of their middle-class and white bosses and the pressures to represent the race and help Black people.

According to Gilkes, many of these women become "rebellious professionals" or "race women" in the black community. These terms refer to women who, despite being professionals—social workers, nurses, counselors, lawyers, or college professors—view their professional status on a moral, not an occupational, basis. In their work they reject professional ideologies that support traditional practices and values operating in white institutions, which they see as "part of, if not the root of, some of the problems they are trying to solve" in the black community. (Sokoloff, 157)

Irrespective of whether she is rebellious or complacent, the Black woman professional continues to be a caretaker whose responsibilities are often ill-defined and effusive. She is supposed to include, represent, defend, counsel, and console both her superiors and those who work under her. She is regarded by those superiors as essential to the functioning of the operation, but prevented by them from wielding any real power. Yet she willingly performs her designated tasks and even takes on extraordinary tasks and particular clients.

The Black female professional is a bonus to the companies and agencies which hire her because she is competent and loyal. She is willing to work longer hours, at lower wages, and do bureaucratic caretaking that whites and males at similar occupational levels would not consider. The company or agency exploits her willingness to serve by not providing her with adequate staff, salary, or resources. One of Dumas's case studies describes the "extra work" of the Black woman professional:

> ... At her office she has an open door policy and people drop in all hours during the day to seek her counsel and guidance or just to sit and talk. She is called upon to support the causes of the low-status groups in the organization and works with them sometimes after office hours to plan strategies and aid them in presenting their grievances to top management ... she is assigned to several inter-organizational committees and task forces to represent her department ... She is frequently called at the last minute to cover commitments that another member of the staff is unable to keep—including those of her boss. Her boss continues to redefine her job to take up slack created by staff attrition." (Dumas, 208–209)

Black women professionals internalize a work ethic based upon that of their slave and domestic foremothers: to be loyal and hard-working employees accustomed to harsh discipline, close scrutiny, and severe penalties for mistakes. Like mammy in the big house, the Black professional woman has become an indispensable but powerless functionary in modern day plantations. "She is overworked because the people in her department believe they can't do without her and she behaves as if they really can't." (Dumas, 208) Her sense of responsibility to the company or institution works against her own and her clients' best interest. She has little time or power to carve out a manageable set of goals which could lead to material success and authority.

Employers and co-workers encourage a mammified style of work which overburdens Black women by keeping them spinning their wheels while standing still. When the Black woman fails to be the expected mammy, she is seen as a bad mother who "is perceived to be deliberately depriving and rejecting, and therefore, hostile and potentially destructive." (Dumas, 210)

Black women should not be criticized or penalized for being effective, nor for attempting to personalize their professional work. Black professionals do "owe" the community and should strive to meet their people's needs. Because they are so overworked, depressed, and anxiety-ridden, however, Black professional women are often unable to discern the best ways to help themselves or their people. Too often an inappropriate pattern of work—mammification—has obscured the possibility of developing strategies for assuming power or transforming systems. Black women must realize that the "bionic woman" who comes to work each day and expertly does her job with all its mammified aspects is a strong Black woman being slowly "murdered by living." (Scully, 58)

V

Those pioneering Black women professionals who have attempted to break away from the stereotypical mammy roles have paid a high personal price. Banging against the glass ceiling in white male institutions such as journalism and the law, Black women have demonstrated the complex and obdurate quality of white male power and their own vulnerability in attempting to survive within it.

Essays by Black woman journalist Leanita McClain capture the tension of having a foot in the Black world, connected and committed to Black people, while also having a foot in the white world as a pioneer professional. "I am a member of the black middle class who has had it with being patted on the head by white hands and slapped in the face by black hands for my success." (McClain, 12) Unable to resolve the tension of living in these two worlds, on June 11, 1984, 32-year-old Leanita McClain committed suicide.

On September 11, 1990, my friend, Denise Carty Bennia, an outstanding attorney and law professor, also took her own life. Like Leanita, Denise was a sensitive and talented Black professional woman. She was also a race woman—a rebel attorney committed to fighting racism and sexism within her own profession and in the society. As a founder and leader of the National Conference of Black Lawyers, she encouraged many Black women to become attorneys. She, however, expressed concern about their personal lives which seemed so devoid of lovers, children, community, or pleasure. Denise was unable to resolve her own personal difficulties as a gifted Black professional woman.

Robin Barnes's tribute to Denise suggests the continual challenge faced by *all* Black women professionals:

> Before Denise died, I assumed that just mustering up the courage to tell the truth about what I see in the socio-political realm would strengthen me enough to complete each task. I surmised that because I knew, better than anyone, all the places which I was vulnerable, I was, therefore, immune to the toll which struggle takes on even those most committed to the cause." (Barnes, 59)

Illness frequently takes a toll on the lives of Black women committed to breaking down racist and sexist barriers in the professions. Marguerite Ross-Barnett, the first Black woman Vice-Chancellor of Academic Affairs at the City University of New York and the first Black person to head a "white" university, died of cancer when she was only 50 years old. The Black woman who succeeded her as Vice-Chancellor at CUNY, Carolyn Reid Wallace, was felled by a serious liver disease.

Black women who become pioneering professionals face personal penalties and consequences often overlooked by those valorizing their accomplishments. While most are not dying or committing suicide, many do suffer from depression, fibroid tumors, and addiction to food, shopping, and alcohol as a result of the stress of their positions. Many male or white professionals also suffer from these well known signs of job related stress. Black women, however, are not often rewarded with their high incomes, upward mobility, and social support systems.

In her remarkable account of her work at the *Washington Post* as a pioneering Black woman journalist, Jill Nelson describes her experiences as "voluntary servitude." Nelson's middle-class background had led her to believe that the "authentic Negro experience" was that of her more downtrodden brothers and sisters. However, at the *Post,* she soon learned that although she was hired as a professional journalist, she was restricted and manipulated in ways designed to stymie her from writing effective and powerful articles. Her tragi-comic account provides insight about the "authentic" experiences of a Black professional woman.

Patricia Williams, a Black law professor has also chosen writing to address the dilemmas of being a professional Black woman. In a book designed to occupy the gap between "theoretical legal understanding and social transformation," Williams has chosen to embrace, rather than choose between, her two realities. She reaches out for connections between "her psyche and the reader's, between lived experience and social perception, and between an encompassing historicity and a jurisprudence of generosity." (Williams, 8)

For many decades the Black community struggled for their best educated Black men and women to enter prestigious professions—law, medicine, and academia—which white males had dominated. Now after having worked within these areas, many Black professionals have discovered that they are required to mute their rage, downplay their abilities, and participate silently in new forms of servitude. These new forms of racism and sexism prevent them from achieving real wealth and power. However, Black women are additionally burdened with a legacy of selfless servitude which they believe requires them to represent the race, mentor the sisters, protect the brothers, and be perfect workers in the eyes of their white superiors.

Those Black women who reject the role of servant professional are using writing, support groups, and organizations to expose racism and sexism's multiple and intransigent nature. The writings of Jill Nelson and Patricia Williams are public conversations exposing the isolation and contradictions of the experiences of Black women in the white male elite professions. By exposing the oppressive aspects and internal workings of these highly prestigious arenas, Black women are making them more equitable and supportive of themselves and others.

VI

In 1981, I began work as an adjunct faculty member and college administrator at the City College Center for Worker Education, a degree-granting evening program for working adults based in lower Manhattan. My students, mainly Black and Latin women, were returning to or beginning college in order to advance in their jobs, usually in publicly funded service work.

We established the Center to meet the needs of working adult students for more personalized services and evening office hours. Our Center provides our students with individualized administrative support for admissions, financial aid, and registration. Staff members, regardless of rank, personally register every student each semester. We are also available for counseling on a walk-in basis.

I am the only Black female of the four-person senior counseling staff at the Center. During my first years of working with students, I became advocate, social worker, mother confessor, and soul sister. My colleagues could see five students for every one who came to me. Not only was I taking care of their academic needs, I was hearing about their personal problems and trying to help with their family, workplace, and other personal issues. Since I was an instructor, I was also concerned about their intellectual development.

I was so busy working with the students, organizing in my community, and raising my children, I had little time to focus on the problems of my work site. Eventually, however, I realized that I was the only senior counselor without a doctorate in a field where the Ph.D. is a requirement for advancement. I learned that I could never become director because I was not a senior member of the faculty, and in order to become a faculty member I needed a doctorate. I served under four white male directors who were senior members of the faculty, but whose administrative skills were not as developed as my own. (The pattern in the university seems to limit the hiring of most Black women to counseling and administration and to severely limit our entry into the professoriate.) I was stuck, because without a doctorate I couldn't move to a faculty line or even advance to other divisions of the university. My "job" on the other hand, had neither boundary nor focus, and women students interpreted my physical presence as instant availability to meet their needs. Although I learned a great deal about Black women's lives, which I later channeled into teaching, public speaking, and writing, I was stymied in my own development at work.

Until I read Rhetaugh Dumas' article on "The Dilemmas of Black Women's Leadership," I had no name for the exhaustion and rage I felt. Her article made me realize that I was a mammy working for other women who, as childcare workers, were also mammies. When I attempted to set professional limits—if I didn't nurture them or always agree to see them—some refused to speak to me. They complained to my white male boss about my lack of attention to their needs. They became personally angry with me. At home I was a mother to four children, and I soon learned my students also expected me to mother them.

I was also expected *to serve* my bosses, who usually gave little supervision, help, or useful direction. Many white male faculty members at the Center often mistook me for a student, or approached me as if I was a personal secretary, even after I had been introduced as a colleague. None of my achievements as a writer, public speaker, political activist, or leader helped to transform my role at the Center. Although white junior faculty members with fewer achievements were mentored and treated as members of the "club," to this day I have been left alone to "toil in the vineyards" helping students. After a decade, my skills and talents would be better used to help further evaluate and develop our program; I should be able to easily advance within the college and university, but I have not.

I share these personal details because they are so typical of my Black female friends within the City University and of other professional Black women I have read about or spoken with. We are all mammified in ways which maintain the status quo, especially at state-run bureaucracies. Instead of being the change agents who were supposed to "make a difference" once we were hired, we have become "colonized" bureaucrats unable to grapple with the overall system's forest because we are too busy "pruning the trees."

Recently, for example, a Black woman was hired to be president of City College, where I work. A newspaper account described the typical work week in her previous position as Vice-President of Academic Affairs at California State University at Dominguez Hills. She worked twelve-hour days and often on weekends. She is married and has two teenage daughters. Though active in sports, she spends most of her time working.

At Dominguez Hills, she helped "countless students to develop self esteem and success in school." She is also active in the community, a frequent consultant on cultural diversity in education, and has developed programs for gifted minority high school math and science students. (McFadden, B2)

Although she should be applauded for becoming President of City College, her style of work seems typical of the mammification of Black women workers who continue to work like mules. It is no wonder that "Black women who are pressed into such positions are faced with problems that challenge their own identity and threaten their inner security." (Dumas, 207) The question is, why, regardless of their education and position, are Black women continuing to work like "mammies"?

VII

I have had discussions with students who are Black workers in childcare centers run by Black women, centers which primarily serve Black families, and which function under the auspices of the Agency of Child Development, which is headed by a Black woman. These discussions made me think about the ironies and possibilities of the three- or four-tiered Black female work site. Although these agencies and institutions seem dominated by Black women, their activities are regulated by "absentee" and abstract bosses—most often, white male policy makers and legislators.

In 1990 Barbara Sobol was named the first Black woman to head the Human Resources Agency in New York City. In 1992, using her vacation days, she posed as a welfare recipient for a total of twenty-three days. (One of the clear benefits of Black women serving Black women is that they can easily go undercover to become one of "them.") The Department of Investigation and Mayor Dinkins knew of her plan and gave her false identities. Sobol the welfare recipient reported that she was confronted with "bureaucratic confusion almost immediately, treated condescendingly and frequently given misinformation." (Mitchell, B2) Her experiment vividly highlights the problems at the three-tiered Black female work site: Black female professionals who supervise Black female clerks who then serve Black female clients.

Sobol, like other Black female agency heads or college administrators inherited an antiquated and inefficient bureaucracy from white males who maintain power from a distance. Now that the clients, students, and patients are mainly people of color, their direct care is relinquished to the willing hands of Black women. In spite of Black males' concerns about Black women taking their jobs, on every level including this one, the job of managing care for the poor and indigent is not one desired by Black professional men. As for White women, they come in and quickly move as far up and away from direct service as possible. There is no power, few rewards, and not nearly enough perks and money in managing a welfare center or even in running the entire system. The Black female professional/commissioner is only given authority to care for those viewed as too dirty, dangerous, or immature for the attention of whites or men.

The second tier of Black women clerks and office workers in these agencies spends its days cleaning up and maintaining the paper trails of clients and the agency. These workers manage payrolls and assistance disbursement. They assure implementation of state regulations and compliance by clients. Often they have the responsibility of working directly with welfare clients, seeing the desperation and feeling the frustration, and sometimes rage, of the destitute. Yet these eligibility specialists have no authority to adjust the regulations or to address the situations of their clients. They are hired to enforce regulations rather than to truly help. Since their bosses are often Black females, they can't even charge racism. Though the "system" seems to be in their hands, fighting against Black bosses to change it feels wrong and traitorous to the race.

Since the regulations which reach these workers by fiat are the real boss, neither the workers nor their superiors have control over the organization of their work. Their rage and powerlessness get transferred to the helpless client who doesn't obey the rules.

Unfortunately, in order to cope, these welfare workers voice the same negative attitudes about welfare clients held by the general society. Many know better because they are closer to the clients than are any other workers in the society. They often live in the same neighborhoods, attending the same schools or churches. These workers, often receiving food stamps and welfare supplements, are only a paycheck away from welfare themselves, but they have little sympathy for its current recipients.

Their rage and shame gets passed on to the Black woman client, who is usually a single mother, a crack addict, or homeless. The client enters the welfare system with trepidation and cynicism, placing her very life in the hands of workers who often look like her, but who cannot be depended upon for support. Lies, omissions, and embellishments are needed to simplify and mold her experiences to fit the requirements of the welfare system. In fact, eligibility is not based on the actual need of the client, but on her ability to produce the correct papers and tell the "right" story.

Just as servants and slaves hid information about themselves from their white masters, welfare clients know that in order to receive the money, they are expected to camouflage details of their personal lives which don't meet the stereotype of the "welfare client."

Unlike the slave plantation, which brought different kinds of workers together in an oppositional community of resistance, today's triple-tiered, Black female work site does not foster community. In fact, the most divisive aspects of Black female interaction are often witnessed at these work sites. As Sobol discovered, Black female clients are treated like "dogs" by Black female workers, who are in turned worked like clerical slaves by Black female bosses, who are in turn held accountable for workplace efficiency and fiscal prudence by invisible, white male bosses executing their domination through legislation and regulations. Similar arrangements occur in hospitals where Black nurses' aides are supervised by Black nurses who must obey Black female hospital administrators and doctors. In daycare centers and elementary schools, Black teachers' aides work under other Black women teachers, who often serve under Black female principals, superintendents, and board members. Even in the criminal justice system, Black female inmates are often kept in check by black female prison guards under the control of Black female commissioners and other managers.

Although occupying different jobs and roles at the work site, each stratum of Black women at work in these institutions shares common experiences as Black females, which offer enormous potential for forging transformative coalitions.

They share common responsibilities as single mothers and as wives. Concerns with schooling, safety, and childcare cross job site differences. High rates of cancer, epidemic levels of fibroid tumors, and eating disorders are shared by Black women workers and welfare recipients. Addictions to eating, drugs, and alcohol have similar roots in low self-esteem and painful trauma.

Black women also share among themselves in their relationships with Black men. They suffer in common the abuse, adultery, and addiction of bad relationships and enjoy the love and support of good ones. Others, as lesbians, have common concerns with "coming out," homophobia, and love and romance.

However, differing roles at the work site prevent Black women from making common cause around the issues they share outside the job. Mutual hostility and distance at work also prevent them from effectively organizing and addressing workplace problems.

The distance is increased when Black women are silent about their personal problems. Supervisors with drinking problems use their education and salaries to separate themselves from addicted welfare clients. Single mother clerks who condemn teenage mothers have not honestly addressed their own situations. Closeted lesbian supervisors subjecting the "out" lesbian client to homophobia need to remove their facade of heterosexuality. Because the Black woman across the desk usually wears our own face, denial and condemnation are forms of self-delusion and self-hatred which prevent us from being effective and healthy.

The differences created by employment hierarchies tend to flatten out when Black women become more conscious and open about their "personal experiences" and the reality of their position. The marginal influence of Black women professionals and the ineffectiveness of agencies with three tiers of Black women is directly related to these women's often unwitting role in perpetuating the humiliation of Black women found in the larger society.

Public discussions about welfare reform, childcare, and healthcare often use coded and distorted perceptions of Black women. Yet, Black women workers and professionals in these areas are afraid to remove their masks and fears of self-disclosure and join their interests with those of their more disadvantaged sisters. If they did so, Black women would have a strong enough base to shape public policy and discourse. Managers could work with scholars to create surveys and ethnographic procedures, which could then create a data base for developing meaningful and effective policies designed to serve the needs of all Black women. Since Black women will, in large part, have to implement these policies anyway, the three-tiered work sites could be developed in ways which could help both workers and clients.

The notion of cooperation across class lines for societal change is not new. Slave "mammies" and female field workers developed strong networks which in turn supported resistance and survival among all Black people. During the segregation era, Black women domestics and teachers joined together to build schools and social movements. Besides, the systems of white supremacy and male domination are so intertwined and strong that class distinctions among Black women are, in reality, thin and weak. But Black professional women alone cannot make changes or even create safe spaces for themselves. Black women clerks alone cannot help becoming cynical and isolated. Working by themselves, Black women remain wheels in the middle of wheels.

In my own situation, I was able to relieve the stress of working as a "lone professional" when I received a small grant to create special programs for the education majors in my program. Figuring out how best to use the money was a test of my feminist convictions in that it made me address the question, "What would I do if I were in charge?" The money was used to build a Black female team. Our former financial aid counselor became my assistant and our former receptionist was hired to replace her. Together the three of us reinforced and supported each other's work.

As our first project, we enlisted the support of some women students to develop a conference for other students. We hired women specialists to address needs that *we* defined as important: handling death and loss while a student, using nutrition to deal with stress, and developing ways to become better organized. When some workshops were badly attended, I reminded myself, "This is only the beginning of our right to define our own work—we will make mistakes."

By stretching our funds in a creative and collaborative way, we were able to strengthen our impact on the students. These changes called for me to let go of the role I had been assigned and the job description I had been given. I could then recognize and receive support for my own feelings of weakness and lack of development because I had other sisters to talk to and lean on.

At the same time, we were beginning to create an effective Black female model of caregiving to replace the mammified one we had inherited. This model depends upon Black women helping each other and using different but complementary skills and abilities to address workplace challenges and problems. As members of a supportive team, Black women workers on all levels can better serve their clients, students, or patients because their own needs are being addressed by their Black women co-workers.

Somehow the presence of Black females in childcare centers, hospitals, schools, and welfare agencies should make a beneficial and notable difference in the existing patterns of caregiving. Most importantly, these changes could provide a model for non-Black women workers and for all clients. They could help develop work sites which reflect the kind of compassion essential to a Black female model of caretaking.

The plea for Black women to "lay down this world" is a call for them to reject all models and forms which denigrate them and keep them from improving their own lives. It doesn't mean that Black women should give up jobs and positions they deserve and worked hard for. They should enlarge, improve, and transform those positions to create insurgent circles of sisterhood. They should also create support groups around common issues such as single parenting, addiction, sexual relationships and violence. Sisters could learn to look out for each other's mental and physical health; they could give each other help with their rage and frustration.

Today's Black women, who run the occupational gamut from fast-food restaurants and hospital laundry rooms to corporate law firms and college classrooms, share a common past and a legacy rooted in nearly three centuries of domestic work. The mammy we carry to work with us is our mothers' ethic, pattern, and dream. The demeaning and shameful aspects of their legacy have to be consciously separated from the memory of their dignity and talent. Black women workers must become aware of the best and worst from our mammy past.

Our foremothers want to know if the price of their hard work and sacrifice was worth it. Our daughters wait to see what kind of legacy we will leave for them. With all our education, wealth, and experience, Black women workers have the power to transform the world.

But first we must reinterpret it. We must see a new world, in which we work for ourselves, self-determined and self-defined. We must break our own chains. We must lay down this world.

4

IT'S A FAMILY AFFAIR

THE REAL LIVES OF BLACK SINGLE MOTHERS

IN THE WEEKS BEFORE I left my husband, ending our seven-year marriage, I celebrated my first Christmas alone with my children, mentally linking arms with past generations of Black parents and kin and vowing to do the best I could to raise my children well. With only $5 to spend on decorations and presents, I resolved always to give my children Christmas as a way of toasting our family's health and well-being. This past Christmas, nine years later, I began the holidays as usual in a frenzy of gift-buying for my four children, close friends, and kin. On Christmas we went to my aunt and uncle's house for our traditional family dinner. The next day we visited one of my closest friends and her daughters, the oldest in from college for the holidays (my friend is also a college student). On Ujima, the third day of Kwanza (an African-inspired harvest holiday celebrated at Christmastime), we had dinner with another friend and her family—her 10-year-old son, her daughter and son-in-law, and their children. Some of our male friends were also there. After we stuffed ourselves on fish, vegetables, and desserts, the children played while the adults sat, talked, and watched television.

All my close women friends and I are Black single mothers, connected to each other by our commitment to our families and to political and community organizations in central Brooklyn. About half of my friends were teenage mothers; nearly all of us have been on welfare. We share similar past experiences of poverty, mental torment and physical abuse, self doubt and confusion. But now we are heading our households and raising our children in well-functioning families.

To most Black and white politicians and social scientists, our families are by definition pathological—"broken," "illegitimate," "incubators of the Black underclass" that perpetuate poverty, teenage pregnancy, crime, and welfare dependence. Since the early 1900s, about 25 per cent of all Black families have been headed by women, but in the 20 years between 1960 and 1980, our numbers almost doubled. A significant proportion of us are teenagers; 45 per cent are poor. These statistics have led to increasing hysteria about "the breakdown of the Black family." During the 1960s, most Black social scientists and elected officials condemned Daniel Moynihan and others who suggested that the "matriarchal" character of the Black family was the cause of continuing racial inequality. But the changes during the past 20 years have so alarmed many of those same Black spokespeople that they now advocate programs to restore the two-parent Black family and accept the conventional wisdom that disparages Black families headed by women. The media reinforce these distorted perceptions by highlighting the successes of white two-parent households while focusing on the weaknesses of Black single mothers and Black fathers. These attacks on Black single mothers occur in the context of tremendous changes in the white American family: a steady increase in female-headed households, a rise in the rate of out-of-wedlock births (5 per cent in 1960 to 14 per cent in 1975), more teenage pregnancy, more households where adults live alone or with one other person, more women who both work and rear children, and a general relaxation of sexual mores. Black single mothers have become convenient scapegoats for the white population's backlash against these changes. Historically, problems in the white family have been attributed to individual failure while problems in the Black family are seen as evidence of collective Black pathology. This is ironic, for American society is dominated by a racial patriarchy—white men who have always used their power over social policy to control and shape the Black family. Black single motherhood began as a response to slavery. The slave master outlawed marriage between slaves, separated parents from their children, and sexually abused slave women and young girls. In opting to have children rather than abort or kill them, in resisting the slave master's attempts to breed slaves like animals and force families apart, Black women consciously chose to nurture those children, either with the support of their mates or, when necessary, without, but always in a supportive slave community. Black slaves struggled for the right to a family centered on an African-like broad network of kin. After slavery's end, many Black men and women, like my grandfather and grandmother, married and stayed married all their lives. They worked hard on the land, and in spite of terror and pogrom made good their commitments to their family and to us, their future progeny.

Today, the context of the struggle to have a Black family is legal desegregation and superficial political gains for Black people, along with high unemployment among Black men, depressed wages for Black women, and public denigration of poor people. The concept of a pathological underclass has become the rationale for continued racism and economic injustice; in attempting to separate racial from economic inequality and blaming family pathology for Black people's condition, current ideology obscures the system's inability to provide jobs, decent wages, and adequate public services for the Black poor. And in a racist-patriarchal society, the effects of the system's weaknesses fall most heavily on Black women and children. Just as Black family life has always been a barometer of racial and economic justice and at the same time a means of transcending and surviving those injustices, Black families headed by women reflect the strength and the difficulty of Black life in the '80s.

In 1980, according to the Urban League, 28 per cent of all Black single mothers were married women with an absent spouse, 22 per cent were divorced, 22 per cent were widows, and 25 per cent had never married, though most of these women had significant, common-law relationships. Whether or not her child's father ever lived with her, the Black single mother usually becomes the head of her household with the same needs as a man in her position. But she's unlikely to have the same material resources or social status.

Contrary to the myth, most Black single mothers are not second and third generation welfare recipients who sit around having babies in order to collect the government's pittance. "Although three-fifths of all Black families headed by women receive public assistance, only one-fifth are totally dependent on welfare," states Robert Hill, formerly director of research for the Urban League. Welfare payments most often supplement Black women's low wages: in 1980, the median income for Black female heads of households was $7425. When welfare is their sole source of income, it's because they're disabled or have no child care. Most poor

Black women reject welfare as soon as they can. As one former welfare recipient I know put it, "Welfare makes you feel that poor people aren't better than spit. So I got off as soon as my children started school even though I made about the same amount of money as my check, once child care expenses were deducted."

Most Black single mothers are the working poor. We do domestic work, sew in factories, and are self-employed as merchants and caterers. We commute daily to city, state, and federal government agencies. As paras, aides, and clerks, we are the backbone of the hospital, child care, and nursing home systems. Although the wages are low and the work tedious, Black women stay with their city jobs for years because they offer stability and benefits.

Black single mothers are the majority of students in many evening college programs. The typical student at the City College Center for Worker Education, a degree-granting program for working adults, is a 35-year-old Black woman who works for the city and heads her household. Higher education will bring her a decent wage, job security, and the hope of upward mobility. Getting a degree is a lifelong goal for many Black women who were forced to interrupt their education because of family and financial pressures. Many who have steady jobs and attend college were yesterday's teenage mothers or welfare recipients. If any of us were frozen in those past crises brought on by unemployment, lack of decent, affordable housing, or trouble with our spouses or mates, we would have seemed destined to live out the stereotype of perpetual poverty and despair.

In fact, after surviving the trauma of losing a loved one through separation, divorce, or death, most Black single mothers slowly stabilize their families. Though social scientists choose to focus on Black single mothers in crisis, they are not in the majority; if nearly half of all families headed by Black women have incomes below the poverty line, as the Center for the Study of Social Policy reports, then over half do not. But housing, welfare and court systems that treat us like social lepers are constantly working to undo our struggle. Black single mothers face discrimination because of our color, our sex, our marital status and, of course, our children; landlords often prefer a family with a male head. In addition, exorbitant rents price us out of most neighborhoods. As a result, Black women and their children are relegated to the oldest and most precarious housing in the city, apartments often owned by landlords who prey on poor families and provide few services or repairs even when their tenants do pay rent.

Black single mothers who work also need child care. But because the number of spaces in subsidized day care centers is severely limited, we spend a great deal of our meager income paying relatives and neighbors to watch our children. We help support other Black single mothers who work sporadically or are unemployed by hiring them to do child care. Some Black single mothers take jobs in community organizations and businesses, like beauty parlors and car services, so that they can have flexible schedules and be near their children's schools or family support systems.

Black women who do need welfare are subjected to a system whose implicit assumption is that it's a crime for men not to support women and children and for women not to force men to support them. That system blames Black women for "allowing" men to impregnate them without benefit of marriage or money. Welfare policies confuse the economic issue of how to support a family with the personal issues of sexuality and procreation, and this confusion shapes the perception of Black female-headed households as lacking men rather than money. Recently the Human Resources Administration in New York City began requiring women applying for welfare to provide explicit sexual information about themselves and the fathers of their children, but backed off under protest from community groups and civil libertarians.

When we see Ethiopians starving we don't feel the need to ask questions about their sexual patterns, the whereabouts of the starving children's fathers, or whether different tribal customs might have provided better ways of feeding them. But when a destitute Black single mother goes to a welfare office, her need for food and shelter is overshadowed by papers that must be signed, questions that must be answered, and moral lectures that must be tolerated: "You shouldn't have let him live with you. Didn't you know about birth control?" She must sit silently because this fool's questions stand between her and food and shelter for herself and her child. No one else is scrutinized so closely or punished so bitterly for making human, if often unwise, decisions.

Most female heads of households currently live in urban centers, although some Black single mothers remain in economically depressed rural southern areas, where poverty is more persistent and prolonged. For nearly a century, rural Black single mothers have tended to migrate to urban areas in search of better employment and educational opportunities for themselves and their children. Both rural and urban single mothers, however, live in rental units which are crowded and inadequate. Few are able to buy their own homes and therefore rarely have the equity, security and comfort of most two-parent families.

Whether a Black single mother is on welfare or has a job, securing adequate housing is the most critical factor in stabilizing her family. She can easily spend her days caught up in her housing crisis. Often she's in housing court because the landlord has not made repairs, and there is no heat or hot water. After a day in court, she goes home to a cold apartment. She and the children sleep on the floor near the stove; she spends the night worrying about accidents from the fumes and the flames, hoping the steam will come up, because she's sick. She boils and hauls water for the children so they can wash up and go to school. She washes halfheartedly, gets on the train, and goes to work in a heated office where paper and machines are treated better than she and the children are. She gets headaches worrying about the apartment. She can't take off any more days to go to court and she doesn't have enough money to move. If she's on welfare, she has to find a decent apartment within HRA guidelines. She tries Family Court, hoping her child's father can come up with some money. The children have gotten sick and sniffly; she takes them to the clinic, where the lines are long, but it's warm. She is trapped in a cycle of begging for help from a system that refuses to recognize the legitimacy of her need or to give her the services she and her family deserve.

Since no one can live forever in this kind of crisis, she is likely to fall backward, lose the apartment and the job. If she can't live with relatives, she goes to the shelters and the hotels and waits, while the city and federal government spend thousands of dollars a month rather than give her even $1000 to find another apartment. Her struggle to secure decent housing has affected everything about her family life: meals, leisure time, work, school attendance. Life in shelters and hotels or even with relatives further demoralizes her and undermines her ability to create a healthy family. Meanwhile, she keeps hearing in church and on television, from Black politicians and social scientists, social service workers and teachers, that her family is "broken" and that she's incapable of successfully raising her children, especially her sons, without a man. She usually feels guilt, uncertainty, and shame, yet she has no choice but to keep struggling.

Homelessness and poverty are not new issues for Black women, but they've been exacerbated by the estrangement and tensions between us and Black men. Since most Black women become single mothers because their legal or common-law marriages break up, all must grapple with the contradictions of this institution, which pulls Black men and women together so easily and pushes us apart with such violence and pain. Once the land and terror of segregation held our marriages together, but the city with its illusions of mobility and individual freedom cannot.

Now, long after the chains have been removed, slavery continues in a new form inside the minds and hearts of Black people. Far too many Black women have become "the slaves of slaves," and their slave masters are Black men. Physical and mental abuse is a major reason Black women leave their husbands and mates. One of the friends I visited for Christmas-Kwanza shared this much too common story: "The children were in the other room. He said sit down and he closed the door and pulled a rifle from the closet, he put it right between my eyes and dared me to move. He called me all kinds of names and promised to blow my head off." After years of such abuse, she saved up enough money and took her three children and left, becoming a single mother.

Mental anguish and depression also hurt our relationships. Wives suffer and suffocate under the treatment of men too prideful to give them emotional support and too weak to respect their feelings and ideas. Too many Black men buy into the master's notions of male superiority, even as they think they are resisting his notions of racial superiority. Once, at a conference, a Black woman who had been married 18 years slipped me a note asking some familiar questions: "How long must any woman continue to be subjected to these abuses (both mental and physical) simply to maintain the family? What good is a family if it's not a happy family?" Most of the separated and divorced Black women have answered, "Not much."

After becoming single mothers, most Black women do not stop having intimate relationships with men. But integrating dating and sex with family, household, and work responsibilities poses serious problems. After carefully and often painfully stabilizing our families, we have learned to weigh every step to make sure that no relationship with a man throws our families into crisis. We have become quite pragmatic and guarded about our finances and our hearts. When the children and the household are a woman's highest priority, she can lose the relationship. If the relationship becomes too important she may neglect or even lose her children. Having both is difficult, and for some women impossible, because a single mother's lover must be flexible enough to fit into her intact family, and must balance commitments to her family with commitments to other children and former mates. Her children must be secure enough to accept her lover into their household. If the relationship exacerbates family tensions, teenage daughters and sons will fight them, fight her, or bail out fast to the streets or their own mates.

These dilemmas and pressures are compounded for Black Lesbian single mothers, who are stigmatized and ostracized by both Black and white communities. A Black Lesbian mother's access to support from her family and from other Black women can be severely limited or non-existent, depending upon the degree of homophobia she faces from these potentially significant sources of help. The society's general hostility toward Lesbians and Gay men is often compounded when it must deal with the fact that many Lesbians and Gay men do indeed have children.

If a woman is not heterosexual, she is considered, by definition, to be an unfit mother. Custody of her children is potentially under threat, not only from the children's father or from his or her family, but from any individual or institution that has knowledge of her Lesbianism and decides to make a case out of it. Women, both Black and white, lose custody of their children every day based upon no other criterion than their sexual orientation. If a Black Lesbian mother doesn't have money and must deal with the welfare system, she is in even more danger of being scrutinized, "discovered," judged unfit, and having her children taken away.

Black women who do not remarry or live with men are likewise seen as social Lesbians, regardless of their sexual preference. Women without men "to take care of them" or take them out are considered freaks in a society where coupling and heterosexual partnerships are the norm. These pressures force far too many Black women into accepting men into their lives without question or demand. The fear of being "deviant" or of failing at child-rearing by not having a "legitimate" family with a father, drives many Black single mothers to casual or live-in lovers, whether or not those lovers meet her and her family's needs.

No family survives without resources and support. Black single mothers, like Black families generally, rely heavily on relatives and friends for help in raising the children and managing a household. When I became a single parent, one of the first people who helped me was another Black single mother who daily encouraged me to look for work. The Black woman principal of a private preschool allowed me to work part-time to offset the school fees of my three children. Black male friends and white female co-workers did child care and helped me shop. My aunts and uncles stood by in case I needed money or babysitting. And most important, my children's father continued his relationship with them.

These new networks and the traditional kinship ties of Black families are the most useful support systems for Black single mothers. Though many believe that they're disintegrating, they remain vital and effective. It is when they are weak or problematic because loved ones are dead, ill, or far away that Black women and their families go into crisis and must rely on the church or social service agencies. Growing numbers of women in central Brooklyn now supplement or replace these supports with help from the Sisterhood of Black Single Mothers, a 12-year-old self-help organization founded and built by Daphne Busby, herself a single parent.

I found out about the Sisterhood while working on my master's degree, when I was still married. I was immediately impressed with the positive attitude of the women in it. A few years later a friend invited me to a conference sponsored by the Sisterhood where men conducted workshops on money, pornography, and relationships for participants of both sexes. I volunteered to help the group and was asked to participate in their Big Sister program for teenage mothers. In 1982, I coordinated a successful 13-week Black women's history series for the Sisterhood. Though I've used its services only informally, I know how well it helps Black single mothers survive.

The Sisterhood's first step in empowering a Black single mother is to encourage her to name her own reality, rejecting negative labels like "unwed," "illegitimate," and "teenage mother" (this last a code for saying you will have a lifetime of misery and trouble). The organization then offers practical support: every day, women come in or phone for help with welfare, housing, protection from violence, health and education problems. It is truly a sisterhood, not a social work agency with paid advocates, who are often distanced from the problems and possibilities of Black women and their families. Daphne and her two-person staff regard other Black single mothers as sisters and peers. Their philosophy is rooted in our past, when Black women supported each other in day-to-day living as well as in helping each other through crisis and celebration.

Daphne's greatest success as an organizer has been with teenage mothers. In 1979, the Sisterhood launched its Big Sister program with a Ford Foundation grant. The big sisters modeled successful mothering, encouraging the little sisters to stay in school, develop healthy parenting practices and self-respect, and maintain good relations with the fathers and their own families. The grant ended, but the spirit of the project has continued throughout the Sisterhood's work. Many organizations with much larger budgets and staffs have tried to duplicate the model but have failed because of their moralism and disdain for the teenage mother's condition;

they feel she will never amount to much and can't help showing it. The Sisterhood's staff, in contrast, knows that support for teenagers before, during, and after pregnancy will allow parents, children, and their families to build more successful lives.

The Sisterhood does not try to keep women in isolation from the rest of the community, but actively supports Black fatherhood. Each Father's Day, the Sisterhood sponsors a program featuring men who best exemplify positive fatherhood: married and single fathers, nonresident fathers, teenagers, and men active in the community. Black men have always been part of the counseling and other activities of the Sisterhood; recently it started a fathers' self-help group.

It's clear that Black single mothers need to influence and shape public policy on welfare, child custody, education, health care, and housing, and the Sisterhood is a natural center for campaigns on such issues. For years Daphne Busby has been speaking about Black single mothers and the Black family and has now joined the New York State Governor's Advisory Committee on Black Affairs and the New York State Commission on Child Support. Black single mothers across the country have expressed a growing interest in affiliating with the Sisterhood because no similar group exists in their area.

In fact, any group of Black single mothers composed of at least two or three sisters who care about each other can break the isolation and help each other survive with successful family experiences. The Sisterhood of Black Single Mothers is based on a model of self-help and self-definition which asserts that sisters who are experiencing single motherhood are best able to help and support each other in their parenting, professional, and private lives. A new group can work on common material needs such as obtaining child support, housing, and child care which can involve agencies, advocacy, and information sharing; or they can work on common personal needs such as loneliness, stress and self-doubt which call for sharing experiences and concerns. The sisters could also plan social events for themselves and their friends such as picnics, theatre parties, and pot luck dinners. Single parent fathers, older and younger women, and guest speakers could be invited to small meetings to share information with and give support to the members of the group. One of the most rewarding experiences of a single mothers' support group can be planning activities for the children such as holiday parties, camping trips, and sports.

The Sisterhood's concerns are not only relevant to Black people. White families have always been held up as the model Black families had to follow. Yet now, as Robert Hill noted, "White families, especially since more white women have entered the labor force, are increasingly adopting coping patterns that historically were used by Blacks."

We know that all families are in trouble: it's hard rearing children in a country burdened with a narrow puritan moralism, racial and sexual stratification, poverty and oppression obscured by selective social visions of national success and material wealth. Focusing solely on the problems of Black single mothers only deflects our attention from the real crisis in the family—the nation's lack of commitment to children's welfare and progressive social policies; the conflicts between men and women, adults and children, that prevent loving relationships.

The scapegoating of Black single mothers makes it hard to honestly discuss the families of poor and working-class Black people. If we criticize the welfare system, we give ammunition to an administration bent on dismantling welfare. If we attack Black male chauvinism, our remarks add to the undermining of young and working-class Black men. If we criticize Black women's participation in their own "sweet suffering," we reinforce those who deny the reality of Black female oppression or disparage Black women's competence. If we speak in public, we are accused of adding to white racist self-fulfilling prophesies of Black failure. Yet if we are silent about the weaknesses in Black families, keeping Black male violence and failure in the closet, we risk further abuse of Black women and children.

Many Black spokespeople would rather lament the increase of Black single mothers than seek to understand its causes; they would rather be alarmed about Black teenage pregnancy than do something concrete for Black teenagers and speak out firmly against the sexual abuse of young women. Since few of the social scientists, public officials, and media commentators of either race who purport to analyze and judge our lives understand the real strengths or difficulties of Black single mothers and their families, their suggestions for solving the "crisis of the Black family" are paternalistic and impractical.

Many, assuming that the major cause of the rise in Black female headed households is Black male unemployment, propose that job training and employment programs focus mainly on Black men. This idea not only condones job discrimination against Black women but ignores the chauvinism that so often causes Black women to leave their relationships in the first place. Appeals to Black men to find their manhood in employment so as to reassert their dominance over Black women can only increase the number of Black single mothers. Many Black men are overcoming their sexist attitudes and seeking loving and equitable relationships with their spouses and children; Black women are also beginning to explore their own weaknesses and problems in establishing positive relationships with Black men. Yet dreams of patriarchal restoration have continued to permeate the Black family debate. If this is to change, Black women must speak truthfully, naming our own reality and vision of the Black family.

The families of Black single women are hardly immune to trouble and failure, and from their perspective on the edge of a new frontier in family living, Black women are conscious not only of the family's possibilities, but of its limits. In a racist and patriarchal system our sons will never truly be their own men and our daughters will be taught to despise all that is wonderful about Black womanhood. We worry that street violence and drugs will claim our male children. We realize that our daughters, like those in two-parent households, are drawn into motherhood and wifelike loyalties to men far too early in their lives.

But in their struggle against those limits—weathering changes from within and without, pitting themselves against social agencies and public opinion—Black single mothers and their families have something to offer us all. By daily demonstrating that they can survive and succeed without marriage, that they may even be better off without it, they challenge the basic patriarchal ideal. My children and other children of Black single mothers are better people because they do not have to live in families where violence, sexual abuse, and emotional estrangement are the daily, hidden reality. They are not burdened by violent sexist nightmares that block their strength and sensibilities at the core of where they live. They know that fathers and mothers are only men and women, not infallible tyrants or gods. They have choices and a voice. In a society where men are taught to dominate and women to follow, we all have a lot to overcome in learning to build relationships, with each other and with our children, based on love and justice. For many Black single mothers, this is what the struggle is about.

5

GENDER IN BLACK

THE LAND BOUND US TOGETHER connecting us man to woman, father to child, child to mother, and everybody to God. We worked the land together, men, women, and children chained by the terror and connected by the beloved community. Slavery outlawed, and then segregation marginalized marriage and the Black family, but an African communal sensibility and a Christian faith in deliverance embraced and encircled displaced and besieged African Americans. After slavery we remained linked to the land, often working the same plots and obliged to the same people: no longer to a slave master, but to a master none the less. Peasant communities emerged in the midst of serfdom, lynching, and the ever-present pogrom.

No matter how connected we were to the land, it belonged to us only in a spiritual sense. The land's ultimate owner was white capital in the person of business men, corporations and companies. These men could and did claim the land at any time, using terror to push Black communities to and fro. Throughout the century children of Black farmers would recount the tragedy of lost claims by the simple phrase, "they took my father's land." Like Mexicans and Indians, Italians and Irish, Black people's push off the land was met by a pull to the city. Capitalist development has always mercilessly dislocated and disconnected people from their land. Each economic expansion and technological innovation turned some groups away, as others were gathered into productive service.

The "imperfect unity" of a distinct Black community was forced to extend itself from the rural south into city life. But after all, hadn't Black people been living in cities for centuries? In every city we settled, Harlems and Southsides blazed anew each day with a flashy, hip, and jazzed up street culture. But even the number runners and whores, the urbane Langstons and Zora Neales were only branches connected to the solid roots of the "center of gravity" of community life. The center was not the intellectual or the hipster, but men and women like my mother and father, who worked, loved and believed in being connected to family and God. In fact, common experiences, visions, and dreams bound Black folks everywhere to each other.

My mother and father came from the land. My maternal grandmother and her sister, both tall and dark-skinned, married two brothers, light-skinned and short. My mother and her sister told me about growing up with a strict father and a strong mother. My maternal grandparents lived and died in the rural areas of a very small North Carolina town. The picture in my living room shows it to be a flat, pale, dry land close to the eastern shore. As a child, I remember the land being sandy, yet full of peanuts and tobacco, fruit trees and farm animals. Everybody Black was kin in one way or another, and some of the white people were part of our family too. We went to town only for candy and sweets; everything else was connected to the land.

My father's family came from a larger farm in eastern Virginia, only one hundred miles away from my mother's home. My father's father lost his land during the Depression and many of his children moved into the cramped quarters of Philadelphia apartments. Unknown to each other, my father and mother both migrated to Harlem during the Depression. There they eventually met and married, worked in private families as maid and chauffeur. Dutiful visits south during my childhood connected me and my sister to the land, although we were born in Brooklyn.

Manhood and womanhood for my parents' generation rested on marriage, family, land, and religion, which all in turn defined and composed our Blackness. Since it was blatantly clear that no one would survive alone on the land in the face of white terror, we stayed together in marriage and family to help each other survive. Courting, romance, sex, and love were all tempered and shaped by mutual need and by opposition to the system of white supremacy.

Black people were proud of being different. It was as if experiencing the inhumanity of whites only reinforced Black humanity. For one thing, Black people distinguished between a person's basic humanity, which must be affirmed, and their undesirable practices, which should be condemned. Black community ethos enabled gay men and lesbians to survive within families and communities which morally rejected their behavior as sin but accepted the person as one of God's children. Other stigmatized groups such as "unwed" mothers, and other deviant activities like prostitution and alcoholism were treated with the same combination of moral renunciation and Christian forgiveness and love. However, no Black child was considered "illegitimate." Deviants and the marginalized were both shamed and embraced as the family and community closed ranks to protect its members from the hands of the white "folks."

Class differences within the community were muted and blurred, because, as bell hooks explains, ". . . it was irrelevant how much money any individual Black person did or did not have because we lived as a community in the same area and, for the most part, under the same conditions. We all went to the same schools, we attended the same church. So one could say, my 'sense' of Blackness was monolithic, I thought all Black people existed in a kinship structure of larger community." (hooks, 68)

Black women were able to enlarge and expand stereotypical and confining gender roles as wives and mothers. Respected as strong women and as hard workers, Black women commanded tremendous personal power while living under men. While many rejected blind obedience to male authority, most Black women struggled to shape and mold that authority to meet their needs. They exposed ruthless male leaders and condemned men who wouldn't do for their wives and children. They used their relationship to God, not man, to strengthen their positions within the patriarchal church and family.

The land and terror which unified us in spite of our differences and imperfections also enraged and silenced us. White violence begat black rage: fathers gone suddenly and temporarily mad with their own insignificance and impotency often beat, raped, and abused their own women and children. Mothers who knew the transgressions of the fathers maintained silent conspiracies and stayed loyal to their men. Southern womanist writers such as Alice Walker and Maya Angelou have pointed to the brutality and pain of being female and black within this beloved community. Testimonies like Nat Shaw's autobiography describe how the land and the terror defined the rage of being Black and male in the south. Children remembered fathers who were publicly shamed by white merchants and bosses.

Black men and women were all these things: invisible, afraid, proud, brutal, and benevolent, living an "imperfect, but prevailing unity."

(Strickland, 4) Above all, the community viewed itself as the shelter from a common storm.

Black workers began to pin their hopes on factories and companies in the north, as they moved toward the better life they couldn't achieve in the rural south because of peonage and the terror of white violence. Industrial expansion during and after World War II favored Black workers. During the 1950s, factories in midwestern and northeastern cities became boom towns for Black farmers who had not left the south until mid-century. Once-closed labor unions were open to Black membership. Migration, expanded job opportunities, and the desegregated armed forces gave new dignity to Black manhood.

At the same time, although Black women began to perform public domestic work in childcare and nursing, their bondage to domestic servitude in private household work was reaching a merciful end. Their daughters began working in prized jobs as clerks for insurance and telephone companies, while their sons became factory and office workers.

Cars, homes, and televisions were bought by Black men and their wives, turning the streets of places like Brooklyn's Bed-Stuy into placid and comfortable sites for black urban children like me. However, in spite of these gains, Black parents in both northern and southern communities realized that unless legal segregation was destroyed and educational opportunities expanded, another generation would be confined and limited. The unique ethos of these Black communities and the strong families of powerful men and women enabled them to sustain a social movement which defeated segregation seventy-five years after it was instituted. They supported the Civil Rights Movement not simply for what it did for them but for what it promised their children. These parents "put their lives on the line so that Black children would not be denied." (Strickland, 4)

Just as Black people were creating families in which men could work and adequately provide for their wives and children, well-paying jobs for working class men began to decline. As Black children were beginning to realize educational and professional opportunities, structural obstacles tempered the promise that these opportunities had held. Just as its culture was developing an effective politics of social change, our Black community lost its power. Just as our "shining princes" were challenging the "system" and our men were walking with pride, they were weakened by war, fratricide, and drugs. As we Black women realized the power of our minds and our labor, we found ourselves disconnected from our men, yet responsible for the major work of continuing families and communities on our own.

During the 1970s, forces outside of Black people's hands shattered and transformed their community and family life. First, the poverty programs and affirmative action legislation which promised Black workers jobs and a safety net of public assistance in hard times were ended or diluted. The racially integrated but gender segregated public sector employed Black women as clerks and administrators and did the same for Black men within the criminal justice and transportation systems. Black professionals moved into high salaried, high profile positions. Black elected officials, movie stars, and athletes constantly "proved" that we had made progress. But more and more Black men and women were poorer and dislocated. The community was wasting away, just as some began to feel we had made it. In fact, the social agenda which linked equality and justice to state-financed programs supplementing Black community-based self-help efforts was derailed before it ever really began. Rising conservatism in both Democratic and Republican parties forced the state to retreat from its direct role in ending racial inequality. By pursuing a policy which shifted both blame and the responsibility for meeting social needs to states, municipalities, and individuals, the Federal government allowed the quality of black community life to erode. Since the Reagan Presidency, it had become even more apparent that no national and collective solution to Black impoverishment and social injustice would be pursued. The notion of a "race blind" social order became a code term for silencing specific Black demands, while limiting progress to those Black *individuals* who could integrate into the white world on its terms.

With the government no longer addressing a Black-created social agenda, the efforts and strategies of the community were subverted. During this same time, the economy rapidly and simply changed its base from industrial to service labor.

Black employment patterns began to resemble those of the pre–World War II era, in which women could find low paying work, while men were more erratically employed in somewhat higher paying jobs.

The very fact that Black women worked as domestics in the first place was caused by the inconsistency and inadequacy of Black male wage work. However, in the past, Black community and cultural power was able to blunt the impact of the vicissitudes of an economy ultimately controlled by white hands. There was no reason to believe that Black men and women could not, therefore, weather the storm of changes wrought by post-industrial society. However, these changes have been accompanied by a more thorough integration of Black people into the market economy as consumers of white culture and products, and of commodified Black culture. Media, schooling, and entertainment have mentally seduced and addicted blacks to a virtual reality version of White World. In virtual reality, the viewer remains stationary but dons an apparatus which vividly seems to transport him or her into other settings. Blacks viewers are mentally integrated into the world created by white media moguls while never physically leaving Black world, with its concrete problems of violence, addiction, poverty and racism.

In the past Black people were physically confined within boundaries created by slavery and segregation. Nevertheless, they interpreted their lives and experiences in ways which promoted opposition and supported community. In spite of shame and destitution, they generated their own culture and ethos.

Black people believed their efforts to promote integration would increase their own community's political and economic power. Instead it undermined their cultural and community life. Some have become so debilitated, they lack an accurate and effective understanding of the source of their oppression and pain. Our collective life is being eroded by Black people overly influenced by media's perception of Black life.

Reggae singer, Jimmy Cliff explains this phenomena this way, "they took the chains off our body and put them on our minds."

My children and many of their generation now live physically segregated from white society, in a Black world which lacks community. The hard won "beloved community" of the past has disintegrated into tribes divided by nationality, class, gender, ideology, and state of mind. We left the certain boundaries of "white only" signs which fenced in our community to live within and across the blurred lines of a fractured blackness formed out of common traumas but lacking collective memory or vision.

The changed social order (which we helped to shape and usher in) has disrupted the manhood and womanhood so painfully constructed by Black hands within the context of a protective family life and community. From a Black perspective, gender can only be understood within a lamentation for the loss of our community and the resulting fragmentation of our manhood and womanhood.

While Black gays and lesbians have been seeking to redefine themselves and their sexuality through the processes of "coming out," seeking lovers, confronting homophobia, and creating safe spaces and community, Black heterosexuals have yet to do more than define their problems in terms of lack of available and suitable mates. In the meantime, our estrangement and despair has increased, and the crisis between Black heterosexual men and women has deepened. Furthermore, this crisis has prevented any meaningful dialogue or rapprochement between homosexuals and heterosexuals. More importantly, since Black heterosexual men and women have no meaningful *social* language or space for coming together, we have no ability to create an oppositional politics or community. Our children, especially adolescents, including gay and lesbian teens, have virtually no powerful examples of loving, mature adults. Our urgency and even desperation is to find out whether black adults can effectively reproduce the best of ourselves in our children, even as we struggle to make sense of ourselves on our own terms within the context of the postmodern world.

> For a group of people one generation out of slavery, gender-defined work and domestic responsibilities were symbolic of their new status. . . . The tension between the ideal of a full-time mother and respect for and recognition of black working women's abilities and contributions to family income existed within a set of attitudes that tended to favor traditional sex roles. (Harley, 170–171)

MEN AND WOMEN

The segregation era's "beloved community" of African Americans resembled tribal and peasant societies worldwide. Gender roles we now regard as traditional reinforced the centrality and cohesion of family and kin in these societies. Manhood and womanhood for them were defined in terms of social roles beyond merely "husband" and "wife." All men were considered father and brother, and all women were mothers and sisters, hence, membership and collectivity was imposed on everyone irrespective of their actual blood lines. Hard work, obedience to God, respect for the dead, and caring for children were also regarded as essential elements of being an adult. Traditional households were built to contain marriage, parenting, and kin under the control of patriarchs. Single mothers, a common phenomena in many societies when married women became widowed, separated, or divorced, were included in households or lived under the protection of male relatives—substitute husbands or fathers.

In most societies, households were organized into gendered separate spheres with women responsible for domestic work, farming, and child-rearing, while men were involved in the controlling institutions of politics, war, and economics. In spite of racial segregation, until the 1960's nearly all Black families, irrespective of class, replicated these spheres.

Although they worked as maids and farm laborers outside the home, Black women were expected to perform traditional domestic work within it. Black men, in spite of severe limitations on their role in controlling the political economy of their community, were expected to head family households, assuming paternity as well as protecting and providing for their women and children.

Separate spheres assumed that women shared the same culture, ethos, and values as their men. In fact, men and women spent a great deal of their time in each other's presence—participating in the rites, rituals, and routines of daily life.

However, in desegregated society, sex, parenting, marriage, and households were radically fractured. Sexual liberation separated sex from parenthood and marriage; the racialized/gendered economics of the market place removed men from the family. Racial integration fostered individual mobility and autonomy for professionals, the intelligentsia and "stars." Media, especially television and music, reframed intimacy and personal relationships with false constructions of fantasy and emotionalism. Violence and addiction intensified the devastation of community and traditional family order. This radical social transformation resulted in men and women living as single individuals outside communal relations and restrictions.

Chronic unemployment and underdevelopment understandably intensify Black male alienation from the family. But many Black male workers and professionals also turn to the non-domestic and non-family oriented aspects of the Black community. Some activities of street culture involve criminal acts, but most are excessive "hanging out" and partying. Men whose lives are centered around "the street" have little commitment to creating households and participate only marginally in family life. Unfortunately their street activities often mask a manhood constructed out of rage against racism, confrontation with danger, and idealism about male supremacy. These ill-conceived notions of manhood block many men from doing more than merely sleeping and eating with their families.

Black women often find their child-centered values and interests in conflict with those of their men. Physical abuse, addiction, and adultery reinforce their differences.

They often become "social lesbians," single mothers who exclude men from having any significant role in their lives.

Black heterosexual couples are unable to create a community with common and progressive patterns for gender socialization of Black children.

Men and women find themselves dancing an asymmetrical sexual boogie, going different ways between dances, while their young bodies slam each other against the wall, grinding and gyrating, ignorant of authentic sexuality or genuine love.

Marriage, sexuality, and parenthood have become separate and distinct experiences in contemporary Black society. Long term, heterosexual mating and social activities are no longer a common experience for most Black people. Although there are increasing numbers of Black gay men and lesbians and more people desiring to remain single, they do not offer explanations for the problems in heterosexual relationships. Numbers aside, there remains a profound and disturbing decline in the quality of the Black heterosexual experience.

BLACK SINGLE MOTHERHOOD

Looking back on this post-industrial, conservative era, Black pundits from the next century will probably discover the noble qualities of "Black single mothers" much as the Black intelligentsia of this generation has discovered the power and nobility of Black slave women. The fact is Black single mothers, in diverse and various circumstances, are almost single-handedly responsible for the survival of the Black family and the rearing of its children. For some, the most frightening aspect of this radical social phenomena is the number of Black single mothers who have successfully raised children "on their own." In assuming this responsibility, Black women must wrestle with a number of profound issues which challenge traditional notions of family and marriage as well as of sexuality and intimacy. In order to meet the daily physical needs of children Black women must either work for wages—holding stressful, poorly paid service jobs which conflict with their parental role—or must negotiate complex systems of begrudging and shaming public assistance bureaucracies. They must also raise children in sectors of cities with old housing stock, inadequate services, and lack of safe recreational areas. Often the unpaid work of single mothering includes negotiating the battlefields of the daily wars occurring in many places in our communities. Black single mothers whose hard work and resourcefulness enable them to better provide for their families are maligned for "taking jobs away from Black men." Although they make the same commitment and sacrifice for their families as male heads of households, the legitimacy of Black female heads are questioned.

Because they are Black, female, unmarried, and have children,

Moynihanian-inspired witch hunts, sociologically constructed distortions, and just plain lies constantly hound Black single mothers. Assumed to be sexually promiscuous and regarded as "ho's" by social scientists and the media, their daily lives and experiences are stigmatized and denigrated.

The majority of Black "single" mothers became mothers as a result of an intimate sexual relationship with a Black man, although the significance of this relationship may have been only in the woman's dreams. (Even never-married teenagers dream.) Some relationships were affairs, while others were "common-law" marriages. Some women became pregnant as a result of rape or sexual coercion. Some mothers lost their spouse or mate as a result of divorce, separation (including incarceration), and death. (Although for many that loss was accompanied by the joyous gain of a better life for themselves and their children.) Few ever wanted to become *single* mothers. Although there are lesbian single mothers, the singleness of most Black mothers is a result of their break with a Black man.

In the past, Black women were trained to place men and marriage at the center of their lives, while being cautioned to guardedly approach that center without being engulfed or dominated by it. Black women were taught to be economically self-sufficient and not to rely on Black male support; at the same time, they were taught to acknowledge and promote those men's authority. Many girls remember hearing their mothers and adult women talk among themselves about man's foolishness and worthlessness, then behave dutifully in their presence. Black female views of Black men were often like the lament of the folk song—"all men are false says my mother, they tell you wicked loving lies, the next evening they court another, leaving you alone to pine and sigh." This lament wove itself through both optimism and expectations of failure when Black women fell in love with Black men. Women romanticized and sang about a "someday he'll come along" kind of lover, but grounded those dreams with a shield of pragmatism and fatalism. Unfortunately, myths about the Black female's strength and sexual promiscuity overlook the impact of her love for Black men. Because she can go on automatic pilot when it comes to wage and family work—she is after all, the daughter of slaves and maids—her vulnerability regarding men is usually hidden.

Many Black couples begin with hope and promise; however, often theirs is a union of unequals: she is a family maker and he is a rapper—a street culture denizen. He wants the party and comfort of her sexuality and domesticity. She wants his protection and maleness. They both want sex and love, but view them through different prisms: she feels emotionally connected and assumes it means long-term commitment, while he feels sensual and sexual intensity, and avoids commitment.

They both use the term "love" to describe these different perspectives, so it takes some time before their differences begin to erode the relationship. In the eyes of Black women, the relationship often declines when Black men commit a litany of misdeeds: misspent money . . . unexplained nights spent away from home . . . job hopping . . . broken promises . . . did not carry out plans . . . didn't take care of the children . . . ignored her needs. His inadequacies feed on her rage, his rage and acting out create her depression and despair. The more Black women complain, the more "it" keeps happening, and after a while she can't take "it" anymore.

However, violence and abuse along with the misdeeds also cause women to move on—male violence is probably the greatest cause of marital break-up. It was always there, contained but never eradicated, within the boundaries of the ironies of the "beloved community." As in most patriarchal societies, violence was kept hidden within families, with some women attempting to help each other and others never telling anyone about the abuse. The debased position of Black men in society evoked sympathy and silent complicity. Black women grew up being taught by other Black women to cultivate self-sufficiency and a tough front, in order to keep Black men from harming them. This was because there was no collective, community-wide response to male violence.

Black male violence is even more poignant because Black men both love and unashamedly depend on Black women's loyalty and support. Most feel that without the support of a "strong sister" they can't become "real" men. Realizing how difficult it is for Black men to work and be respected in white society, Black women feel obliged to stay at their side in spite of abuse and fear.

Black women's rationale for remaining with violent husbands and lovers is the same one given for the violence: Black male economic and social marginality. Some feel the male's violence is a direct result of his woman's employment and his own lack of a job. Others feel his marginality is reinforced by women who are not duly deferential and respectful. The "perceived" success of Black women versus Black men who do have jobs or get into school is another rationale for the violence.

The fact that violence occurs against Black women irregardless of whether they are respectful and supportive, or whether their men are prestigious, well paid, and educated, is ignored. The Black male victimizer's denial continues to be aided by the silence and defensiveness of the Black community, which is responding to white society's negative stereotyping and treatment of Black men. Black women find themselves defending Black men against these distortions by denying their own victimization. Meanwhile the violence and abuse itself leaves Black men remorseful and bitter, and sisters injured and unforgiving. Since no one acknowledges the crime of violence against Black women, their men have no place to go with their rage or "guilt" and hence, no systematic way of being healed or forgiven. Black men usually leave the situation attempting to deal with their pain and rage by themselves. While social scientists ponder the reasons for so many single mothers, cycles of violence and abuse which rip apart Black couples go unnoticed.

But the break-up of a couple, doesn't end the dilemmas and problems of Black men and women. Following society's expectation and their own socialization, men and women are almost forced to couple and mate in order to be considered normal. Black single mothers feel compelled to search for a father for their children and a man for themselves. They try to manage intimate relationships along with the responsibility of motherhood, hopefully in an environment in which sexuality is freed from patriarchal bonds.

"Sexual liberation" has, however, become a contradiction in terms because to be sexually expressive and casual in the midst of male chauvinism has meant anything but "liberation," especially for young Black women. Nevertheless, it was considered liberatory for women to be free of the sexual restrictions of the "beloved community," where modesty and primness defined the way women dressed and carried themselves. Kinked hair, loud colors, and bare legs and arms were the forbidden emblems of prostitutes. Open discussions or displays of sexuality were considered sinful according to the puritanical community. Sex between unmarried men and women was considered a taboo, although children from such liaisons were not illegitimate, and both hard working, repentant mothers and providing fathers could redeem themselves.

However, the release from the confines of their father's house has plunged Black women into forms of serial monogamy, casual sex, and emotional exploitation which seem to confirm the rationale for the very rules their father upheld. In trying to negotiate the territory between sexual desire and prohibition, Black women find themselves "liberated" but playing by a set of sexual rules which reinforce male lack of commitment and responsibility. Women are often left more alienated and estranged than when they lived under the restrictions of their father's house. They have traded the sexual restrictions of the patriarchy for casual sex, but their bodies have become casualties of sexuality dominated and defined by male desire.

In spite of such sexual precariousness, heterosexual women continue to vie with other women for the supposedly scarce commodity of a "good man." Because children are an obstacle for the woman and a burden for the man, single mothers sometimes have a disadvantage in competing for men. Relatives, usually mothers, often help dating single mothers by caring for the children. However, some men actually prefer the stability and domesticity associated with women who are mothers and heads of household. As one brother quipped, "single mothers always have food and a clean house."

However, men dating single mothers are not simply coming into a personal and sexual relationship with a woman who happens to have children, but interacting with a family which implies domestic routines, caring for children, and negotiating for time and space. However, few men have the social skills, trust, and patience necessary to manage a relationship with a woman and her children in her household.

What has priority when she, for example has to do domestic chores with her children on Saturday mornings and her lover wants her to stay in bed with him? Black single mothers find themselves frequently making choices between the needs of their man, and the needs of their families.

The situation becomes even more complicated when marrying or making long term commitments because the man now has a defined role as husband *and* father, whether he desires it or not; he has become responsible, in part, for the family and the household. Most men mistakenly read this responsibility as simply being in charge of, or the head of, the household. The single mother, rightly or wrongly, wrestles with whether she should allow him to parent her children and head *her* household. She might be reluctant to place her children in emotional or physical jeopardy by allowing him to father them "his way." Should she indeed relinquish her power as head of household, or can it be reshaped to include him? Can a man legitimately head a household he has not emotionally, financially, or biologically created?

Complicating this issue of power in the family are the woman's specific and concrete roles as mother and homemaker, which automatically make her central and essential to family life. However, men usually remain on the periphery of and therefore feel excluded from family life. Withdrawing from rather than moving toward it, he remains a marginal guest and visitor in both the family and household. He reinforces his isolation by barking orders or pouting in silence. Once again caught up in the continual, asymmetrical dance of the heterosexual relationship, the single mother is poignantly forced to choose between her household and her relationship with a man.

In order to successfully continue, there is a point at which single mothers must accept themselves as the legitimate heads of families and households which are complete without a father or husband. Although ending the preoccupation with finding a man doesn't preclude intimate relationships, single mothers must begin to focus on the priority of building a life and family with her children.

Rejecting an intimate life with a man as too fraught with danger, pain, and confusion, many Black single mothers become "social lesbians." Neither sexual preference nor feminist choice, "social lesbians" have not chosen to spend their social lives with other women. But since they work in gender segregated jobs, rely on support from other women, participate in churches and social organizations dominated by women, their lives are homosocial.

The "social lesbian" is often full of rage about being single and blames her particular experiences with Black men on all Black men. To mask her rage about being hurt by Black men, many "social lesbians" make defensive and lofty public statements supporting them. Privately, they trash and condemn Black men. Often their only contact with men is that of casual sex.

Because they do not have an ongoing relationship with a man, "social lesbians" believe they are inadequate women. These feelings of inadequacy and rejection reinforce a unique form of homophobia which causes them to also reject close relationships with women. "Social lesbians" rarely honestly confront their "singleness" or engage in realistic relationships with either men or women.

Being heterosexual and without a mate is complicated by motherhood, but Black single mothers needn't view themselves as outcasts. Their responsibilities as heads of households and as mothers are legitimate. The daily needs of self and children are crucial, taking precedence over bad heterosexual relationships. Black single motherhood is an opportunity for women to create close and honest nonsexual relationships with both men and women. Their condition and status imply a new way of being heterosexual and "single." These new ways for creating and prioritizing relationships are essential for building a community based upon neither bitterness nor compulsion but upon love.

FATHERHOOD

For every Black single mother, there is a non-residential father—a man cut off from his children by distance and emotions. Fathering from outside a household, especially without money, is admittedly difficult, but the non-residential father often visits and thinks about his children, even though he has not committed his life to them. Unfortunately, he is usually involved in behaviors, sometimes addictions, which alienate him from family life and children. Often frustrated because he can't measure up to the power of the mythical or actual patriarchy, the non-residential father gives up all forms of serious parenting, but longs to be a patriarch.

These Black men want to be heads of households where women and children do not question their authority and judgment. They believe that their female companion is "their woman" and hence, required to be obedient and docile. These would-be patriarchs often view Black women's wage earning work as a threat to her traditional domestic role in the family. However, since in many instances he is either unemployed or has only meager financial resources, her wages are necessary for maintaining the household. The would-be patriarch's dilemma is his inability to establish and maintain a household without his "woman's" financial contribution. Rather than create a cooperative family leadership with his companion, he clings to intimidation to maintain the dominant role in the household.

However, our fathers and grandfathers, who had even fewer material resources than contemporary Black men, earned the respect of their wives and children. Although their wives worked, Black husbands and fathers were regarded as heads of their households because of their commitment to marriage and family. In spite of working in low-paying and often demeaning jobs, they were committed to and involved in the daily life of the family. When they couldn't find steady work, they did odd jobs.

In addition, Black male authority at home, "was backed not merely by individual force but also by mechanisms of social control enforced by ruling classes, churches, and the state." (Mann, 155) It must also be remembered that this authority or patriarchy was restricted by Black male subjugation under segregation. Many Black men of that era were violent and abusive toward their women and children. Others had "women on the side" and though they fathered children out of wedlock, the Black patriarchal culture demanded they acknowledge and care for whatever children they fathered. Many Black men simply could not support their families and often left to become "roving men."

However, in spite of these problems, Black men of the past *defined* their manhood in terms of fatherhood, marriage, and maintaining a stable family; many Black men of my generation do not.

Many now non-residential fathers once lived in households with children and their mothers. These would-be patriarchs often absent themselves physically or emotionally from the carrying out of duties necessary to being respected fathers and husbands. Not having wage work makes it difficult for some men to perform these duties, further estranging them from their families who, paradoxically, should be a motivation for them to work and avoid the pitfalls of streetlife. Then, undoubtedly with a great deal of pain and anguish, these men allow their children to be reared solely by their mothers. Without authority or habit, the men remain estranged from their children—visiting strangers who have given up on ever being fathers to their children.

Although appearing to be "single," the non-residential father may date or live with single mothers. He often has fathered children with other mothers. Alienated from his biological children, he finds that bringing them to even visit with the family of the woman he is currently "seeing" is often difficult and tense. While single mothers parent all the time, the non-residential father's skills at parenting are undeveloped and uneven. He limits his role to picking up "his" kids from their mother's, bringing them to "his woman's house" to be cared for along with her kids.

He often has an exaggerated and distorted need to be recognized and respected by the women and children he lives with. However, he seems uncomfortable living with children at all. His misreading of children's emotions, and the feelings of inadequacy that follow, make it impossible for him to parent in a way which commands, rather than demands, respect. He is jealous and resentful of the mother because she must devote time to housework and childcare. This kind of "single" man continues to drift from woman to woman, sojourning but never fully participating in either the family he's in or the one he's left behind.

These men continue to use the excuse that they need emotional and physical distance and avoid responsibility to their children. They believe that lack of money and contentious relationships with their children's mothers prevent fathers from "seeing their kids." But they don't provide financial or emotional support for the family they live with, either. They unsuccessfully attempt to become a powerful patriarch without assuming fatherly responsibility. False bravado often masks feelings of failure and inadequacy from not being a better father.

However, there are growing numbers of Black men who are realizing, sometimes too late, that successful fathering is intertwined with their becoming a man. These men understand that being a father requires constant demonstrations of love and concern. The child's needs take precedence over male chauvinism or ego. Many are discovering new ways of being non-residential fathers by sharing responsibility with their children's mothers. The best aspects of the Black patriarchal tradition are being reclaimed when men, who often lack money, continue to redefine their roles as fathers.

CONCLUSION

> Oh that my head were waters, and mine eyes a fountain of tears, that I might weep day and night for the slain of the daughter of my people.
>
> Jeremiah 9:1

Jeremiah's lamentation about the destruction of Jerusalem informs my own concerns about the complex relationship between the decline of the "beloved" community and our present crisis in heterosexual coupling and the struggle to create families. The power of individual mothers and fathers stands in contrast with the powerlessness of the Black community as a whole. I wonder if contemporary Black adults will gain the power to reproduce the best of our selves in our children? Will our children continue to be intellectually, emotionally, physically, and spiritually slain by the loss of community and the weakening of family? How long can Black men and women continue to exist in separate cultures which place them at risk for a kind of emotional AIDS, which thrives on their nihilism and alienation?

While the intelligentsia celebrates the power of the erotic and unearths powerful identities within the social construction of sexuality, Black youth and their counterparts across the country are constructing a sexually destructive and, indeed, pornographic way of life. The drugs, consumerism, violence, and music which feed that sexuality are controlled by economic strings which go beyond youth communities. Irrespective of their backgrounds, young people are seduced and enraptured by sexual symbols. The values and culture of individualism and alienation are fostered by the marketplace, which has appropriated Black cultural forms and artists. If integration meant the movement of Black workers into the economic mainstream, offering educational and occupational opportunity for Black children, then the culture which came with "social" integration was not only unanticipated, but functioned to subtly undermine that movement.

While Black communities were undergoing changes in sexual behavior, there were similar changes in the larger society. Casual sex among college students, movie stars, and the upper classes was promoted as an emblem of personal liberation. Sexual liberation during the 1960s was informed by the anti-patriarchal Playboy culture which connected with a more sexually permissive intelligentsia and which merged with Black working-class blues culture. Superseding the restrictions imposed by church and family, the marketplace and media packaged and sold sexual liberation to adolescents as symbolic of rebellion and evidence of adulthood.

Among many contemporary Black adolescents, sexuality has become a "lethal weapon." Sex has been a central theme in rap—a Black adolescent cultural form. The oppositional aspects of rap have become the perfect vehicle for promoting violence and sexuality. Neither the majority of rap artists nor the democratic poetics of the form is at fault. Rap's Black youth origins enable record companies to commodify, package, and sell "sex" and machismo back to Black youth like so many crack vials.

"Vulgar rap," an extremely scatological form of rap, reproduces and represents sexual confusion, demeaning Black men and women. Unfortunately, sexual behavior on the street, in the schools, and even in the home replicates the messages of vulgar rap. Black girls attend schools in which the rap-inspired idea that Black woman equals "ho" prevails. As recent reports indicate, they are daily sexually harassed, poked, and touched, in ways Anita Hill could not even imagine. These girls have grown so accustomed to being called "vulgar names," they use them to refer to themselves. When a curious melange of white conservatives, Black nationalists, and feminists opposes vulgar rap, freedom of speech is invoked. But how can the right of the rapper to free speech be upheld if its based upon the denigration of me and my daughters?

Vulgar rap is only a part of the decline of Black community control over the behavior and morality of its youth. It is indicative of the inability of adults to create safe public spaces free of violence or obscenity. Because patriarchs of my father's generation controlled the behavior of young men within and outside their families, Black men were forced to treat Black women with respect in public places. (Although they maintained private places, such as brothels and bars, where they could enjoy "immoral women.") In the absence of patriarchal power, today's adults are not able to contain the behavior of young men. Contemporary Black women freed of patriarchal restrictions about their dress, mobility, and sexuality are considered "immoral" or "ho's". The challenge is whether Black men and women, be they socialists, nationalists, or womanists, can create communal control over their young people's social behavior—

without the patriarchy.

The contention between heterosexual men and women of my generation over issues of power, chauvinism, and sexuality has immobilized our ability to gain moral authority over our teenagers. Our confusion has enabled our community's sexual values and behavior to be overtaken by the culture of adolescent rappers with their white, playboy managers and agents. Sherley Anne Williams notes that Black youth "listen only to each other, and have such contempt for us they hardly listen to a word we say (and barely understand what they do hear)." (Williams, 170) These are simply new forms of bondage which must be decidedly rejected . . . but by whom? If the sexual legacy of adult men and women is so confused and impotent, then how can our children learn to become men and women?

The Black intelligentsia, including my womanist community, continue to produce radical books which do not reach the hands of Black youth in any systematic way. We engage in radical discourse about the past but never make consistent contact with the young people who are our future. The sisters and brothers on the block are not helped by the intelligentsia's endless debates among ourselves about gender and male chauvinism.

Influential Black leaders who could promote an authentic and respectful sexual ethic and a gender-political agenda for the Black community are reluctant to speak out too loudly lest we discover their own improprieties and vulgarity.

Not all playboy rappers are Black, adolescent, or male. Many are included in the professional classes, the intelligentsia, and the conservative and liberal leadership. They publicly pimp off of condemning Black teenagers and single mothers and adolescents while engaging in sordid sexual games and indulging in pornography. Although the rap is different, the playing is the same. Tragically, their leadership fails to help those attempting to build successful families, and reclaim their community.

Fortunately for this generation of Black children, many Black women accept the responsibility for their care. Black women's almost habitual efforts, however, have exacted a high price, often sapping their energy and health. There are limits to Black women's strength. As noble as the efforts are to mother at any cost, women can not raise children alone.

While the sexual and marital choices of Black women are not beyond critical assessment, policies designed to encourage marriage or to limit childbearing as solutions to her problems do not adequately address her needs. Black women shouldn't have to raise children without sufficient material resources and community support from concerned and bold Black men and women. As an African proverb says, "It takes an entire village to raise a child." All men and women in the village are mothers and fathers, implying roles which authorize them to watch over the community and all its children.

Single or two-parent families cannot control the social reproduction of their children without collective social and political power. Black parents can save and sacrifice to put their children through college, but, by themselves, they have no power to determine what they are taught in those colleges. Black parents can teach their children to be moral and law abiding, but they can't individually contain the culture of violence and vulgarity.

In the Black community, gender is about collective power and control over social reproduction. Black people need a gender agenda which emphasizes the protection and care for Black children; which meets Black teenagers' need for tough love and support; and encourages dialogue and healing among and between Black men and Black women.

Across the country Black parents and organizations are unknowingly working on particular elements of this larger gender agenda; however, there is no conscious analysis and plan nor overall leadership. Resources exist for sustaining a broader, more politically driven gender agenda and for organizing more systematic programs in the school systems, at worksites, in the prisons and on the streets. However, a drug-free and nonviolent Black community is needed in order to carry out this agenda. This agenda is a tough love applied to ourselves as Black adults: a leap into another kind of maturity—to act like grown men and women and reclaim our community.

Black heterosexual men and women must have an erotic, intimate sexual sphere: it is our human right. Forced celibacy or addictive sexuality is not healthy or desirable. We need spaces where we can dance with each other. Women must feel safe enough to make a leap of faith again with men who have become worthy of their trust, who recognize their humanity and can become converted to family.

However, a liberating sexual life is an integral and necessary part of our social and political liberation. In turn, our politics and vision of liberation have always been connected to our belief in God. In our community every great Black leader, every good mother and father, every lover has always claimed an intimate walk with God. Those of us who want to live and love and want our children to have a good life can not prevail without the power of God. Collective and spiritual power enabled the "beloved community" to prevail in the past, and are necessary for our current survival.

The gender agenda acknowledges the pernicious role of the white world within our psyche and community, but requires that we suspend how and what white society does to and for us, in order to grapple with our own survival. I assume that since most Black people love and live with each other, we need to view our selves and the spaces we occupy as a community in opposition to white supremacy and its market economy. We may have to earn our money from that market, and live in a society dominated by white power, but we don't have to succumb to its presence in all aspects of our lives.

We can build a community which contains the best of our southern and African past and the most significant lessons learned from our present attempts at family and community. We can envision a future which will not be contained within a Black world, but which can not exist without its sensibility and ethos. We must build villages to raise our children and a new "beloved community" where Black men and women can dance together at their own healing pace and by their own loving rhythms.

PART II

INVISIBLE TO THE NAKED EYE
BLACK WOMEN
AND THE ACADEMY

6

THE SILENCE AND THE SONG

TOWARD A BLACK WOMAN'S HISTORY, THROUGH A LANGUAGE OF HER OWN

SHE WAS CENTRAL TO the slave economy which was central to the development of the Americas, north and south, and critical to the intimate and personal dynamics of the white families for whom she worked. She was at the center of the struggles and the whirlwinds, the ups and downs of Black life: its families, its churches, its organizations, and its ideas. She dared to walk union picket lines, sign antiwar petitions, begin schools, and stand up for the downtrodden and less fortunate. She has danced and sung her way across the Americas and Europe for at least a century. And she has been writing books, making speeches, and creating poetry for more than two hundred years on this continent and since the beginning in her homeland. Yet there are no history books that tell her story on her own terms, few history books that sing her songs.

Colleges and universities have promised to teach white men, and recently white women and men and women of color, universal truths and useful knowledge. The very universality of their claims have always been false and their "truths" and "knowledge" have been most often used to oppress and silence most of the world's people. Black women attending colleges have been taught to instruct, but not to teach, to learn but not to know, to research the works of others, but not to create their own. Though there have been noble attempts by Black women to succeed—to break through and overcome these barriers against creating new languages, new perspectives and knowledge—the unique voice of Black women and their experiences has been silenced.

History books and social scientific studies about Black women have yet to capture, touch, or transmit their historical experiences and visions with the truth and depth of the poetry, songs, and novels written by Black women about Black women. The Black woman is certainly a historical being, but where is her history? Where are the books for high school and college reading that tell her story? Where are the lengthy discussions about her political philosophy, her religious theology, her sociological methods? How did she become so central, yet so invisible; so outspoken, yet so silenced?

A pioneer Black woman historian of the eighties writes:

> Despite the range and significance of our history, we have been perceived as token women in Black texts and as token Blacks in the feminist ones. Most of the books that focus on Afro-American women are of the "contributions" type: the achievements of Black women, who despite double discrimination and oppression, were able to duplicate the feats of Black men or White women.
>
> What I learned by reading these texts was important and illuminating. But it wasn't enough. For Black women have a history of their own, one which reflects their distinct concerns, values and the roles they have played as both Afro-Americans and women. And their unique status has had an impact on both racial and feminist values.
>
> So I set out to write a narrative history on Black women, tracing their concerns—and what they did about them—from the 17th century to the contemporary period. It is thematic in approach, using a broad canvas to illustrate the nature and meaning of the Black women's experience.[1]

In writing *When and Where I Enter*, a narrative history of Black women, Paula Giddings has begun our search for our own historical language. She has built upon the documentary histories of Gerda Lerner, Bert Loewenberg, and Ruth Bogin; the historical surveys of Angela Davis and Jeanne Noble; and the more distant legacies of diaries, speeches, papers of Black women.[2]

Inevitably, Black women's history will fully emerge only when Black women become "griots" speaking and creating a historical language of their own. The Black woman griot historian actually is not a reflection of the "griot's" historical role in West African traditional society, where they were usually male, and attached to the courts to praise royal lineage. Here the "griot" is a symbolic conveyor of African oral and spiritual traditions of the entire community. A "griot historian" is a scholar in any discipline who connects, uses, and understands the methods and insights of both Western and African world-views and historical perspectives to further develop a synthesis—an African American woman's social science with a unique methodology, sensibility, and language. The "griot historian" is and must be a warrior breaking down intellectual boundaries while destroying the political limitations to her people's—and, indeed, all humanity's—liberation. She is a challenger to the university's way of operating. She carves out new lands of the mind while reaching back to her spiritual and cultural sources, the major one, of course, being Africa, with its rivers and memories. One river named for the African orisha, Oshun, a symbol of female power and sensuality, is a guiding power for the griot-historian's quest.

THE SILENCE

The African woman had been baptised. Since the beginning of time, the power of woman came through her. The lives of men and of women were seen through her eyes. She sang and danced their story. But then she was raped and became chattel and then she became silent. First she dared to moan from memory the songs of her African mother. She sang out in her own words the tunes she recalled. She moaned and sang while tending fields, washing clothes, preparing food, and caring for her kin. Some dared to write diaries and letters. Some spoke out against the pain, "but none but Jesus heard." Her sisters heard her whisper. Her brothers heard her sing the blues, white others wailed out in spirituals.

Black women poets and writers heard all of them and combined their voices into books and poetry. Black women fought against the silencing. A few tried to tell the history and moved toward being a "griot" while remembering the river where the first African woman had been baptised long before the horror of her sentence of silence.

Before a new language which captures the experience of Black women in the Americas can be created, the griot-historian must "break de chains" of Western thought which controls the methods and visions of the historical process. The Black woman griot-historian must be baptised by some force outside the tradition of Western civilization and become submerged in the waters of Black women's pain, power, and potential. In order to tell their story, the griot-historian must acknowledge and reach beyond the shame of being the embodiment of the "underclass" and the mother of the "teenage mother." She must overcome her fear of the stigma of being the daughter of Aunt Jemima, the granddaughter of "negra wenches," and the great granddaughter of Africans called "primitive and animal-like." Seeing the woman beyond the shame affirms the use of historical truths, to sing praise songs which resurrect the lives and experiences of the orisha, the warrior, and the "drylongso" Black woman.

The history, study, and writing of Black women is shaped by two conflicting paradigms existing within the United States of America; a culture and a nation that she and her brother unwillingly helped to create and that they both willingly struggle to transform and change into a more humane society. The Black woman griot-historian must be shaped by an African world-view which evolved within democratic/consensus tribal societies where the oral tradition of transmitting information and knowledge is interwoven among music, art, dance, and crafts, and everyday activities intermix with communication and connection with both the spiritual world and the ancestral past.

Rites and rituals, along with intuition, feelings, seeing, speaking, and singing embody a tremendous repertoire of historical methods. The griot-historian who recognizes and uses these methods as well as reading and writing is in opposition to the paradigm of Western intellectual history and its civilization. The ways of knowing which have developed in the West betray an obsession with rational thought; an inability to connect body, mind, and spirit; and a preoccupation with domination based simultaneously upon violence and impotence.

Since the nineteenth century, history has been the most powerful discipline within the academy, spawning all other social sciences-psychology, anthropology, political science, economics—and shaping their conceptual framework and methodologies. The control of history and the writing of history is the means of controlling how people think about themselves and their place in the world and in time.

There have been three significant developments in the discipline of history during the last hundred years. First, German historian Leopold von Ranke helped establish history as a discipline in the universities, making it the "Queen of the Sciences." He promoted the concept that all "sound history must use primary sources and rigorous scientific methods." Second, Karl Marx's historical method, which relies on materialism as a basis for explaining the development of nation states from "primitive [sic] commu-nalism," examines the contradiction of class under capitalism. Third, dur-ing the twentieth century many historians have broken with traditional history to study social history: the everyday experiences of average men and women. Social history evolved from the protests and movements of the working class, people of color, and white women in Western societies.

In the West the scientific approaches of both social and natural scien-tists are based upon isolating and concentrating on data, atoms, and facts. Placing the observer in an ivory tower with pen and pad, telescope or books to observe the comings and goings of the lowly is at the locus of Western thinking. Western thought, especially in the social sciences, rests upon reading, writing, and thinking, in an ivory tower removed from human distractions. The function of distance is to enable the observer ostensibly to objectify, but actually to dominate the observed. In this manner, the observer-scholar has become connected to the conquistador and the slave master, for his observations become useful data for explain-ing and justifying the domination of the observed. As subjects of Western scientific research, the African in the New World is transformed into an entity who constitutes the silent and the missing of history—the slave, the negress, and the nigger. For nearly four hundred years, including the contemporary present, Black women have been used by white men simul-taneously as slaves and servants and as whores and workers. The accom-panying history and other social sciences of the West are preoccupied with racist pathology which views Black life and history, when it views it at all, as problematic. Thus, a Black woman historian of Black women is not merely a contradiction in terms, but an ontological impossibility, for all Black women within the academy are regarded as nonbeings and therefore without a history outside of the white world.

Black women who attempt to study Black women using the discipline of history are students in an institution whose entire raison d'être, philos-ophy, methods, purpose, and history have never allowed her voice to be heard, her body to be respected, or her existence to be recognized. Black women writing Black women's history outside the academy are unduly pressured and, at least, influenced by the academy's definitions and meth-ods of "doing history." The authentic historian of Black women, therefore, cannot reside in the ivory tower or its shadows trying to see Black women through her master's telescope. From way up there, all the observer will see is a shadow. She will not be able to hear Black women moan and sing.

Black women scholars in the shadows or the rooms of the ivory tower get caught too tightly within their training to see and feel the serious involvement of their sisters' and mothers' scientific commitment to the past and the future (because their science is derived from traditional African, Indian, and women's culture which uses and combines information about mind and body, feelings and thought, the seen and unseen into a holistic understanding of the world').

Most Black women scholars have been trained by white men or by people who have been trained by white men. At first, a Black woman student gets overtaken by a passion to become scholarly to please those who have trained her, then she develops the scholar's love of learning, the search for truth, and the concern with "objectivity." She spends long hours in the library verifying her every instinct and thought. Seminars and lectures are religiously attended and she takes copious notes. Books and sources are read and reread; papers are written in that precise and professional style in which the "I" and "me" and "she" have been changed into a discussion about subjects, clients, and "theys." After all, she is competing in the white man's world and must prove herself to him in order to pass the course, get the job on the faculty, get her grant funded, receive a book contract, or simply to justify all that time spent studying and postponing her life.

Black colleges and institutions of higher education which have housed and educated many Black scholars have also failed to produce significant Black women griot-historians—scholar-warrior-women who could liberate Black people as well as defend and produce Black intellectual and cultural traditions. Black colleges influence Black public opinion and policy through their training and recognition of Black social scientists in Black periodicals, journals, and other publications. Black historians, both male and female, have been confined to a vision usually concerned with restoring Black manhood and pride by demonstrating the equality or superiority of Black "civilization" to white "civilization." In nationalistic, patriarchal, and bourgeois terms, they chronicle Black contributions to American society usually in terms of "great" Black male leaders who have uplifted the race out of poverty into the middle class. Furthermore, increasing numbers of Black female social scientists in both "Black" and "white" publications have focused a considerable amount of their writings on Black male-female relations and the Black family in little more than idealistic lamentations of the passing of the patriarchal family. Their historical writings have documented the legacies of supposedly "exceptional" Black women, most of them, like Mary McCleod Bethune, who pulled themselves out of poverty into powerful, middle-class positions, or women like

Mary Church Terrell, strong middle-class fighters for Black social justice. What about the nameless members of Ms. Bethune's National Council of Negro Women? What about Black women domestics and labor leaders, blues artists and mothers? What about those extraordinary, ordinary Black women of the past and present who are our mothers, our sisters, and daughters? For although Black women have been professional social scientists, instructors, and students in Black colleges for over a century, the Black academy and the Black church have taught Black women to devalue their sexuality, African philosophical perspectives (especially spiritualism), radical culture and politics, and "low class" women and "no count" men—that is, the poor and working class. They learned to write and study with and about Black men and viewed Black women from that vantage point, neither particularizing Black women's experiences nor taking them seriously enough to institutionalize Black women's scholarship. Could that be why Zora Neale Hurston died a forgotten woman in an unmarked grave? Or why it took Spelman College, a Black female institution of higher learning, over a century to develop a Black women's center for research and study?

No institution of "higher learning" and few publications and magazines allowed the Black woman to speak, to write her own story in her own way. Daughter after daughter, both inside and outside the academy, grew up ignorant and mute about themselves. They always deferred the more important historical places to their men. They wrote histories and documented experiences of themselves that were incomplete, and dulled by years of silence. They forgot the griot-historians that came before them and their sister scholars were unknown to them. They omitted the blood of their sister's abortion, their sister's lesbian lover, the gele-lapa wrapped women, the warriors who became "sick and tired of being sick and tired," the singers who shouted in church and the silent musings of dancers, teenagers, and workers. They could not hear their own hearts and voices. The academy had successfully trained Black women against herself and her sisters.

And unlike her brothers, Carter G. Woodson, Arthur Schomburg, W. E. B. Du Bois, Ivan Van Sertima, and John Henrik Clarke, she had little room to collect the facts and write books telling her story. For even with a degree she was first a worker and a mother. She had no companion to type her records, save money for books, to care for the children so she could study, or to cook for her while she wrote and thought. Her life was caught up in babies and work and men and struggle. With few exceptions her story would remain silenced and unwritten, or if written unpublished; *except for Zora Neale.*

The Black woman griot-historian in the West, even more so than her brother, had to fight for the right and the time to think and to know, the right and the time to learn and to be literate, the right to come together with her sisters in serious discourse about themselves—examining, analyzing, criticizing any and all aspects of the world. She had to struggle for the right "to see" what she saw, and to speak about it in her own way.

THE SONG

> *The woman stood up with ghosts on her shoulders . . . she reached inside and a voice rose up and a story came through her which spoke of our past . . . and the old people tapped their feet while the eyes of children shined . . .*

The Black woman griot-historian must wrestle herself free of the demons of the discipline of history which deny her. Eventually she must break the fetters of the academy and its shadow on Black women's thought. She must retrace the steps of our people, allowing the capacity of her dreams and her struggle to guide her through the raw material and data of our history. She must embrace the men and women of the past who push their voices into her body and mind, ignoring time and death to do so.

The Black woman scholar faces the index cards of facts and references as she sits down to write, and the voices of the academy come to haunt: "Bad history are those set of assertions which cannot be verified with primary sources." "Your language is too subjective." "Quote from authorized sources!" "Demonstrate how this is significant to the entire society, not just Black people." "Don't be a generalist!" "Your work is too rhetorical, too lyrical." She sits immobilized, caught between those voices and the voices of her mothers and fathers. Her writing becomes paralyzed and stunted; stillborn within her psyche.

Yet Black women novelists, poets, activists, dramatists, artists, singers, and dancers use their ancestral voices, serve them, and allow them to become a medium for "brutal honesty" about the Black experience. Their honesty and passions enable their readers, in turn, to use the Black experience as an explication of the struggle of the human spirit to be free. The Black woman's cultural and literary renaissance of the 1970s and 1980s has demonstrated the model for Black women in social science, especially historical writing. These "wild women" have been able to use a combination of historical voices, spiritual consciousness, liberation politics within creative mediums and works designed to empower and enlighten. Their example should urge social scientists to use simultaneity, multiple consciousness, and diverse approaches in their work.

Dialogues, letters, and family histories are some of the tools historians use to build their theories of human movement through time and space. In the hands of Alice Walker, Gayl Jones, and Toni Morrison these tools take us straight into the insides of Black women, drawing attention to the immediacy of their pasts with their "twists of fate" and the incredible sense of justice going and coming around.

Many renaissance women use slavery as a reference point—the "slave within us" as a present place of confusion and limitation while emancipation, the "laying down of the world," comes from reliance on feelings and passion. That holocaust can never become objectified. It is always remembered in the way they touch it gently with lines from spirituals and memories of chains. The father's ravishings in *Corregidora* and the slave love of *Sally Hemings* are not allowed to become self-righteous and simplistic, but rather human dilemmas and tragedies brought about when human beings become sexual chattel. The holocaust of the renaissance woman is a personal, not merely a political statement of enslavement.

Using the language of the people of everyday Black life without apology or adherence to the "underclassness and poverty" of Black life, renaissance writers and singers reinforce the dignity of Black women as brilliant, insightful philosophers and commentators on the human experience around them. The responsibility of the chronicler is to hear what people truly are saying about their experiences. To use their rhythm and cadence of expression to define and describe and not delete it from the retelling. The retelling should not be blindly copied. The language of the people should become shaped and honed into a conscious statement of both the writer and her people. The words must become musical notes and beats in the hands of the musician who can then put all the parts together.

The language of the social sciences tends to be mechanical and fraught with fear because the words do not have life. So much of the research material is dry and lifeless, few can or want to read it unless they are forced. Social science information repeated in magazine articles is vivid, but hardly accurate and, in no way is it "brutally honest." The people they discuss get lost in charts and data, overshadowed by language constructs designed to hide their humanity rather than illuminate and celebrate it. The people who need the truth the most, for example Black women, get turned off because there are few social scientists who are trained to translate and write clearly and passionately of their lives. Articles by Black women social scientists that are committed to eradicating poverty and strengthening the Black family are often passionless discourses unlike the music, poetry, and writings of Black women of the renaissance of the 1970s and 1980s.

Many of those renaissance women rely upon African culture-orisha power, rites, rituals, colors, and sounds. Toni Cade Bambara's description of the dialogue between the healer and "her old hag" beautifully illustrates the work and the world of the spiritualist in the African tradition. Many Black artists stand in awe of the great human mysteries which can't be explained in rational terms. (Just how did Harriet manage to free all those slaves?) The reliance on the spiritual center for answers, explanations, and focus is the strongest opposition to Western social and natural science. All questions can't be answered through objectivity, and certainly the Black woman's power and knowing can't be understood without a knowing of her spirit and spiritual life. Black spiritual and gospel music seems to impart the most perfect notes to match the internal rhythm of Black women's prayers and visions. Wasn't it the prayers of Black mothers that placed Black daughters in the academy in the first place? And once there, Black women were able to push these mothers aside for the first time in their lives and became lost and confused without them. Social scientists in their search for reasons, theories, themes, and explanations of human history have always dismissed the concept of inner spiritual life as a force in a material world, though any truly scientific understanding would have to acknowledge it. Resurrecting those prayers and dreams is the most difficult wrestling Black women scholars have to do . . . though it is all too necessary for any sensible understanding of the world and Black women's place within it.

Renaissance women blaze a path of spirituality and sexuality which moves us all to defy the limits placed upon our lives, especially upon our gender, our race, and our heterosexuality. The biomythography, poems, and essays of Audre Lorde implore us not to use the master's tools anymore, but to seek the power of the erotic along with other powers of our liberation. These artists defy our mothers' fear of sexuality and its power and force us to link sexual freedom with liberation politics. As organizers and activists altering movements for social and political change, the renaissance artists have renounced the thoughts of the white and Black patriarchs. Their political warriorship infuses their writings. They have also worked in myriad low-paying, demeaning jobs to survive. Many have been secretaries, waitresses, maids, and lonesome travelers from city to town, seeing and learning. As pioneers they painfully had to create the space to stand. Like Nina Simone and Miriam Makeba, they had to create ways to sing their own song. Nothing was given to them. They had to expand their reach by recalling the powerful Black women of the past as they drew strength from their sisters in collectives, friendships, love affairs, and organizations. Many were escapees from the ivory tower, thrown off paths of legitimacy to become word warriors and documenters of the Black woman's world.

To be thrown off the path to and from the ivory tower is no longer stigma, but part of the baptismal needed to empower Black women and to demystify the West's way of knowing. And once outside in the "real world," they discover there can be no scholarship or writing on behalf of the oppressed unless it points toward liberation, no real writings except those which lead to revolution and freedom. Justifications and rationalization of oppression without a class stand with working people without affirming Blackness and the language, history, and cultures of other people of color, without explicitly loving women and telling their story and without using common sense and our mothers' wit about life, is an inexcusable travesty of both scholarship and politics. Yet the writings of Black women social scientists who, meaning no harm, uphold whiteness, maleness, and privilege, do harm, furthering the oppression of their sisters. Black women who author historical studies which use whiteness as the model and reference point when discussing the suffrage movement, radical organization, and education, demonstrate the poor training and lack of consciousness of these sisters. Yet the politics of the renaissance women teach us to "lay down that world" and embrace the downtrodden and speak fearlessly of our people, our sisterhood, and the richness of our spirit and culture.

There are far too many lost legacies and sheroes whose stories lie obscured and hidden. The problem of publishing these works is another story of prejudice and jealousy. Clearly, Black women novelists have demonstrated the commercial success of Black women writing about Black women. Yet publishers still frown upon and reject social scientific writings by Black women about Black women. Our tasks as social scientists are to discover alternatives and possibilities, as well as new ways to speak to our sisters, while we fight the academy's partners in silence—the print and broadcast media.

Like gospel singers, the griot historian stands with her sisters, and those shadows of past women and men stand behind her singing words in her ears. She writes about the moving women, the warriors, and the silent women. She stops writing to go outside to march with her sisters and brothers, shaking their fists at the madness of those who enslave. She anonymously writes a leaflet for the march. She passes it out, separated from her authorship and ownership of the words. She meets with the others to plan, to cheer, to worry about the next time and the next time. She puts the children to bed, waits for her lover to come in, make love, and fall asleep. Then she returns to the typewriter and Zora Neale is there waiting for her—soothing her and urging her on. She, fighting the fatigue of her body with spirit energy, writes the history of what was and is. While writing about the slave, the words become the moans of women, sounds from the mourners bench in southern churches. She suddenly remembers why there was a bench and why her grandmother got up early to take her with her to sing and moan there in that old-timey way. Her grandmother was a slave and the words she writes and reads about slavery are about her, and she strains to remember the face of the oldest person in her family, for the story of slavery is in her blood, not just in the books. And the white men can never know it or teach it because it is in her beyond the words and the footnotes. The next day our griot walks to the store and hears Black girls clapping the same rhythm as African drums. The girls look her up and down with disdain, and seeing how she's dressed and how old she is, they go back to sing and rap some more. These sisters, with their tough street selves, await her words in some future time and she must leave the words for them and their children's children. Each precious word becomes something for them and the time capsule Black women and men will need and seek.

She becomes multilingual. She understands and speaks the oppressor's language—Europeanese. She also speaks with Du Bois and learns. She speaks along with Bessie Smith, and Dinah Washington, and Billie Holiday. She does research using the poking-around method of Zora Neale. She interprets and translates a speech into a story which becomes a political program in the hands of some, a bedtime story for the mother, the document and scholarly paper for the library and conference, the legal defense of the fugitive, and all these forms become the song. And all of it becomes history, the recording of those who are, what was done, and will be done.

And when the sister griot writes these words which touch so many, especially other sisters, they become a part of her words and part of her grandmother's moans and the girl's clapping. They all smile after she hits the right chords, verifying and amening with the poets, the singers, and the dancers. Others translate her history into their own languages, and they further the story, and the songs become extensions of the sister griot historian.

Her historical method is to take the melody and spread it to the singers in the chorus behind her, and as each one sings the melody and improvises upon it in her own way, the sounds come together. Each one becomes a griot, a storyteller of the past and future. They all learn to create a song loud enough to end the silence.[3]

7

ORIGINS

THE ROOTS OF THE BLACK FEMINIST INTELLIGENTSIA

> It is impossible for Black female intellectuals to blossom if we do not
> have a core belief in ourselves, in the value of our work, and a
> corresponding affirmation from the world around us that can sus-
> tain and nurture.
>
> bell hooks (161)

THE EMERGENCE OF A Black feminist intelligentsia is one of the
most important developments of the desegregated era of American life.
This intelligentsia is a social phenomenon which profoundly impacts
both the production and reproduction of knowledge as well as the social
and cultural development of African Americans and, more generally,
American society. Since the 1960s, enough Black female intellectuals have
emerged to create an intelligentsia with several distinctive forms evi-
denced in books, articles, speeches, and plays, as well as in the visual and
performing arts.

The social origins of the contemporary Black female intelligentsia are
broader than the distinctive collective experiences Black women share. In
order to write about ourselves in relation to the intellectual structures of
history, power, and knowledge, a group of Black women had to be
"thrown off" the normal course of Black female experience. It was neces-

sary for a group to have the time necessary to develop a conscious aware-ness of themselves within a supportive climate and with a supportive audience for their works. The Southern Civil Rights Movement provided the necessary environment and condition for creating a Black feminist intelligentsia.

bell hooks refers to Terry Eagleton's *The Significance of Theory* for a def-inition of an intellectual. "Clearly he considers it essential that intellectu-als be creative thinkers, explorers in the realm of ideas who are able to push to the limits and beyond, following ideas in whatever direction they might take." (hooks, 152) An intelligentsia is "a systematically constituted group bound . . . by common perception dispositions, practices and insti-tutions that account for the systematized nature of their intellectual pro-duction while simultaneously allowing for different discursive strategies within the intellectual field." (Franco, 504)

Often, elitist ideologies obscure the material conditions of intellectual work. Both producers and consumers create myths about the social ori-gins and contexts of such work. Western intellectual traditions for exam-ple, usually claim racial, male, and cultural superiority as a rationale for their ascendancy. While every culture has gifted thinkers and wise men and women, here social rather than innate conditions create and sustain intellectual production. All intellectual work and its producers, even Black feminist ones, first develop from specific social contexts, practices, and arrangements. Then the work and its creators become abstract and symbolic representations. After being written, codified, printed, repro-duced, and distributed, they (especially those works that survive after the intellectual's death) take on a life of their own.

In the West, intellectual work has traditionally been the property and purview of a privileged intelligentsia of wealthy, white males, whose con-trol over knowledge production has depended in part upon silencing and exploiting others, especially unpaid and poorly paid women. Usually, women (as maids or mates) cook, clean, and wash for intellectuals and their households. This labor enables intellectuals to have the necessary time and space for reading, writing, and thinking, because they have the privilege of being excluded (in precisely the ways that women are not) from biological sustenance and reproduction of themselves and their fam-ilies. Only a few white women, usually daughters, wives, or lovers of male scholars, have become intellectuals. Most were limited to supporting and encouraging their men. Much of the work these female intellectuals pro-duced was appropriated by male scholars.

In spite of the educational advances of women during the twentieth century, male intellectuals not only continue to depend upon the private labor of their spouses and female family members, but also use a largely female clerical workforce to type, file, process, and reproduce their work.

However, women of African descent were prevented any connections with male intellectuals—their own men were excluded from intellectual production and white men relegated Black women to domestic or farm labor.

However, since the colonial and slave eras in the United States, there have been many talented Black female thinkers who were writers, public speakers, and political activists. Yet under oppressive conditions, when the center of white male intellectual discourse was the question of whether Black people were human and therefore capable of thought, there was little wide distribution or systematic reproduction of their ideas. The antislavery movement did, however, foment an outpouring of tracts, articles, and speeches by both Black women and men describing and analyzing slavery.

There were abolitionist communities which produced and distributed the works of these Black thinkers, but Black women pursuing the world of ideas on their own terms were rare.

Zora Neale Hurston's life, represents the difficulty of being Black, female, and intellectual. While she produced "over a dozen published stories, 2 original musicals, 1 libretto for a folk opera, several articles on voodo, several on language and lore, 2 major collections of African American folklore . . . 4 novels, and 1 autobiography," (Bambara, 8) she was always patching together subsistence for herself. In spite of her college degree and distinguished awards, she died in the same obscurity and poverty as other Black female intellectuals and artists. Only the post-war feminist movement, especially the Feminist Press, rescued her from this common fate. Her works, now widely published, are considered seriously as pivotal for the creation of a Black female literary tradition.

While Black male writers and intellectuals also had difficulty with their works being adequately compensated or recognized, especially by white audiences and Black colleges, by the time of the Harlem Renaissance, a Black male intelligentsia was firmly established. The fate of the Black male intelligentsia did not rest on single or individual intellectuals but was assured an important community of fellow thinkers and an audience for their work. However, these Black men routinely ignored and silenced Black women intellectuals and writers. "Traditionally the World of Black Literature in the United States has been a world of Black men's literature.

The 'fathers' and purveyors of Black writing have been men. There have been no recognized 'mothers' of Black literature." (Herndon, 38–39) The renaissance and flowering of a Black female intelligentsia during the 1970s and 1980s is significant because those most silenced and impoverished by race and gender, and most marginal to the intellectual arena, began to speak in the name of race and womanhood, using their own experiences and voices to explain and explore the human condition.

Hence, the development of a Black female intelligentsia not only radically alters the traditional roles of Black women, but presents a unique opportunity for understanding theory and insights from those who have been most jeopardized by race, gender, and class oppression. As Collins observes, "the unpaid and paid work that Black women perform, the types of communities in which they live, and the kinds of relationships they have with others suggests that African American women, as a group, experience a different world from those who are not Black and female," and that these experiences "stimulate a distinctive Black feminist consciousness." (Collins, 299–300)

Gender symmetry structured West African women's and men's participation in the political, economic, and cultural life of their societies. Women were expected to marry and mother but also to be members of women's groups, organizations, and networks, inside and outside of their kin and family groups. Women could work individual and communal plots of land, keep the profits from trade and commerce for themselves and their children. From their own spheres women could become leaders over other women as well as have increased societal prestige as they aged or engaged in notable acts. However, somewhat contradictorily, women were also often expected to recognize and defer to male privilege in traditional rituals and customs and in their marriages and households. (see Sudakarsa)

In spite of the harshness of slavery and colonialism which removed political, economic, and social autonomy from them, African captives continued to shape and bend their own traditions and culture within the restrictions of bondage. Women continued the African tradition of strong female support networks and fulfilled lineage obligations by maintaining extended family systems. They also continued to exercise political and social leadership within their own communities and in resistance to dominant groups. In spite of continuing and increasing tensions between the Western model of gender relations and those of West African culture, African American men and women survived and struggled under a "prevailing unity."

This unity was demonstrated in mixed gender organizations such as the church, the NAACP, and the UNIA; and in gender-specific organizations such as the National Council of Negro Women. Gender-mixed organizations further divided their work along gender lines. Women were the backbone, the behind-the-scenes organizers and power brokers, while men were spokespersons for and representatives of the entire group, especially to white authorities. Sometimes women representing their gender-specific groups were part of coalitions and joint actions with mixed gender groups under a prominent male spokesperson. An individual woman could be a member of a woman's organization and of a mixed gender organization. Hence, Black women in the Civil Rights Movement had no single organization: they worked with and under other women, with and under men in their common struggles for racial justice and community self-determination.

The Montgomery Bus Boycott presents a good example of Black women's varied organizational roles. Rosa Parks, a leader and officer in the local NAACP chapter, initiated the boycott. Joanne Robinson, an English teacher, produced and distributed leaflets making it a community-wide news event. As a leader in the Women's Political Caucus, she was also a member of the team from the Black community which negotiated with the bus company. Ella Baker was a membership organizer for the NAACP, the founding executive director and administrator of the Southern Christian Leadership Council, an organization started during the boycott to coordinate the activities of southern civil rights ministers, and founder of the Student Nonviolent Coordinating Committee. However, Baker remained relatively unknown, while Martin Luther King became the famed "leader" of the boycott and the chairman of the Leadership Conference. In addition, Black women domestics supported the boycott by staying off the buses and supporting the leadership of Robinson, Parks, and King.

By ardent participation in the civil rights movement Black women were attempting to provide their children with a decent education which enabled them to achieve without stigma or prejudice. Women also saw the movement as an opportunity for Black men to obtain well-paying jobs in order to properly provide for their families. Black females held political as well as emotional views of marriage and motherhood. The intimate domain of family and sexual relationships were a part of the struggle to protect and sustain the private sphere of Black life from the encroachment of white racism. Black mothers felt an obligation to improve their children's lives and to protect them from the harshness of segregation.

"Taken together, the outsider-within perspective generated by Black women's location in the labor market and this grounding in traditional African-American culture provided the material backdrop for a unique Black woman's standpoint on self and society. As outsiders within, Black women have a distinct view of the contradictions between the dominant group's actions and ideologies." (Collins, 11) The rigid structures of race and gender relegated nearly all Black women to domestic work in the private households of white families. Their "outsider" caste position made them a poorly paid cheap and demeaned labor force. Being "outsiders" inside white families offered Black women an opportunity to compare gender roles between themselves and their men, white women and men. They measured their own competencies and courage against that of the white families they worked for. Black women bore witness to the restrictions of the white woman's private pedestal and compared it with their own, more autonomous situation, which could be restricted by the brutality of Black men, who were in turn abused and contained by some of the same white male bosses. At the same time, Black women were "insiders" within African American families, organizations, and communities, where their participation, leadership, and creativity gave them a distinct view for measuring their group's humanity and inhumanity against the inhumanity of the dominant group's systems of racial oppression. Yet as "outsiders" within the intimate and private realms of white power, Black women could critically observe its personal forms and contradictions. The unique "standpoint" of Black women as insider-outsiders developed from the simultaneous divergence and intersection of these experiences. Managing these complex experiences fostered their organizational skills and talents. Black women consequently developed an ability to do many things at once: work as cleaning women, while planning their own household work, while working on songs for the church choirs they led, while listening for information useful to their community, while helping white women resolve their problems with child raising. Later, this simultaneity of experience was easily translated into theories of multiple consciousness, the linchpin of Black feminist thought.

Black women's daily work consisted of systematically converting raw materials into "use value." Their work as cooks and homemakers for white families taught them how to organize and implement the plans of large, complicated events. They, in turn, used these skills to develop programs and organizations within their own churches and families. These skills helped Black women become effective community organizers, activists who could plan demonstrations, marches, and rallies with few financial resources. Their marginality and silence at the work place was translated into a very "large" voice in the community. Taking care of white people's needs, in spite of these people's claims of racial superiority, taught Black women to look beyond the facade of false ideologies and focus on the "real deal." This focus gave their militancy a pragmatic hard edge and critical stance which, when combined with skills and discipline, made Black women formidable "movers and shakers" of the Civil Rights Movement in the south.

Although African American women participated in all battle-fronts and campaigns of the movement, local Black female leaders who encouraged community-wide support for activists were most admired. These women often overruled reluctant and hesitant Black male church and civic leaders to support radical, young civil rights workers from the sit-ins and freedom rides. These local women leaders, in turn, gave the students and freedom fighters a radically different model of womanhood.

Fannie Lou Hamer of Ruleville, Mississippi became the most important local Black female community leader of the movement. She was fired from her plantation timekeeper job and beaten in prison for the "radical" step of asserting her right to vote. She then organized and encouraged Mississippians to challenge the white Democratic power structure by developing a Mississippi Freedom Democratic Party. The delegation she led eventually received nationwide support and media coverage at the 1964 Democratic Convention. But Ms. Hamer, a mother and wife and a poor woman without formal education, was also an astute political scientist and courageous "warrior." To many college students, she seemed more educated about power relations than their own professors and more courageous than any woman they had ever met. While epitomizing the life of an ordinary Black woman, Ms. Hamer offered a powerful example of womanhood which reached beyond the norm. Like many Black women local leaders she maintained traditional domestic life as wife, wage earner, and mother, while doing radical political work.

Ella Baker, "the fundi" of the movement, was another model of a radical Black woman leader. Ms. Baker was a college educated, single woman, without children, whose "career" was creating organizations, leadership, and an arena for protest politics among Black communities. Ms. Baker was an activist intellectual, who consciously developed a unique "standpoint" for college-educated, Black and white men and women in their relationship to the Black poor and to the white power structure. While Ms. Hamer represented a leadership whose constituency was a traditional community (or in her case, communities throughout Mississippi), Ms. Baker was a unique "wild woman" whose talent and full development as a social theorist and political activist created a unique community. Ms. Baker was able to move, experiment, and reproduce herself in a community of young movement activists. These activists became articulate, courageous, and mobile movement "warriors" working full time at supporting southern Black communities.

The movement enabled Black and white, male and female activists to work and live together on a day-to-day basis outside traditional work, family, and academic life. Activists generated political acts and intellectual discourse while evaluating, re-evaluating, and planning more political actions. White activists became colleagues rather than a dominant force. Confrontations with white racists furthered a sense of community because Black and white activists protested, demonstrated, and were even jailed together.

While many women were relegated to supportive office work, its radical context and communal settings still "threw women off" the traditional expectations of their gender roles. In these settings traditional sex roles between men and women were relaxed or suspended. Women were more likely to be lovers, friends, and comrades than wives, mothers, or maids. Intense social relations among movement participants connected men and women across racial lines as well as within their own race and gender groups. The movement gave them a collective oppositional perspective as well as distinct "standpoints" and world views.

Movement participants identified with poor and working class Black people who were courageously struggling against segregation. While mobilizing and organizing protest and voter registration campaigns, movement activists received an education about the subtexts of political power, and of hierarchical class and race relationships. The role of economic control was exposed, and the facade of liberal democracy was stripped away. Students rejected the elitist values and sentiments of the professional and educated classes and accepted the "standpoint" of the Black poor as their own. "Let the People Speak" became the students' motto as they attempted "class suicide" by consciously limiting their own privileged voice. The movement experience taught its activists that an interlocking "system" of power, corruption, and hypocrisy, held in place by elite white men, conspired to oppress and exploit poor Black people. The system profited by keeping Black people second class citizens, while it maintained ideological control over all society—especially keeping blinders on college students, which prevented them from "seeing" the true nature of power and racial relations.

The system's maintenance of institutionalized racism prompted activists to establish an alternative. They challenged the educational system by creating freedom schools in the South and the "free speech" movement back on their college campuses. Their voter education drives challenged national party politics. Legal and medical establishments were challenged by their free clinics and daring legal strategies. The movement became a laboratory for its participants to create ways of addressing social problems within a democratic organization of rich and poor, Black and white, men and women from all over the United States. These participants learned to critically examine all institutions, and to value individual freedom of inquiry within a sometimes quarrelsome community.

The movement brought Black men and women together and facilitated the development of a Black nationalist consciousness. Its Black members saw themselves as citizens of the African American southern community which was linked internationally to other African communities and nations. Their nationalistic prism, however, increased awareness of the patronizing attitudes and behaviors of some white movement participants toward southern Blacks. They saw an increase in competency and power when these same Blacks were supported and helped by Black activists. As they steeped themselves in the messages of powerful leaders like Malcolm X, nationalism grew in the movement.

At the same time, the feminist consciousness of white women also increased. White women were the "insider-outsiders" of the Civil Rights Movement, in which they felt marginal to the inner circles of leadership, but respected and effective in community based projects such as freedom schools. Their position enabled them to develop a gender lens for examining the differences between males and females in leadership positions, work assignments, and personal relations.

Freed of the restrictions of middle class norms which dominated the lives of most college educated Black women—and freed of the "burden" posed by work, family, and marriage for working class and poor Black women—these activists saw themselves as autonomous freedom fighters. They grew used to sharing political and social ideas with each other, and with white women, and with men. Later, these practices of analyzing and theorizing helped Black women become feminists as well as nationalists on their own terms.

Black women in the movement established a pro-Black, nationalist, and strong womanist identification with the poor, while celebrating their own unique ability to overcome hardship, rejection and institutionalized racism. Not surprisingly, Black women activists also became intellectualized and used their own "standpoint" to make sense of their experiences in the world. The movement gave Black educated women an oppositional location in which to use their knowledge and their commitment to both critique the society and change their proscribed place within it.

While the movement was teaching Black men to emphasize a macho nationalism, and white women, a white feminism, it also taught Black women to validate and spread their own voice. Fannie Lou Hamer's theme song, "This Little Light of Mine, I'm Going to Let It Shine," inspired Black women to stand proudly at the crossroads of race and gender rather than subsist under the political or intellectual domination of either.

As the movement developed and expanded beyond its connections to southern Black community issues, it began to fragment and move in many diverse directions. One fragment moved toward nationalism, which focused on Black male political and personal power. Another fragment emphasized community based organizations of Black men and women such as the Black church. Another part of the movement emphasized white male radicalism, the New Left. White women rejecting this masculinized radicalism founded second wave feminism, which both excluded and was rejected by Black women. In fact, none of these fragments was able to either contain or reflect the expanded consciousness of Black women activists (although many women continued to participate in nationalist struggles and organizations). Black feminism developed from the experiences of a core of Black women—college educated Civil Rights Movement activists who felt "thrown off" and out of a vital place in that movement by Black men and others who were their former lovers and comrades. This throwing off forced Black women to use the same intellectually and emotionally transformative processes they had learned in the movement on themselves. These women, in turn, influenced and inspired post-movement Black women intellectuals and activists.

Each fragmented direction of the movement (except community based struggles)—nationalist, feminist, left, and Black feminist—produced its own distinct analysis, literature and viewpoint, which, in turn, eventually led to the development of its own intellectual culture, creating of course, its own intelligentsia.

Community-based struggles were framed around activism and reforms which sought to maintain traditional institutions such as the family, school, and church. Those who became members of the intelligentsia were usually college graduates and professionals who were alienated from these traditional groups. Feminists, nationalists, the left, and Black feminists were able to become members of the intelligentsia because they had the privilege and time to write and speak, while community-based organizers were frequently unable to do so because of their pressing commitments to family and work. The intelligentsia were able to garner resources and develop skills to promote themselves and their ideas with the media, publishers, and other intellectuals.

Post-movement American society swung from industrial to service employment, a swing which increased and changed Black women's labor force participation. Aided by affirmative action and their own expertise, Black women became administrators, professionals, and teachers. The diminished capacity of the patriarchy to limit women to motherhood and marriage increased their determination to expand and explore their own consciousness and experiences. While it further alienated the most impoverished Black people, the unevenly desegregated world which the movement had ushered in offered more resources and access to educated Black men and women desiring a life of the mind. Lesbians and gay men, formerly closeted during the movement, came out with their own intellectual explosion. Claiming some of the most admired Black writers as their own, they challenged standard ideas of both Black identity and sexuality.

These shifts afforded Black women the motivation and the resources to support the work of Black women writers and intellectuals. For the first time in American history, significant numbers of Black women had the time to read, purchase books, attend the theater, purchase art, and to write. Black working women were better educated and more literate than their foremothers and could now become a market for the works of other Black women. Some Black feminist writings were also becoming an integral part of college curricula, especially in women's studies courses

In spite of the continuing poverty and marginality of large numbers of Black women, and in spite of the movement's decline, there is a strong material base for the development of a financially sustained feminist intelligentsia. In this area, a remarkable number of black women can support themselves by their intellectual and creative work.

The Black feminist intelligentsia has had its greatest impact upon the development of scholarship and a popular literary movement which gives voice to the specific and diverse experiences of Black women. The most significant Black women writers, Alice Walker, Toni Morrison, and Audre Lorde, lived and worked in the Black community, chronicling its history, social movements, and daily life. Darlene Clark Hine, Joyce Ladner, and Patricia Hill Collins have significantly challenged the social sciences to include the perspectives of Black women. In the thirty years since the civil rights movement, Black women have written themselves into the literary and scholarly discourse in the same way they have attempted to transform the social order which had so brutally silenced them in the past.

8

A BLACK FEMINIST PEDAGOGY

A BLACK FEMINIST PEDAGOGY is not merely concerned with the principle of instruction of Black women by Black women and about Black women; it also sets forth learning strategies informed by Black women's historical experience with race/gender/class bias and the consequences of marginality and isolation. Black feminist pedagogy aims to develop a mindset of intellectual inclusion and expansion that stands in contradiction to the Western intellectual tradition of exclusivity and chauvinism. It offers the student, instructor, and institution a methodology for promoting equality and multiple visions and perspectives that parallel Black women's attempts to be and become recognized as human beings and citizens rather than as objects and victims.

Three issues form the context of my thinking about Black feminist pedagogy: the clarification of the source and use of power within the classroom, the development of a methodology for teaching writing skills, and the need for instructors to struggle with their students for a better university. *[handwritten: 3 issues]*

POWER AND AUTHORITY IN THE CLASSROOM

Picture an evening college in New York City: The students are typically nearly all Black women, the faculty nearly all white.

During the late 1970s, I became an adjunct instructor on one such campus, the urban campus of a suburban college. The campus offered only evening classes and employed only adjunct instructors to meet the needs of its working adult student body. A close friend who was already teaching at the urban campus told me about a job opening for a Black woman to teach a course on Black women. The Black women students had requested such a course, and since I was completing my master's work on Black motherhood, I was hired immediately, with minimal college teaching experience. I accepted the job reluctantly because I already had a full-time job with a national women's organization and was a Black single mother of three school-age children.

I developed a course, "The Histories and Experiences of Black Women," which gave a historical overview of Black women's lives and then considered contemporary issues facing Black women in terms of work, family, and community. All my students were Black women in their thirties and forties. I immediately regarded myself more as a sister than an instructor. Like many Black working-class women and most of my students, I had worked as an administrative assistant, typing, filing, and phoning all day. For many years I had been the unemployed wife of an erratically employed Black man. My condition and position in the society were (and are) sociologically and economically the same as my students'. We shared the same rural, recently urban parentage and lived in the same kinds of communities. Since my students were my sisters, it was difficult for me to teach them because I was fearful that I would be arrogant and judgmental. However, I had recently learned some Marxism, so I tried to teach Black women's history from a Marxist perspective. I ignorantly spoke about primitive societies, bluffed my way through imperialism, and skimmed the Industrial Revolution.

At one point in an early course I stopped in the middle of my lecture and looked at the students. There was silence, every eye was on me. I was terrified. The students wanted—hungered, really—to know more. They wanted me to teach them, not just to be sisterly and befriend or rant politics at them. They gave me automatic deference and respect, and in fact, were too respectful to question me closely. Much of the time I literally didn't know what I was saying. And the task to know more about my subject, Black women, was made even more difficult because there were few available works about Black women, almost no courses taught about Black women in the academy, and even fewer Black women college teachers to call upon for help. The best part of this course, discovered during my desperate search for resources and support, came from oral history interviews. On the last day of class, one of the oldest women interviewed

came to demonstrate her handiwork and encourage the students to continue to learn. I discovered a sisterhood in our mutual experiences as
Black women that I had not explicitly encouraged and had failed to draw
on or explore as the centerpiece of the course.

For the past five years, I have been working as a counselor, administrator, and instructor at the City College of New York Center for Worker
Education, which offers BA degrees to working adults during the evening
at off-campus sites. Although there are now more resources to call upon
in teaching about Black women than when I first began, questions of
power, authority, and relative priorities in the classroom continue. Like
myself, the average student is a thirty-five-year-old Black working woman
who heads her household and is employed in one of the city agencies.
However, because of the privilege afforded intellectuals and college
instructors, even Black and female ones, I have continued to feel confused
and challenged about my egalitarian values and my contradictory class
position in relation to the students. I am just like my students in relation
to white male privilege and white female and Black male status. We also
share a common cultural and historical heritage. But as an employed
intellectual who uses my mind and my skills to instruct others, I have
greater status than my sister students in the classroom and in the society.

At first I denied these differences in status between myself and other
Black women students. I continued to wallow in liberalism and was
blinded to the power differences among Black women and between Black
women students and teachers. The differences have remained, of course,
and have permeated my teaching and scholarly concerns. Last year, these
contradictions around class and power became more apparent for me in
the context of the issue of literacy, partially as a result of having shared the
concerns of my colleagues, most of whom are white men, about the
inability of many students to write well. I felt even more dismay when
these Students were Black women who had not achieved the intellectual
levels of literacy I expected from college graduates. I told a group of feminist educators, mostly white women, that when I began teaching I
regarded the writing problems of my students as the "problems of sister
victims without opportunity" and that, alarmingly, I now also regarded
some of my sister students as "dumb," implying an inability to do college
work. One educator, Claire D'Amio, pointed out, "Barbara, you just feel
ashamed of their ignorance, because they are a reflection of you. You see
yourself in them and get angry when they don't measure up."

The students also reflected my own complex and contradictory marginality within the white-male-dominated academy. I suspect that the same colleagues who share my concern about poor student writing have probably also dismissed my own writings and insights. I have felt that, as a teacher, my position of power within the classroom has involved the risk of allowing feelings of shame and marginality among my students; yet I could also use my marginality to identify even more with my sister students inside the classroom.

The issues raised by these experiences are central to the development of a Black feminist pedagogy, with significance for all pedagogy within the academy: first, the contradictions that emerge between students and instructor around their similar and disparate experiences of race, gender, and class; second, the tensions that evolve between student expectations and the instructor's sense of student needs, especially concerning literacy; and third, the context and politics of learning in institutions of higher education. The rest of this essay explores and suggests some of my ways of constructively confronting these issues.

TEACHING WRITING SKILLS

When I am teaching history and politics, my students can bring their experiences, insights, and questions to classroom discussions. I assist them by adding the factual, analytical, and contextual information that illuminates and expands their insights. This method works well to empower students, drawing them out, helping them to make sense of what they already know and have experienced. The creation of an intellectual partnership, a mutual sharing of information and experiences, lessens the power imbalance and class differences between instructor and students, yet reinforces the knowledge that can be received from the instructor, the readings, and the discussion. My role as clarifier—almost consultant—to the students' learning process has become politically and pedagogically comfortable and consistent with my task of imparting the course content and creating a learning environment that frees the minds of Black women, and the minds of others about Black women.

However, when I assign a scholarly paper, I must assume the politically problematic role of evaluator. My standards of judgment are dictated by the purpose and rationale of a college education: to produce students who can enter the professional and managerial class because they have and can communicate useful knowledge and information. When students fail to write and read up to par, they become nonstudents, incapable of participating in the very medium and work of the academy. In the past, these students, i.e., Black working-class women, never came into the academy unless they had exceptional literacy skills. Literacy itself has further class connotations because it also means having the time and space to read and write, usually in isolation from one's family and kin. Literacy necessarily distances and separates people: the learner from the doer, the scholar from the worker. But the challenge of a Black feminist pedagogy is to use literacy to connect people with ideas and histories across racial, gender, and class boundaries and to further connect Black women to each other and to their unique history. By making available knowledge of their own history as well as that of the ruling elite, knowledge of men and women and Black and white people, we can give students a sense of their worth and their power to affect their position and condition. The worker can become a scholar who does not have to abandon her class in order to become educated.

The process of evaluation, of correcting and measuring the written and spoken skills of students, has usually been used in racist and sexist and elitist ways, which serve to diminish students' integrity and humanity. But a liberal feminist stance should not be used to deny the students an honest appraisal of their learning and skills. I used to err on the side of liberalism and promoted sisterly rapport instead of directly grappling with the difficulty of teaching scholarly writing skills and critical thinking. Such skills can assist Black women in gaining an overall and coherent way of analyzing the information they receive in the classroom and from the experiences of their lives.

In attempting to avoid making Black women students feel uncomfortable, I tried to protect those who wrote poorly and analyzed superficially from feeling a sense of failure. In the beginning, I assigned papers but did not rigorously grade them, satisfied that students expressed themselves and tried hard. Then, I gave double grades on term papers: one for ideas and one for grammar, stupidly separating content from process. When my grades accurately reflected their work, I felt that I had abandoned all my sisterly values. The double grade process, however, protected me from guilt about grading their papers at all, and helped me avoid the truth about their writing skills and course performances.

By avoiding the struggle to face the weaknesses of my Black women students, I also avoided the essentials of the learning process. All teaching and learning involve tensions and discomfort, as students unlearn and replace old ideas and limited understandings with newer, and, one hopes, better information. The solution lay not in attempting to remove the discomfort and tension, but in creating a learning environment where Black women could feel safe about making mistakes and taking chances. Students have to be taught to honestly evaluate failure and turn mistakes into lessons as they face the difficulties associated with learning mathematics, history, paper writing, or speaking in class.

THE STRUGGLE FOR A BETTER UNIVERSITY

Many educators are struggling with developing a progressive pedagogy for women and working-class students, as if the issues involved can be isolated from the larger politics of the colleges and universities in which they work. Some are aware of the political implications of open admissions, affirmative action, and the effects of changes in student populations upon classroom instruction. But rarely does an instructor have the opportunity to interact directly with the political direction and framework of the university—an experience that would force the instructor to translate that learning experience back into the classroom and her or his teaching.

Until 1982, like most instructors, I was concerned and knowledgeable only about my own teaching and my own program. In March 1982, students at Medgar Evers College, a predominantly Black college, with 78 percent female students, within the City University system of New York (which also includes the college where I work), began to call for the resignation of the president of the college. He had refused to meet with student leaders or to consider student demands, which included childcare for the children of students, an end to sexual harassment, and support for Black studies.

The university was undergoing tremendous demographic changes that challenged its status quo, its curriculum, and its structure of power. Two-thirds of the overall university student body are people of color (those of African descent—from Africa, the Caribbean, Europe, and the United States; Latinos from within the United States and from Central and South America; Asians from every country). A majority (60 percent) of the students are women, typically Black women. Most of the faculty of the university's twenty units are white males, and the control and running of the university are in the hands of white men.

Some friends of mine worked at the college, so I was kept informed of the growing struggle at Medgar Evers, but I was unprepared for its direction. During April, I was asked to speak at a student rally, following which the students marched to the president's office and began a sit-in protest. The sit-in lasted for four months. During those months, I talked with participating students, most of whom were Black women. Some of them were on welfare and younger than the students at my center, but they shared the same hunger and desire for a good education. In the halls of Medgar, usually late at night as I "sat in" with them, I began to better understand the context of my own dilemmas as a college educator.

When Black students "sat in" at Medgar, demanding a president more responsive to their academic and social needs, they were signaling to the university that its students were not willing to settle for an old educational arrangement that did not reflect their reality and the realities of most of the students. The connections between what I was attempting in one part of the university and the sit-in in another illuminated the different ways of empowering students, using new methods, new course content, and a new political understanding.

If students transform the learning process until it becomes the study of themselves by others like themselves, they can transform their institution and overturn those who have imposed a "foreign" understanding of the world upon them. My struggles with sisterhood and literacy, with power and knowledge sharing, which seemed isolated and eccentric, were part of a more critical inversion process that began when I, a working-class woman, began to teach women's history to Black women like myself. I was teaching Black women about themselves and their history in an attempt to rescue and liberate *both* of us from silence and oblivion, making us historical beings who had the power to move away from the margins of the university, as well as the bearers of legitimate knowledge to its cutting edge.

THE EMERGENCE OF A BLACK FEMINIST PEDAGOGY

The struggle at Medgar Evers College revealed the responsibility of Black women academicians to develop the meaningful content of a pedagogy that makes rigorous academic demands and has the political aim of liberating working people, especially Black women, from ignorance and powerlessness. Then, along with those students, Black women academicians must struggle for the power to implement their pedagogy. Black women instructors and students who participated in the Medgar Evers College sit-in have developed the framework of that pedagogy: a Black feminist set of academic themes that centers on the research, study, and development of Black women.

In order to assume power in the urban areas of the United States, which are increasingly populated by women and men of color, the continually exploited and oppressed peoples, especially Black women, must develop the skills to take over and run urban institutions. In order to transform current conditions and positions of powerlessness, those people must have the capacity to run them differently and humanely.

The development of these leadership skills requires that students learn differently within a liberatory classroom environment. Classroom instructors must be more like consultants to, rather than controllers of, the learning process. Although some educators advance a pedagogy that proposes to do away with all structures such as course outlines, the absence of structure leaves students without a clear sense of where a course is going. It is like telling students to drive to California from New York without knowing how to drive very well and without a road map. The instructor, on the other hand, has many maps and drives very well. No one can teach students to "see," but an instructor is responsible for providing the windows, out of which possible angles of vision emerge from a coherent ordering of information and content. The classroom process is one of information-sharing in which students learn to generalize their particular life experiences within a community of fellow intellectuals. The breadth of material students receive about the diverse perspectives of women and men all over the world should give them new ideas and new models of scholarship. This is especially critical for Black women students, since Black women's experiences and Black female scholarship are seldom placed within the syllabi of the academy's courses.

Without an explicit pedagogy, Black women and all other working-class students will continue to be disregarded as participants in the learning environment. They will learn in a fairy land, with the good fairy godmothers (who are Black) giving them solace and approval without wisdom, and the bad fairy godfathers (who are white) denying them both humanity and useful information. Neither fairy godmothers nor godfathers can be equal partners with students engaged in a political struggle to learn enough and know enough to transform our mutual futures within and without the academy.

9

INVISIBLE TO THE NAKED EYE

A CASE STUDY OF BLACK WOMEN STUDENTS AT THE CENTER FOR WORKER EDUCATION

AFRICAN AMERICAN WOMEN have a curious way of turning disadvantage around to make "it" work for themselves and their families. They have attempted to make social spaces for their own intellectual development in the margins of colleges and universities while struggling against combined systems of oppression. Their presence in the academy is unrecognized witness to the blindness of traditional scholarship as well as testimony to their perseverance against racist/sexist schooling.

Perhaps only tenacity can explain why mature African American women workers are so often students in urban college programs. Black women students make up the second largest cohort group of students in the City University of New York and the "typical" student at the City College Center for Worker Education. Founded in 1981, the Center for Worker Education, (CWE) is an evening program providing equal access to a liberal arts education for New York City workers, especially service workers employed by the state. The Center offers regular counseling sessions and administrative support. At one point an internal survey indicated that the typical student was a Black single mother in her thirties. Most of the Center's curriculum consists of traditional liberal arts courses taught by white male professors. Students indicate a great deal about their particular ethnic and gender experiences in their comments during the few Black or women's studies courses offered. Many Black students bring to college painful memories of segregated schooling along with their enthusiasm and commitment.

Black women students remember early education interwoven with the emotional and physical violence of segregated schools in the south. One student recalls,

> I would like to reflect back on my experience as a young person growing up in South Carolina during segregation. I felt the impact of segregation more in the school system than anywhere else. Not only were the schools in my hometown segregated, they did not begin the school term at the same time as the white schools. Black children always began their school terms two weeks later than the White children. The reason for this was that the Black children were needed to finish picking cotton for the white man.
>
> The school the Black children attended was nothing more than old run down framed buildings, which our parents referred to as TB camps. While the Black children were making fires in the heaters in the classrooms of these old run down buildings, the white children were comfortable in their nice brick building.(Gumbs, 3–4)

This student also bitterly recalls,

> I shall never forget the words that were stamped on the inside front cover of my books as long as I live. These words were, "For use in Colored schools only." This meant that once these books were used by Black children, they were not to be returned to the white school. Our parents paid for these books while the white children got their books free. (Gumbs, 4)

Parents of southern students also paid taxes for public education, which disproportionately favored white children. Many CWE students remembered protests against legally segregated schools during the civil rights era.

> Desegregation was the primary thing on our young impressionable minds as we sat in High Street Church singing at the top of our lungs,

"We shall overcome, we shall overcome . . . some d-a-a-aay." What an exciting and eventful spring and summer we had in 1963, in my home-town, Danville, Virginia. Ninth grade had been such a challenging time, our first year in our pretty "colored" high school . . . A new wing had been added and we had an excellent shop department and Home Economics Section but just a few blocks over, they were adding new business machines and computers to the all white school. We knew who they were preparing for the business world, it was not us. (Fuller, 1)

Even libraries were segregated. "Three blocks up the hill was the 'col-ored' library on Holbrook Street. More like a little cubby-hole and we were constantly bumping into each other trying to maneuver our growing bodies down the tiny aisles. About six blocks away on Main Street sat this great big beautiful library where we could not go and check out books or use to do our research papers." (Fuller, 2)

Students educated in the north also recalled the impact of racial segre-gation on their lives.

I played on streets with prostitutes a few feet away from me. I re-member the stale food being sold for twice the amount that wealthier neighborhoods paid. As a child I woke up many nights to the sound of glass breaking and screams as my people out of anguish tried to pro-test some injustice committed by rioting in their neighborhood. (Wedderburn, 6–7)

She accompanied her mother in protesting racism in Harlem,

In the 1930s my mother was the first Lady Vice President of the UNIA [United Negro Improvement Association] . . . I walked with her as a child on 125th Street protesting white owned stores that did not employ Black people. My sister and I played around judges' chairs as my mother alone fought landlords in courts. (Wedderburn, 5)

Black students in many northern schools recall how white teachers demeaned and taunted them, and how white children harassed and mis-treated them because of their color. When asked what their earliest mem-ory of racism is, most Black students, from the north or south, describe school experiences.

Proud, hard-working parents believed schooling offered their children opportunities based solely upon their abilities. They provided physical, emotional, and even political support for their children. The schools were supposed to provide physical space, curriculum, and instruction in an equitable and just manner. Parents assumed their objectives were in tandem with those of teachers. Unless there was blatant racism by white teachers, parents paid little attention to the classroom experiences of their children. In fact, in conflicts between students and teachers, parents usually sided with teachers, especially when those teachers were Black.

Most Black teachers in segregated settings encouraged their students to overcome the negative impact of segregated schooling. They tried to "help youngsters by demonstrating the norms of appropriate behavior and by making explicit the situational contexts, including roles and relationships under which particular behaviors are acceptable." (Holmes, 19) Black teachers also tried to "reinforce black cultural values and norms, and . . . exhort young people to do and be things they might not have imagined possible." (Holmes, 19)

However, childhood memories, observations by writers such as Langston Hughes, and studies of educators reveal that Black teacher-pupil relations were sometimes difficult.

A study by educator Ray Rist revealed the ways a teacher can replicate class biases within her classroom. Rist conducted a two and a half year study following a single group of Black children from kindergarten to the second grade. In this school, "all the administrators, teachers, staff and pupils were Black." (Rist, 417)

During the first week the teacher divided her kindergarten class into "groups expected to succeed (termed by the teacher 'fast learners') and those anticipated to fail (termed 'slow learners')." (Rist, 414) Since no formal tests had been administered, Rist concluded that the teacher used information about the children's socio-economic background to place them into their learning groups. "She made evaluative judgments of the expected capacities of the children to perform academic tasks after eight days of school" (Rist, 422)

She created the groups using information about the parents' employment, welfare, and marital status. She further defined which children would learn quickly or slowly by their "ease of interaction among adults; high degree of verbalization in Standard American English; the ability to become a leader; a neat and clean appearance; coming from a family that is educated, employed, living together, and interested in the child; and the ability to participate well as a member of a group." (Rist, 422) After dividing the children into learning groups which mirrored their class, she proceeded to systematically discriminate in favor of the fast learners who received much more encouragement, praise, instruction, and privileges from her. While the slow learners were far more often controlled and ridiculed.

Because the slow learners received less and poorer instruction from and more negative interaction with the teacher, they *became* slow learners. One of Rist's most poignant descriptions is that of a young girl attempting to get the teacher's attention and participate in the activities of the first group; she eventually "gives up" trying. (Rist, 17–18)

Physical appearance and class background of Black girls are viewed by many teachers as more important than their academic abilities. Even before attending school, family members have used skin color, hair length and texture, body size, and African-ness of features to evaluate Black girls. The physical appearance of Black girls is a key determinant of whether teachers, community residents, or even parents recognize and encourage their academic achievements. (Okazawu, et al., Russell, et al.)

Adult Black women recall that heavier and short-haired girls received more negative feedback from family members about their looks and personality than lighter, thinner and long-haired girls. Large, dark girls are often taunted and ridiculed by peers, and eventually ignored at home and school by adults except when performing chores.

Educator Sara Lightfoot observed that in poor families, domestic chores such as childcare, food preparation, laundry, and errands often take precedence over school work. Lightfoot observes that these responsibilities influence the behavior of poor Black girls.

> They are more competent, aggressive and more adept at organization. They are more apt to be seen as assertive and bossy rather than submissive and cuddly. . . . They are alien to the activities, appearance and attitude of the little girls that researchers are used to, so that it may have become easier for them not to deal with black girls at all." (Lightfoot, 22)

Black girls enter school with at least two sets of experiences which differentiate them from other girls and Black boys: a heightened sensitivity about their physical make-up and the fact that they have been doing domestic and household work.

In spite of these gender disadvantages, educator Jawanza Kunjufu assumes that Black girls are more successful students than Black boys. Black girls do not succumb to "a fourth grade syndrome plague" as readily as Black boys.

> In primary grades blacks progress and thrive at the same rate as their white counterparts until the third grade syndrome. I found after the third grade, the achievement rate of blacks began a downward spiral which tended to continue in the child's academic career. The classroom environment was transformed from a socially interactive style to a competitive, individualistic, and minimally socially interactive style of learning. (Kunjufu, 6–7)

But according to Jawanza Kunjufu, Black girls are able to be successful students because they are raised by their mothers "to be academically aggressive." Their mandatory attendance at worship service and the intimacy established between mother and daughter and her friends help to develop an emotionally secure person." (Kunjufu, 19) Hale says that Black girls "adjust naturally to the female sex role model of primary school." (Hale, 66)

> Girls . . . are, in a sense, locked into cumulatively reinforcing cycles of conformity, docility, and dependence and many eventually come to accept receptivity as the proper stance for learning. While schooling might be a more benign experience for girls than for boys over the short run, boys usually resist full indoctrination to receptive modes of learning. The long-term implications of the typical girl's relatively easy accommodation to pupil role are probably counterindicative of her ever becoming a fully active learner. (Lee and Voivodas, 111)

Although boys and girls are both expected to follow the appropriate pupil role behavior, there is a "relative poor fit between pupil role and sex role for boys which leads to on-going stress and conflict in the educational setting." Boys "act out" their rebellion in disruptive and unruly behavior, while most girls "act in," that is behave correctly, but repress their rage and rebellion. (Lee and Voivodas, 111)

Black girls, because they are female, are expected to reflect traditional sex roles of passivity and obedience. However, because they are Black, they are invisible to the teacher as serious learners. In fact, one study demonstrated that Black females were the least likely students to be reinforced by the teacher. "The failure of teachers to give encouragement and rewards to Black girls seemed to reflect a negative image which teachers had of these children." (Reid, 144) Since girls have not even been "awarded the negative and pejorative stereotypes that correspond to their black brothers" (Lightfoot, 3), few scholars have bothered to study the impact of triple oppression (sexism, racism, and class) upon the educational experiences of Black girls.

In addition, as girls mature they are also treated primarily as sex objects by their male peers (and teachers). Recent reports revealed that high school girls are routinely verbally and physically harassed because of their gender. (O'Brian, 7)

It is also significant that pregnancy is the main reason Black female students leave school. One expert says that teen pregnancy is often followed by truancy and boredom. (Robinson)

Effective learning demands articulation and engagement, not passive acceptance of one's sexual place. The active learner interjects her own ideas and questions into the learning process. Since little is expected intellectually of Black girls beyond being quiet and attentive, their love of learning becomes stunted.

Though more Black girls complete high school than Black boys, most have been rewarded for passive learning rather than intellectual ability. Black girls, like Black women students, are rewarded not for being smart but for being "good" and "trying hard." Although schooling stifles the intellectual development of Black girls, it has not entirely destroyed their desire to learn and think. Black women still seek esteem and accomplishment through education.

Black women students bring to college sophisticated skills learned from living in the "real world." Stretching meager financial resources to provide basic necessities, advocating for dependent family members, resolving conflicts, solving problems, and planning, organizing, and executing tasks are areas where Black women excel. Black women students are at their intellectual best when, outside of school, they brilliantly interconnect thinking and doing.

A college degree represents a reliable way for a Black woman, whether married or single, to sustain her family because it increases her assets in the job market. The degree enables Black female heads of household to stabilize their incomes. It enables wives to increase their financial contributions to the family.

Irrespective of their present marital status, Black women at the Center for Worker Education come from traditionally structured Black patriarchal families where the needs of husbands and children have superseded their own. Black wives and mothers are expected to work for wages, perform domestic chores, do kin work as well as provide primary childcare for infants and young children. Black husbands are expected to provide economic support, overall leadership, and direction for their families, performing only secondary domestic and childrearing chores; in other words, to "help out" with the children if they desire. However, relationships between Black husbands and wives tend to be more egalitarian than in other working class families. (Billingsley)

Male students often have the added support of a wife or girlfriend and do not have the domestic responsibilities that female students do. Unlike the college valedictorian who thanked his wife for typing all his papers, adult female college students have to do it all themselves: wage work, childcare, domestic responsibility, homework, as well as typing their own papers.

Because of their multiple responsibilities, it's not surprising that Black adult women may have made several attempts to attend college. Marriages or divorces, births and childrearing, deaths and illnesses, medical and financial problems as well as family violence cause Black women to drop out of school.

Black women students are often the leaders in their families. They are the daughter their mother always calls upon for help. They are the ones responsible for aging parents. Others are raising grandchildren for addicted or ill daughters. Some students have chronic physical ailments which hamper their education.

The "kin work" of family life also interferes with women's schooling.

> By kin work I refer to the conception, maintenance, and ritual celebration of cross-household kin ties, including visits, letters, telephone calls, presents, and cards to kin; the organization of holiday gatherings; the creation and maintenance of quasi-kin relations; decisions to neglect or to intensify particular ties; the mental work of reflection about all these activities; and the creation and communication of altering images of family and kin vis-à-vis the images of others, both folk, and mass media. (Di Leonardo, 443)

In addition, Black women students are usually active in many community, social, and cultural activities. Nearly all of them are devoted church members who contribute a great deal of time and money. These students often volunteer for voter registration drives and political protests. If not active in the PTAs in their children's schools, they provide recreational and cultural programs for children and young people in their community. I also discovered that many Black women students at the Center were semi-professional singers.

Hence, an adult Black woman's college education must compete with many other demands on her time. She must juggle school work along with the needs of her family and community. However, college work presumes that a "fault line" is laid down between lived reality and thoughts about reality. Students are usually required to immerse themselves in the sedentary activities of reading, writing, and speaking in a way that is structured by certain racial, gender, and class privileges. The student/scholar usually has his material needs met by the labor of others. Young working-class students who are intellectually gifted are able to totally submerge themselves into college work and culture because of their parents' support. Ironically, many CWE students provide support for their own children to attend college full time, thereby making their own education more difficult. However, there have been social changes which encourage Black women who are older and more working class than traditional college students to seek a college education.

Black political demands have helped to create more flexible admissions policies, especially at the public colleges. At the same time the marketplace has increased its need for a better educated work force. The combination of open admissions and workplace demands has created the opportunity and context for college education to become accessible for mature working Black women.

Many Black women workers enroll in college as a way to advance from their low-wage employment in the secondary labor market as nurses' aides, clerical workers, and childcare workers into the primary labor market as administrators and professionals. With a college degree, for example, a daycare worker can become a public school teacher and increase her income by at least $4,000 annually. When they graduate from college, clerks on the lowest employment levels in governmental agencies can advance to managerial and administrative positions.

By the early 1980s nearly all of the major unions in New York City, especially those with large numbers of Black women workers in public sector employment, offered college education programs for their members at convenient, off-campus sites. Building on Otto Feinstein's Wayne State model to bring education to the workers, these programs have been housed in office buildings, community centers, and union halls.

Many colleges such as Fordham University and Marymount College have developed special programs for mature students. The College of New Resources, a model evening college program with several satellites in New York City, was established by The College of New Rochelle during the late

1970s. The SUNY Empire State College's Center for Labor Studies recruited its students from its union affiliates. Our City College Center for Worker Education program, in fact, grew out of the liberal arts program of the Empire State College's Center for Labor Studies. And Black women have been the most likely students at all these programs.

The Center has been able to successfully combine aspects from these programs: evening hours, individual counseling, registration, and financial aid services. It has recruited students from several large unions such as Communications Workers of America, Local 1180 and District Council 1707. Through the use of the parent college's liberal arts faculty and curriculum, the Center has become a replica of it. The CWE offers worker students the stability and status of a traditional liberal arts education in a non-traditional setting.

The state's need for skilled service workers, preferably female, the union's need for legitimacy in offering its members the tangible benefits of a college education, and the academy's need for increased enrollment have all merged in college programs for working adults.

One of the current crises facing the union movement is its weakened ability to improve the material conditions and wages of union members. DC 1707 is a good example of the dilemmas involved in offering college education as a benefit to union members. 1707 represents workers in public childcare centers, offering them tuition reimbursement toward BS degrees in education, which many seek at the Center for Worker Education. However, workers who receive the degree usually transfer to public school teaching or daycare supervision which offer better wages and working conditions than their current jobs. Hence, the union's educational benefits indirectly fund upward mobility at its own expense, because upon graduating, workers often leave the union

The various centers for education demonstrate how well the academy and unions have collaborated to provide adult workers access to a college education. However, because no explicit attempts are made to link the meaning of student workplace experiences with their schooling, class consciousness and solidarity are undermined.

These students enter a college culture which reinforces values of meritocracy, individuality, and paternalistic social intervention. Students receive a language and mindset which equips them to adopt the perspectives of ruling elites and bureaucracies regarding social issues such as welfare, education, and housing. The unions fail to demand that the academy provide an education appropriate for improving workers' lives, one which encourages them to think about class consciousness, racial tolerance, or non-sexism. In fact, these college programs remove working adults from their working-class origins.

The program I coordinate at the Center for Worker Education offers a BS education degree which prepares childcare workers to become certified teachers. However, the degree program is nearly identical to an existing campus degree program. Both the academy and the union support a traditional set of liberal arts and education course offerings which meet the state's requirements for licensing teachers. (Thus, the very agencies which in the past have been the sites of challenges to the state now uncritically endorse the state's credentialing requirements.) Unions and schools facilitate the status quo rather than expanding their own radical social change tradition. In addition, most union member students graduate without ever learning about labor, the history of workers' struggles, or radical education traditions. Thus, what gets reproduced from the Center's BS education program are teachers unprepared to engage in serious intellectual discourse within the complex and combative environment of the public schools.

These programs offer Black women students access to a college education while teaching them to become even more ignorant of the significance of their own histories and experiences. Though present in large numbers, Black women students remain "invisible to the naked eye" in the classroom.

Since so much of successful teaching is based on the instructor's ability to "see" and reach the student, if the instructor cannot look into the face of a Black woman student, and see her, then how can she teach her? If all the student senses is the instructor's discomfort with her outward physical appearance, then how can she learn?

While discussing the social construction of beauty in the Sociology of Black Women course at the Center, I heard confirmation of Black women's being judged, labeled, and limited by the way we look. Often we are not "seen" as intelligent because of our physical appearance.

The physical features of Black women—big lips, broad noses, large bodies, nappy hair and dark skin—are considered ugly by this country's standards of beauty. In attempting to foster positive responses in spite of their physical appearance, many Black women become "invisible," silent, and hopefully nonthreatening. Others move loudly through their spaces, using their aggression and size to protect and "hide" themselves, especially their vulnerability, sensitivity, and inner thoughts.

Black women usually learn in a "chilly climate where the instructor's behavior communicates discomfort and lowered expectation through ignoring, interrupting, maintaining physical distance, avoiding eye contact, or offering little guidance and criticism." ("The Classroom Climate," 12) One Black woman student at the Center told of having to stand up in order to get the teacher's attention. She "only called on the few white students in class and ignored the rest of us."

Black women who have difficulty with college work feed into our culture's stereotypes about the inability of women and Black people to learn and think as well as white men do. It's often as difficult for the instructor to encourage her as it is for the student to "shake her dumbness."

When the teacher is repulsed by a student's color and her sex—separation and distance become the medium of classroom interaction. Those left out will never "get it," because they are not seen or taught. The greater the distance from Euro-American standards of beauty, the greater their invisibility as intellectual beings.

Black women students adapt a pupil role model of overcoming obstacles with quiet perseverance which they also successfully apply to their family, wage work, and community activities. In spite of this model not fitting the critical thinking and literacy requirements of the academy, Black women sit through courses and complete the requirements, remaining passive and disengaged from intellectual work. Many adopt silence, including written "silence," as a strategy for avoiding any close scrutiny of their thoughts and work. Their writing is superficial, aiming to please their instructors, rather than expressing their own thoughts. I call this writing a form of silence because, although she does her writing assignments, the student avoids communication. In this way, the writer's thoughts are never challenged or scrutinized.

These women, however, can and do express themselves within their families and community groups, at work, and when negotiating complex bureaucratic systems. Comfortable with the narrative of daily routines, recounting experiences, commenting on personal and immediate dilemmas, some students have never been required to reflect and write. When they have been, their thoughts were dismissed and ridiculed. Any critique of their college work is experienced and interpreted as shaming and scolding.

Students with poor writing and reading skills try hard to do what they're told, but the power derived from performing in the formal language of the academy eludes them.

I have also observed that many Black women students suffer a kind of "post traumatic dumbness," because they are too overworked and fatigued to think and perform effectively. Physical and emotional crises as well as the stresses of everyday life can foster this "dumbness."

Many Black women who don't perform well on exams, complain of "freezing up" with stress, confusion, and fear. These students are not academically deficient, but have lost or never found a confident and powerful intellectual voice. The academy's formal and intense linguistic culture, designed to awe and intimidate, causes many Black women to feel like outsiders in the college environment. This outsider status is reinforced by the absence of Black women as subjects within academic disciplines and the dearth of Black women scholars and instructors.

Mature Black women students with intellectual talent are also marginalized and unseen. Because being intelligent has not gained them very much, they have learned to remain silent about what they know. Viewed as "uppity," articulate Black women are not adequately mentored. In fact, mentoring often follows race and gender stereotypes. A gifted Black woman student who graduated from the Center was hired to be its financial aid counselor while less gifted whites were encouraged to go to graduate school and hired as adjunct instructors. A gifted Black male student was so successfully mentored, he was awarded scholarships for an ivy league graduate school. Once again, the Black woman gets programmed for "mammified" helping work while others get support for intellectual and academic work.

By failing to provide a dynamic and rich learning environment, adult worker education programs like the Center reinforce the intellectual and cultural baggage students bring with them into the classroom: low self-esteem, severe achievement anxiety, veneration of authority, religious and cultural conflict, limited access to intellectual culture, and poor literacy skills. (Kuppersmith) Black women like all working class students are blocked from their own intellectual cultures, which would connect their school experiences to a familiar frame of reference and process. Such a connection would assist them in participating more fully in the academy. They would no longer stand in awe and fear of Western intellectual culture, overwhelmed by its supposed internal logic and grandeur. As partners and not subordinates, they would be able to dissect and critique the intellectual process from a place of power and safety. By learning about their own intellectual cultures, working class student-teachers would be able to reproduce them for their own students.

Because centers for worker education merely replicate the traditional liberal arts curriculum, using standard pedagogical methods, what they have produced are the same old technically skilled bureaucrats and teachers who lack intellectual breadth and imagination. Only this time, they are Black women.

Schooling offers Black women the most tangible and reliable opportunity for economic and social advancement because their agency and determination has forced education to pay off. However, the specific strengths and lessons of African American women must be acknowledged and taught in order for either educators or students to be intellectually transformed and empowered. In the past most Black women have been miseducated by schools which have demanded they learn a highly stylized and rigid academic language which silences and demeans rather than improves and expands their own voices. They have been mystified and overwhelmed by the symbolic language of mathematics and an allegedly objective scientific methodology divorced and abstracted from its social context and meaning. They have been misled by an idealized and false social science and a version of the past which glorifies domination and white supremacy.

A critical transformation of the intellectual culture of schools—curriculum, pedagogy, and organization—is essential for improving the education of Black women (and the education of other working class and ethnic men and women as well). Elimination of gender stereotyping and sexist structuring of knowledge and the active incorporation of the experiences and lives of students (irrespective of age, race, gender, or class) within the educational process is necessary.

Changes in schools, especially in higher education, will occur when Black women realize the value of their own experiences and *demand* an authentic education which incorporates their presence into the curriculum and the classroom. If Black adult women college students begin to see the classroom as a space for authentically reproducing themselves as well as a place for learning about the world, they will rise out of their undevelopment, demanding the incorporation of their intellectual traditions and lives within the schools.

As long as Black women remain silent and invisible, the currently inadequate learning process is maintained, but if they ever get any sustained glimpse of their own power and intellectual community, then all the rage, the pain, the joy and creativity they contain would force the academy to radically change.

10

THE LION'S ROCK SPEECH

IN 1986, THE LATE *Marguerite Ross-Barnett was appointed Chancellor of the University of Missouri, leaving her position as the first African American woman Vice Chancellor of Academic Affairs in CUNY. A group of her Black female colleagues and friends gave her a farewell luncheon in the Lion's Rock Restaurant. We adopted its name for the network of Black women we started. She urged us to continue meeting and supporting each other. The following remarks were made to the group in 1991 at the celebration of Dr. Josephine Davis becoming President of York College.*

> I would like to propose that the lack of black female power in academic fields of knowledge production like literary criticism (of course, the same is even more true of anthropology, history, linguistics and so on) participates equally in this hegemonic scheme ... in which black women as a class, are systematically denied the most visible forms of discursive and intellectual subjectivity.
>
> I have been preoccupied with the question of how black women figure in American culture. In particular, I've been concerned to comprehend their high *visibility* together with their almost total lack of *voice*.
> —Michele Wallace, *Invisibility Blues: From Pop to Theory* (New York: Verso, 1990), p. 215

My presentation explores the tension—perhaps contradiction—between the extraordinary production of literary works by women of African descent during the last two decades, the substantial body of social scientific studies by and about women of African descent and the virtual absence of any significant presence of African American women in teaching and producing the knowledge base within the academy. Furthermore, this problem of high visibility and lack of voice is even more problematic when we consider that African American women have been college students for nearly a century, having been admitted into the newly formed colleges for the freed people after the Civil War. African American women have also been instrumental in creating and teaching in primary and secondary schools for Black people until the post civil rights era. If Black women have been so involved in education for nearly a century, why do they continue to be so marginalized in college teaching?

This problem is further confounded by the large enrollment of Black women in public and community colleges across the country. In the City University of New York (CUNY), Black women are 20.6 percent of the CUNY student body and 24.6 percent of all community college students. In the fall of 1988, Black women were the second largest cohort group of students in the senior colleges and the largest cohort group among the community colleges.

In spite of their significant physical presence at City College, where they make up 20.7 percent of the student body, there are only two courses in the catalog which deal specifically with their experiences. In 1989 there were only 38 Black women faculty members at City College out of 620 full time professional faculty and 66 lecture/instructor positions.

While some of this is due to the lack of "qualified" Black women faculty in the university and the dismal presence of African American women in the country's doctoral programs, I argue that the low numbers of African American women in knowledge production as college professors is reinforced by the invisibility of African American women as intellectual and historical beings within Anglo American academic traditions.

The City University, like all universities and colleges, has a sharp division between its intellectual and administrative functions. The intellectual function is to produce and reproduce knowledge, in essence to reproduce a certain world view and practice in its students and graduates. The administrative function is to serve the intellectual. African American women are plentiful in the administrative service aspects of CUNY where we admit, test, register, counsel, and give financial aid advice to students. We file, type, and keep records of student for the faculty. We staff the special initiatives for "needy and minority" [sic] students. We are even admitted to upper level management of many of the colleges as deans, college presidents, and university vice chancellors. We have had two Black women vice chancellors of academic affairs. There are also Black women on the CUNY Board of Trustees.

However, Black women rarely do research, teach, or develop the academic directions and policies for the college's curriculum and departments. There are virtually no African American women in the university who teach. Medgar Evers College (MEC) and Borough Manhattan Community College (BMCC) have the most Black women faculty. It's understandable that MEC would have large numbers of Black women faculty because it was established as a Black college. It is located within a Black community and has a 98 percent Black student base. BMCC has the largest number of Black students of the CUNY community colleges. There are more African American women teaching in the community colleges than at the university's four year colleges. However, if we did a head count of Black women (or men) teaching history, English, sociology, psychology, political science, art, or music in either community or four year colleges, we would be embarrassed and humiliated by their absence. It is almost more painful and enraging to count the numbers of Black women (and men) teaching the sciences and math.

During this post-civil rights, post-industrial era African American women workers and professionals have been re-mammified. Most of our mothers, grandmothers, and female ancestors were mammies—the domestic servants of white families or worked in the kitchens, laundries, hospitals, and nurseries of white establishments. They were hired to take care of the personal needs of white people. Many of these "mammies" were intelligent, efficient, and hard working women. They often took care of two or even three sets of families: the white families, their own spouses and children; and helped with the care of their parents, siblings, and grandchildren. They oversaw the budget and planning of white family life. They were the emotional support system for many white children and women. They sometimes had great status and recognition in the personal memories of white families, but had no power in the society. They ruled and worked by whim. They were easily fired, demeaned and demoted.

We, their daughters, although college educated, were socialized by these women to be dutiful and efficient workers. We have carried over these attributes of mammification into the public sector employment we now enjoy in the university. We take care of the students and manage the academy.

We cannot determine what students will learn. We have little to say about the kind of workers or professionals our students will become. We, for example, are part of a university which prepares 60 percent of the public school teachers in the city. However, Black women make no determination about the kinds of teachers our students will become because of their absence from decision making roles in departments of education.

We are part of a movement which has created a powerful literature about Black women's experience but do not have the power to offer this literature to Black women students. We can not give Black women students any body of knowledge created by Black men and women. We can not say whether they should have an African centered, multicultural, or any other kind of curriculum, because we have no power to determine any curriculum. We have visibility as administrators but no voice in the university's primary function to produce and reproduce knowledge.

We can see vividly the white male domination of our university in our graduate school, because it does not have the veneer of a racially mixed student body to obscure their power as it does on the undergraduate campuses. Only 8 percent of the graduate school students are people of color, most of whom are foreign students. There are three Black women faculty—all hired within the last few years. One of the women has now been "promoted" to the administration. There are virtually no courses offered on Black women. (During the Spring 1994 semester, a course on Black feminist thought, taught by Michele Wallace, was offered.)

It's as if we as Black women hardly exist. We are nearly invisible to the curriculum. No history and no sociology reflects our experiences. What is the meaning of our being so visible as administrators and so absent from the teaching and shaping of the outcomes of education?

If we continue to serve this university as mammies, we have disserved our legacy and abandoned our responsibility to the future of Black women. We are the daughters of Ella Baker and Fannie Lou Hamer. We are Assata's sister. Winnie Mandela is our contemporary warrior and shero. But we do not have the power to even teach about these women in any serious way in the university. We can not even safely bring Winnie or Assata here—invite or protect them. We have no power because we are well educated, sophisticated MAMMIES and will remain without any voice until we coalesce our forces, and demand our rightful share in *controlling* knowledge production in this university.

Some will be concerned immediately about our connections with Black men and other women. I say to them we must first rise up on our own behalf. We must stand up for Black women, and when we do, many Black men will benefit and will join us. In the past, when we have fought for our own rights, other women of color have been inspired and encouraged by our leadership. But first we must stand up.

Others will, of course, bring up our university's budget crisis. But the financial crisis of the university is a political crisis with economic ramifications and manifestations. The budget crisis is a way of winnowing and prioritizing the agenda of public society. Because our university is 2/3 Black and Brown and mostly female, we are the state's lowest priority. Just as Black maids in former times were given bread pans and clothes instead of wages by wealthy and stingy bosses, when Black men and women are given any authority, we are handed a meager budget to "live with" instead of the money and resources we need. We have become Cuomo's and Clinton's servant girls. We dutifully complain and then proceed to implement whatever budget or directive we are handed.

Since we have no financial or political agenda of our own, we can be impressed to serve without question or protest. If there is enough money to pay the salaries and expenses of white men in this city and university . . . to bail out Trump and other millionaires, then there is enough money to reduce tuition for Black women and other students and to pay decent wages to its workers. If there is only a small amount of money, then Black women should be a priority because of their pivotal and valuable contributions. Black women are among the most productive citizens because their unpaid and paid labor serves and helps other people and institutions such as CUNY. Why then are our needs *always* last? Where is *our* voice of rage against the entire process?

When our students protested against tuition increases, we refused to support them. Many took work home, passed through student pickets, and even helped to end the protests. Although many student leaders were young Black women, we did not give them the baton that Ella Baker gave protesting Black students two decades before. We kept saying we disagreed with their tactics of shut down and boycott, but we gave them few alternatives. A powerful group of Black women workers like The Lion's Rock was needed to give the CUNY protesting students our love or our support.

But we cannot effectively address any issue because we do not have a collective plan, or an agenda for agitating, advocating, and demanding. She who sets the agenda determines the policy. If we continue to merely serve the university and do not attempt to transform it to serve the needs of Black women, we have abandoned our legacy and our responsibility.

We are the daughters and beneficiaries of Black women who took their meager material resources and enormous courage and faith and mixed them together to give us what we now enjoy—access, opportunity, status, and significance. We are the daughters of Ella Baker and Fannie Lou Hamer. What would they have done during the student strike? What words of courage are they whispering to us now? Can we guarantee that the messages of sisters in struggle reach the ears of our daughters and granddaughters, Black teen girls and young women struggling to find meanings in their own lives from watching our own?

What tools and instruments do we offer them to build a new world for our people and our species? What kind of knowledge will we have given them about the world? What will their experiences as young Black women say about how our positions of influence helped them? What kind of ancestors, my sisters, will we be?

Following is a list of demands addressing the concerns of Black women students, staff, and faculty.

DEMANDS, CONCERNS, AND GOALS

1. We call for free tuition and open admissions and full funding to support it, especially for adolescents at risk i.e., teen mothers and fathers. I am suggesting that Black women develop an impact statement on tuition increases and Black women students and families. We should then develop a tuition relief package to supplement financial aid.

2. We call for health, immigration, legal, and AIDS clinics to be ongoing aspects of student support and services. Many colleges already do this, but it needs to be an operating mandate of all colleges, linking the day to day concerns of our students with their college work. Community groups might be organized together to institute and staff the clinics. We also need to pay more attention to the housing of our students.

3. We call for full funding of the Medgar Evers College Center for Women's Development and the development of other women's centers on other campuses. The only women's center begun by Black women students, led by Black women staff, and serving Black women and other students, should be replicated throughout the university.

4. We call for full examination of the admission, remediation, and assessment procedures as they impact on Black women students.

5. We demand a career ladder for secretarial and administrative staff which includes explicit procedures and opportunities to become faculty members and top level managers in order to develop an in-house pool of Black female faculty.

6. We demand an increase in Black women faculty in all departments as well as increases in Black studies and women's studies and courses which include the experiences of Black women.

7. We demand graduate and undergraduate concentrations in Black women's studies.

8. We demand exchange programs and study-abroad programs in Africa, Latin America, and the Caribbean—everywhere Black women live on the planet.

9. We demand a Black women's research center and library to collect and house primary documents on Black women's experience.

10. We demand all colleges become safe havens for Black women where they can meet and voice their needs and demands. We especially want to be able to invite young Black women to our campuses.

PART III

PRAXIS AND STRUGGLE

11

ELLA'S DAUGHTERS

I WORKED WITH ELLA BAKER during the summer of 1964 at the Washington, D.C. office of the Mississippi Freedom Democratic Party (MFDP). She was already a legend in the Civil Rights Movement as the advisor to the radical and committed young activists in the organization she founded, the Student Nonviolent Coordinating Committee (SNCC).

Our Washington MFDP office staff included Ms. Baker, Walter Tillow, a white SNCC worker from New York, and myself, a recent college graduate who had been a part time worker in the New York SNCC office. We were to gain support for seating the delegation from the MFDP instead of the regular Mississippi Democratic Party delegation at the National Democratic Party presidential convention in Atlantic City. We coordinated volunteers who lobbied Democrats on the Hill and raised funds to support MFDP activities.

Although a college graduate, I was so inept and anxious, most of my time was spent trying to deal with my newly discovered sexual freedom and autonomy—and marveling at Ms. Baker. She was everything I was not: self-assured and brilliant. Ms. Baker was able to easily communicate with and gain respect from "ordinary" people, young activists as well as powerful white men such as Attorney Joseph Rauh, a leading Democratic Party advisor. She immediately took command of every situation while I floundered and stumbled through the simplest chores.

In August, the bodies of three missing civil rights workers, Michael Schwerner, James Chaney, and Andy Goodman were discovered. Andy had been my classmate at college and I had recruited him to participate in the

Mississippi Freedom Summer Project. Because of his lynching and the gravity of the efforts in Mississippi, that summer my identity as a woman became intertwined with becoming like Ms. Baker, an effective and respected organizer. Fighting injustice and oppression, making sacrifices for social causes became, for me, the indicators of true womanhood or manhood. However, as the Civil Rights Movement waned I became absorbed in personal journeys and travels, and then in marriage and motherhood.

However, my interest in Ms. Baker and my quest to emulate her was reawakened by my relationship to the women's movement. I was thrust into the heart of second wave feminism, not by choice or politics—I was a staunch nationalist at the time—but because I worked for white feminist organizations. In the mid-70s, I became the co-coordinator of Women's Survival Space, a 40-bed battered women's shelter located in Brooklyn, and then an administrator at the Women's Action Alliance, a national women's organization and resource center founded by Gloria Steinem and others.

The feminists around me constantly spoke about the roots of feminism being derived from books by Betty Friedan and Simone de Beauvoir, which raised women's consciousness and began a "second wave" of women's activism. Few acknowledged the contributions of white and Black women civil rights workers, or the critical role of the Civil Rights Movement, in general, to the material conditions which made the women's movement possible. The reality that much of Black and white feminist praxis and social theory came from the work and ideas of Ella Baker was ignored.

By the time Ella Baker founded SNCC, she had already been a full time organizer for the NAACP in the deep South from 1938–1946 and an executive secretary of the Southern Christian Leadership Conference. In 1943 she was named director of NAACP branches, in charge of establishing and maintaining the local chapters. At considerable risk to herself and her constituents, she traveled throughout the South enrolling southern Black people in the NAACP, an outlawed organization whose members were often harassed, tortured, killed, and run out of town. She helped community members identify local leaders and issues for struggle against segregation. This political work confronted the real possibility of torture and death because at the time the South was ruled by legalized apartheid. Not unlike police states and dictatorships worldwide, protesting Black southerners were "disappeared," their homes were bombed, or they were, at the very least, imprisoned. However, Ms. Baker was relentless and courageous in her determination to extend the mutual support and collectivity of Black communities to include active resistance to segregation.

In 1958, after living in New York for 12 years, Ms. Baker returned south at the age of 55 to become the executive secretary of the SCLC, founded by Martin Luther King, Jr. The conference was a network of Black ministers in southern cities who assumed local leadership of mass movements fighting segregation. One of Ms. Baker's assignments was to organize a meeting to mobilize the diverse and disparate groups of students who, during 1960, had "sat in" protesting segregated lunch counters and bus stations. Ms. Baker was outraged and walked out of a meeting where ministers mapped out plans to isolate students by region and pressure them to become part of an SCLC-dominated youth organization. Rejecting these high handed pressure tactics, Ms. Baker held that "that those who were under the heel were the ones to decide what action they were going to take to get from under their oppression." She encouraged the protesting students to establish their own organization, the Student Nonviolent Coordinating Committee (SNCC), and became its advisor, working part time for the Atlanta YWCA to support herself. She hired Jane Stembridge, a white student from Georgia, and Bob Moses, a Black high school teacher from New York, to become SNCC's first field secretaries.

SNCC became a racially mixed group of male and female field secretaries who from 1961 to 1966 organized voter registration and anti-segregation campaigns in Black communities throughout southwest Georgia, Alabama, and Mississippi. Its ambitious Mississippi Freedom Summer Project, organized with nominal support from the NAACP and SCLC, and in active partnership with CORE, brought hundreds of northern students and volunteers into the state from 1963 to 1965 to organize Freedom Schools, medical and legal clinics, cultural programs and the MFDP.

Representing the fullest expression of Ella Baker's social praxis, SNCC and MFDP were more political collectives than organizations in the traditional sense. Ms. Baker's social theory and praxis is based upon face to face political work involving dialogue, where the organizer/initiator listens to the concerns of "local people," who articulate what they know, receive feedback about their ideas, and offer their own remedies, strategies, or solutions. From a series of dialogues held at people's homes or job sites, the organizer/initiator gathers together several people and calls a meeting—usually at a church. The meetings are usually accompanied by song and prayer, which continue earlier discussions, develop mutual courage, and enable members to resolve to execute an action to change some aspect of their political condition—a voting card, a traffic signal, a new policy. The activity must be decided upon by the consensus of those who will execute and be affected by the action.

The organizer is an "outsider" actively seeking anonymity and no personal rewards, while serving to facilitate the meetings and actions of local leaders and community members. The organizer without domestic or career ties is "called" to social action rather than employed by the civil rights organization.

Although many social theories and movements share Ms. Baker's approach to organizers and communities, hers is one of the few which emerged from an African American ethos of mutual aid and support. "Where we lived there was no sense of hierarchy, in terms of those who have, having the right to look down upon, or to evaluate as a lesser breed, those who didn't have." (Canterow, 60) An organizer's success depended upon "both your disposition and our capacity to sort of stimulate people—and how you carried yourself, in terms of not being above people." (Canterow, 71)

This ethos was expanded to include the collective power to challenge segregation and make social change in communities which were made up of "people from various and sundry other areas . . . who had to learn each other . . . and begin to think in terms of a 'wider brotherhood.'" (Canterow, 61) Class and gender, and even racial differences were muted in this kind of organizing. White men and women SNCC workers became part of the community by rejecting their own racist backgrounds and communities in order to live and work among and *for* Black people.

Ms. Baker was not overtly ideological. She spouted no pre-packaged party line. She was not a Marxist, although she stood with the working class and the poor. She was not a professed nationalist, although she was deeply rooted in the African American ethos and community. Likewise, she was not a declared feminist but modeled for young Black and white women a powerful womanhood that was not tied to traditional domestic social roles. Ms. Baker was a "liberated" Black woman radical whose genius was her ability to develop democratic and activist political organizations and communities.

In giving students permission to organize on their own behalf and define their own role in the movement, Ella Baker transformed American politics. The organization she birthed, SNCC, took on a life of its own. Her philosophy affirming the right of Black poor people to organize gave rise to a political culture which is now commonplace. The idea of "grassroots" groups of ordinary people organizing to protest, petition, as well as develop their own agendas was enlarged and expanded by Ella Baker to empower organizers to meet the needs of anti-segregation struggles in the deep South. She developed a network and apparatus among alienated and disparate community leaders during her NAACP organizing years. She connected activist ministers during her SCLC years, concretizing King's vision and enabling him to be a leader among other ministers in the movement. She produced young student leaders who became the movement's "shock troops." Unencumbered by family or jobs, they could go into southern towns and give local people inspiration and technical assistance.

Bringing white and Black college students into SNCC enabled Ella Baker to influence and train leaders who became part of national movements promoting changes in the academy, including the free-speech movement, and protesting the Viet Nam war. The white men she mothered brought the New Left Movement into being. The white women she mothered in the movement inspired others, creating second-wave feminism.

Many white students attribute their political evolution and enlightenment to SNCC, not realizing that SNCC was Baker's creation. Bob Moses, Jim Forman, Ruby Doris Smith Robinson, Dorie Ladner, and other admired SNCC members worked closely with Ms. Baker in *their* formative years.

Her Black daughters combined and took from feminism, nationalism and the New Left, adding their own unique notions, to birth womanism. During the late 1970s and 1980s, a network of Black feminists or womanists in central Brooklyn emerged to carry on the traditions of Ella Baker. These daughters developed organizations and campaigns in spite of sexism and antifeminist sentiments within Black nationalism and the Black community.

During the 1970s most politically active women in Black communities were connected in some way to the building of nationalist institutions and groups. At the heart of many of these efforts was the construction of more explicitly "African" cultural forms. Outwardly signaled by African names, attire, music, and religions, cultural nationalism rejected the "White World" and its values. Many women were attracted to the ideals of nationalism which affirmed their "womanhood" and beauty. However, male nationalists attempted to confine "womanhood" to mating and motherhood. In spite of the significance of Assata Shakur and Angela Davis, most women found themselves restricted by the rather narrow definitions of their role in nationalist organizations.

Many nationalists believed "the struggle" should restore the traditional gender roles destroyed by slavery, colonialism and racism: strong patriarchal warriors with supportive wives who mothered their children. Although some nationalist men believed women should be co-warriors in restoring the Black nation, ultimately their place would be caring for the home and family. Nationalist men sought to restrict women from leadership roles, though they continued to need Black women's labor, creativity, and resourcefulness.

Nationalist women often saw themselves as "warriors" in their own right. Among themselves, sisters balked at being mere supporters and complained of male chauvinism—while maintaining a united front with men against white racism. Many didn't realize that Black women in the past, especially radical organizers such as Ella Baker and revolutionary woman around the world, were battling the same two colonialisms: patriarchy and white supremacy.

Although Ms. Baker and other SNCC leaders understood that the struggle was really about creating a more equitable and just society, its immediate goals and forms were straightforward. The issues were there in Black and white: politically powerless Black people fought against the white power structure for the franchise, access to opportunity, and for equal treatment before the law. Such a movement required unity and sacrifice among a critical mass of people to show collective resistance for even a brief and defined period of time—the time it took for a demonstration, protest, or campaign. In this sense, the combination of Ms. Baker's work empowering local people (using students as their legs and arms), NAACP legal strategies, and King's spiritual and inspiring leadership was successful: Blacks have gained the franchise, and access to public facilities. But the movement unearthed other issues: free speech, sexism, peace. African Americans were radically changed because as the high points of the southern movement were ebbing, new forms of nationalist politics were being formed.

Both Ms. Baker and Martin Luther King became overshadowed by Malcolm X's post-civil rights message, which offered an alternate paradigm to citizenship for Blacks. His message of Black self determination, anti-colonialism, and transformed identification forced Blacks to look at what kind of society they were struggling to become citizens of.

Inspired by the possibilities of nationalism, two of Ella's sons: Kwame Toure, (aka Stokeley Carmichael) and Jamil Abdullah Al-Amin (aka H. Rap Brown) abandoned her grassroots, passive resistance strategies for a more militant and ideologically confrontational politics in the Black Panther Party. The Panthers' nationalist positions and radical rhetoric demonstrated their break with the methods of the southern struggle, although they grew out of the party of the same name in Lowndes county, one of SNCC's Alabama projects. Ella's sons rebelled against her model, her philosophy, and her name. The nationalism of organizations and groups founded by nationalist men did not allow women like Ella Baker to participate in their leadership.

In spite of the domination of men, Black women remained active in Black nationalist organizations. Their sisterhood and connection to each other strengthened both their own commitment to all Black people and their definitions of nationalism. These organizations fought police brutality and racist schools while building alternative schools and cultural programs. They helped to foster "community" among those viewed as fragmented and brainwashed by white culture.

The East, founded in 1970 by Jitu Weusi, was the major nationalist institution in central Brooklyn. It began as an outgrowth of an alternative school for Black students expelled from a city high school after staging a tribute to Malcolm X; the protest had been viewed as anti-Semitic and militant by the school authorities. Uhuru Sasa, the East's Freedom School, soon drew hundreds of students supported by parents frustrated and angered at the racism in the public school system. It soon expanded into a cultural institution which included an annual street fair of Black merchants and craftsmen/women, musical concerts, and community forums.

"It is our belief that the most crucial work for this particular era of African existence is the building of Revolutionary Nationalist institutions. By 'institutions' we mean schools, political parties, cultural centers, military units, presses—all those programmatic structures that enable a people to see beyond survival; in short, the elemental ingredients of a viable nation." (New Africa Education) The East, at its height, was an internationally known model for this kind of vision.

Women such as Martha Bright, Abimbola, Atchuda Barkr, and Aminisha Weusi demonstrated that strong Black women continued to organize during the cultural nationalist era. Their hard work and strong women's circles enabled them to be effective in spite of male chauvinism. Ironically, most male leaders, needing skilled and loyal workers, expressed admiration and respect for "strong sisters." Some nationalists such as Kalamu ya Salaam and his wife Tayari attempted to address Black male chauvinism through a nonsexist practice involving study, seminars, and pamphlets. They were also some men in the East community who were struggling against their own sexism and its effect on the movement. In fact, during the late 1970s, Segun Shabaka encouraged me, a Black feminist and radical activist, by publishing my articles in the *Black News,* the East-sponsored journal he edited.

When I wrote those articles, I was a single mother of three children, working full time as an administrator at the Women's Action Alliance and part time as an adjunct in women studies at a local college. As a result of my own search for an effective and hospitable political community, I threw myself into a flurry of activism. In addition to writing for *Black News,* I worked with white leftists, primarily in supporting normalized relationships between the United States and the People's Republic of China. I learned about Marxism and nationalist theory by attending meetings of many radical groups. In 1979, I was in a Black women's study group which included Susan McHenry, one of *Ms. Magazine*'s earliest Black woman editors, and Michele Wallace, when she first published *Black Macho and the Myth of the Superwoman.* I was also active in the Sisterhood of Black Single Mothers and the Women's Committee of the Black United Front. I demonstrated against and protested police brutality and South African apartheid. I spoke on feminism and activism to any group that asked me. I was trying very hard to be like Ms. Baker. Soon I kept meeting other activist Black women such as Daphne Busby, Safiya Bandele, Arlene Parker, Andree McLaughlin and others who could also claim to be Ella's daughters.

In 1972, Daphne Busby, a young single mother, founded the Sisterhood of Black Single Mothers, perhaps the first Black feminist grassroots group of the post-civil rights era not connected to any Black male organization. The Sisterhood always identified itself as a Black and female organization. By supporting Black single mothers and refusing to become embroiled in either feminist or nationalist ideological debates, the Sisterhood opened an entirely new arena for Black women's social activism. The Sisterhood was one of the first organization to legitimate the connections between personal issues, such as sexuality and motherhood, and Black female consciousness.

Established to counteract the slandering of women who were regularly called "unwed mothers" of "broken homes" with "illegitimate" children, the Sisterhood defended and advocated for Black single mother families. Daphne Busby's pride in declaring herself the head of a "family that works" challenged critics to examine their own prejudices and sexist assumptions about Black single mothers.

The Sisterhood offered consciousness raising, social services, and social activities to diverse Black single mothers: professionals, welfare recipients, middle age divorcees and teen mothers. As one of the first groups to work with these younger mothers and with Black single fathers, the organization pioneered in social policies and programs concerned with the Black family. While perfecting the white feminist movement's concern with connecting the personal to the political, which was merely a restating of Ella Baker's notion of dialogue, the Sisterhood deepened the Black community's traditions of self help. Interestingly, the Sisterhood was able to simultaneously gain the respect of white feminists, Black nationalists, and Black single mothers, in part because of the timeless energy of Daphne Busby's outspoken and no-nonsense leadership, and in part for its tangible help for Black single mothers.

For nearly 20 years, the Sisterhood attracted scores of sisters like me who were searching for an authentic place to deal with our personal needs as mothers and women and who needed concrete help with our families. Safiya Bandele was one of the first women to answer Daphne Busby's call for interested Black single mothers to join her. Safiya worked steadfastly along with Daphne, and eventually became the Chair of the Sisterhood board.

By the mid 1970s, Safiya and I began to find ourselves at the same meetings of the Sisterhood, the Black United Front and other groups. She eventually became my closest *companera* because we both were searching for a sisterhood which had the feminism and supportiveness of the Sisterhood of Black Single Mothers and the militancy and resistance politics of the Black United Front.

The Black United Front (BUF), founded in 1976 by Jitu Weusi and the Rev. Herbert Daughtry, was a multi-faceted political organization which mounted responses to police brutality and racial injustice, opposed apartheid, and supported radical international movements and human rights organizations.

The BUF women's committee was the largest and best fund raiser of the dozen committees of the organization. The committee was composed of women from the church, from the general membership of BUF, and activists like myself. Together we organized buses to demonstrate in Washington D.C., protesting attacks against affirmative action. We sponsored programs for the general membership and developed strategies for reforming the public schools.

While I worked in the women's committee, Safiya was an officer on BUF's executive board. In spite of the respect given the work of the women's committee and Safiya's executive position, women's leadership in the organization was resisted. Frustrated and restless because of our marginal roles in BUF, both of us also worked with Daphne at the Sisterhood and for a myriad of other causes, conferences, and campaigns.

During this period, Safiya and I learned a great deal about the patterns of male chauvinism and the subordinate position of women within nationalist organizations. Across the country, challenges to Black male chauvinism were increasingly made by Black women whose expertise and experience had been downplayed by dominant males. By the end of the 1970s virtually every Black organization or initiative seemed to break down over the appropriate place of Black women in its leadership. Some organizations, such as the National Black Independent Political Party (NBIPP) tried to create a formal approach by requiring that Black women co-lead with Black men in each of its chapters.

Safiya and I continued to straddle both the Sisterhood and BUF, striving to do work which would give sisters an authentic political voice while defending Black people against injustice. We encouraged each other, but grew increasingly dissatisfied, observing and noting male chauvinism while continuing to lend our labor power to the work of their organizations.

In 1991, I called together five Black women activist friends, including of course, Safiya, to develop a Black female response to the missing and murdered children in Atlanta, whose mothers were being maliciously attacked as "unfit" in the media, yet whose murderers were not being actively sought.

Since white men were reportedly implicated in the ritual murders of the children, many Black groups began rallying support for community patrols and more effective police activity. Newspaper accounts, however, repeatedly stated that the murdered Black boys were hanging in the streets late at night unsupervised because they came from "broken homes" with "unfit mothers"—meaning from families headed by Black women.

Some mothers of the missing and murdered children called press conferences and rallies to respond to these negative attacks on their families.

Our group in Brooklyn wanted to demonstrate solidarity with the mothers of Atlanta's missing and murdered children. We gathered more Black women together and formed the Coalition of Concerned Black Women. We decided to have a Mother's Day march to highlight the plight of the children and their mothers. Over 300 people marched on Mothers Day, May 10, 1981, nearly two miles through Brooklyn in a demonstration supported by 54 organizations. It was one of the first political marches organized solely by Black women and featuring a significant number of

Black women speakers on the program. Organized in 6 weeks, the march was a bold step in which Black women decided upon a goal to go forward and do something together and did it.

A year later, in 1982, I received a small grant from the Sisterhood to develop *The Rising Song,* a 13-week lecture series on Black women's history for the community. Held at the Restoration Corporation, a Brooklyn based community development corporation, the lecture series attracted large audiences of community members. Week after week, noted Black women historians, activists, and poets provided information and vision about the historical accomplishments and achievements of Black women. The lecture series presented speakers such as Professor Myrna Bain speaking about the unremitting toil of African women's labor, the late Audre Lorde discussing sexuality, and poet Hattie Gossett showcasing Black women writers, singers, and "wild women."

While the lecture series occurred, protests were intensifying at nearby Medgar Evers College. Among faculty and student concerns were the competency of the college president and the lack of adequate support services and academic programs for the predominantly Black and female student body.

Medgar Evers College was founded in 1971 as a result of strong demands by the members of the Black community in Brooklyn that the City University of New York create "a new experimental and innovative institution which meets the needs of the community in which it is located and the needs of the City which it must serve." Once established, the college received little support and few resources from CUNY; its neglect and the lack of adequate leadership created a climate of discontent which erupted during the spring of 1992 into a four month long sit-in in the President's office, carried out by students and a few faculty members. The Student, Faculty, Community Coalition to Save Medgar Evers College was founded to rid the college of its president and rebuild the college in the image of Medgar Evers, the man. The movement at MEC was eventually responsible for removing the President, for getting the Board to authorize new facilities and for establishing a woman's center. At the end of the four month strike, a childcare center named in honor of Ella Baker and Charles Roman, a former professor at MEC, was started in the former President's quarters.

Embodying Ella's democratic notions of consensus, the sit-in's student, faculty, and community members argued, debated, and developed an agenda. The agenda presented the group's demands and set forth policies for governing the school. Because Black women students, faculty, staff, and community members performed support as well as leadership roles in all of its levels, the sit-in at MEC was perhaps the first political struggle in the post-civil rights era which connected an explicitly Black feminist praxis to a Black community struggle.

Unlike the students in the Civil Rights Movement, MEC students were workers and parents. The movement at MEC was sustained by women who were forced to strain the limits of their extended kin networks to get care for their children so they could be on the frontline. Some women brought their children with them, sleeping next to them on the floor and in chairs.

Four out of five officers of the Student government were women. The main security area in front of the President's office was staffed by a woman who at times literally put her body across the door. Women were prominent in maintaining a 24-hour watch down the halls and corridors from the office.

Inside another office, students ate together, slept together on the floor and shared resources and information. The domestic chores of cleaning, cooking, answering phones, which had been traditional roles for women in other political movements, were shared by all. Decisions were hammered out and executed democratically.

The militantly democratic nature of the protest, as well as its feminist and nationalist ideology, was insured by the powerful experiences of its Black women faculty leaders: the student movement experience of Professor Andree McLaughlin, the political experience of Professor Zala Chandler, and the community and Black women's movement experience of Professor Safiya Bandele. Their role was matched by the dedication and power of women students such as Sharon Smith, Alice Turner, and Rhonda Vanzant. Students such as Trevor Belmosa, Norman Coward, and Vincent Manuel demonstrated that Black men could work along with strong Black women. Not needing to dominate or cower, these men demonstrated the potency of a truly united effort among equals.

The Sisterhood, the Black United Front, Black Veterans for Social Justice, and other community organizations lent their support and expertise to the sit-in. I became a community representative to the Medgar Evers College Coalition which was created to support it. The MEC struggle brought many groups and individuals together in much the same way that the sit-ins and freedom rides had brought Black college students to SNCC decades before.

During the 1970s, the East and BUF were centers of male-dominated Black nationalist thought and practice. Black women were tentative in their search for an authentic place for their practice and ideas. After the struggle, Medgar Evers College became the center of explicit Black feminist concerns and womanist praxis.

A major issue of the sit-in at MEC had been the lack of support services, information, and scholarship which specifically addressed the needs of women students. Courageous women from the struggle demanded a women's center.

Directed by Safiya Bandele, the Center for Women's Development (CWD) opened its doors in April 1983. It has been one of the only women's centers in the country directed by a Black woman and established by Black women students. The center offers both individual and group counseling, especially for those who are depressed, battered and under stress. The CWD is also a referral service offering information about health, welfare, housing, and other support services. The CWD has sponsored and co-sponsored conferences, forums, and programs which reflect both the international and personal concerns of the student body. In 1985, the Center organized a delegation to attend the United Nations Decade for Women's Meeting in Kenya.

In 1985, Professor Andree McLaughlin, as coordinator of the Women's Studies, Research and Development "piloted a Cross Cultural Black Women's Studies Curriculum" (Jackson, 2) which grew into a series of International Cross Cultural Black Women's Studies Summer Institutes. "Convening annually in different nations, the Institute is a world assembly of women activists, theorists, artists, writers, peasants, and workers who are concerned with learning about each other's realities to enable themselves to better control their destinies." (Jackson, 1)

Since its inception, the group has met in Zimbabwe, New Zealand, Berlin, and New York and discussed "Women and Communications," "Women and the Politics of Food," "Human Rights and Indigenous Peoples in the Information Age," "and Black People and the European Community." "This think tank for women and women's concerns has decided it is crucial to continue to address the legacies of colonialism and feudalism as well as the realities of patriarchy and imperialism which impact on their everyday existence in real ways . . ." (Jackson, 8–9) The Institutes, primarily led and developed by Andree McLaughlin, have created an international community of Black women which, like the anti-colonialist Pan African conferences at the beginning of the 20th century, will undoubtedly have a major impact in global politics in the future.

In addition to the exciting potential of this international work, by the end of the 1980s Black women in Brooklyn had institutionalized many womanist-inspired programs and institutions. In 1989, the Sisterhood founded Kianga House, a residential program for homeless teen mothers, one of the first places to institutionalize Black feminist approaches to this issue. Martha Bright, formerly of the East, joined with Esmeralda Simmons and others to develop parenting groups and legal services at the Medgar Evers College Center for Law and Social Justice. Alice Turner, the heroic student leader of the MEC struggle, after receiving her MSW degree, returned to run the Center for Women's Development counseling unit, developing and expanding its program.

In 1985, the CWD sponsored a Black Women's Conference with over 500 participants. The conference planning committee, composed of lesbians and heterosexual sisters, had hoped it would heal wounds among Black women, and create a common and on-going agenda. However, homophobic participants rejected lesbians who spoke openly about themselves and their issues. Although the conference failed to develop a true sisterhood, it encouraged CWD to do more intensive work on personal issues of sexuality and identity.

Gwen Braxton of the New York City Black Women's Health Project, a member of the conference planning committee, helped the CWD develop an agenda for its own members' health. The motto "if you are not working on yourself, you are not working" informed support groups and "internal work" among Center staff. The Center has implemented the self-help/support group/mutual-help model of the Black Women's Health Project, which emphasizes coming together to give and receive help, "*not* as expert, social worker, psychologist, organizer, physician, teacher, paid helper, and needy paying client helpee." (NYC Black Women's Health Project)

One of the women who helped the CWD institutionalize this approach is Arlene Parker, the first Black woman to receive a degree in Black women's studies from CUNY. Before working at the Center for Women's Development, Arlene worked at the Bedford Stuyvesant Restoration Community Development Corporation as Assistant to the President. Arlene brings a unique approach to her work by attending to the well-being of Black women. She affirms and connects women to each other by using the traditional approaches women have used to maintain kinship relationships: sending cards, phone calls, celebration of holidays, and birthdays. Arlene has fostered a sisterhood among the women at the Center for Women's Development.

The Center's special approach to Black women's self-help was consolidated in a series of workshops, "Healing Women Warriors," which grew out of an unpublished article I wrote with Andaye de la Cruz, a Latina activist and therapist. Both of us were recovering from our own "burn-out" and overextension as activists, workers, and mothers. We looked around and saw that many of the women activists we worked with were themselves "sick" and overworked.

The "Healing Women Warriors" work enabled me to critically confront one of Ms. Baker's motto's: "She who believes in freedom cannot rest," a powerful yet dangerous message for overworked women activists. For more than a decade, I and other women were trying to work for the people and the sisters while we also worked for wages and raised families. Not only were we "burning out" and suffering from the same tragedies as other Black women—murder, rape, cancer, and depression—we were often neither effective, nor sisterly. Many of us realized that we could not remain wedded to a politics which tried to hold back the tide of diminishing political community, waning activism, and the avalanche of new and complicated social and personal issues, without strengthening and healing ourselves. Ella's daughters had to learn to rest and carve out time to recuperate. We also needed on-going support groups to in order to be effective women and organizers.

Ms. Baker worked behind the scenes of major political organizations, doing the unrecognized toil of meetings and campaigns. Although she claimed not to want to "be in front," the tensions between the male authority in power and the authority she embodied were just below the surface of Ms. Baker's problems with SCLC and the NAACP. While Ella worked around gender issues in order to "contribute" to the Civil Rights Movement, today's Black woman activists are compelled to focus on them—especially violence against women, women's development, homophobia, and challenges to male chauvinism.

Some of Ella's daughters have replicated her role as the "woman in front," the pioneer and initiator. The woman in front "puts her body into the movement." She, like Ella, is found working long hours, squeezing in family obligations and sacrificing personal pleasures. Policy, programs, and work evolves from and is most often initiated by her. Andree McLaughlin, founder and leader of the Cross Cultural Black Women's Institute, and Daphne Busby, founder and director of the Sisterhood of Black Single Mothers are examples of the "woman in front" leadership model. In fact, because of the rise of such womanists in the Black community and in Black women's consciousness, more are daring to become "women in front."

Ella Baker's adherence to democratic collective work has inspired another womanist leadership model—the woman leader "in the circle." Groups of Black women work together on projects, campaigns, and programs and maintain friendships and personal relationships beyond their work. Safiya Bandele at the CWD has used this model in her work, empowering the women on staff to work on themselves as well as on the Center's tasks.

As Brooklyn's Black womanist community matures, it becomes clear that these two approaches—"woman in front" and "woman in the circle"—are not mutually exclusive. The "woman in front" leader often becomes "burned out," feels isolated, and truly needs to share her work and responsibilities with sisters in support groups and networks.

However, without the daring actions of these "women in front," women's circles can become overly concerned with raising the consciousness of their members. We, as Ella's daughters in central Brooklyn, have developed a praxis that uses and develops both kinds of Black women's leadership. Each woman in the group is encouraged to work on herself and her dreams, and somehow they all become part of the Center's mission and work.

Our Black womanist praxis is a process which utilizes the social distance between Black men and women to raise feminist consciousness. It enables women to see the social character of their personal and private oppression. It exposes male chauvinism and sexism as being detrimental to all Black life. It is a social movement concerned with the physical, emotional, political, and spiritual health of all members of the Black community. Our praxis attempts to bridge differences between lesbians and heterosexual women and tries to work and participate in an international sisterhood of Black women.

The Black Women's Health Project advocates resistance to all forms of oppression, and the complete elimination of oppression as essential to the Black Woman's struggle for and achievement of well-being. It considers violence a public health issue and seeks to eliminate the physical, institutional, psychological, and ideological violence perpetuated against Black women.

Furthermore, this social praxis is developing in the midst of a literary renaissance and an explosion of studies by and about Black women. More and more Black women who want to help their sisters and do something about the destitution and despair in the Black community are becoming leaders of unions and schools, owning their own businesses, and running for elected office.

There is a also a transformation within the Christian church because of the pro-woman praxis of Black women, laity and clergy. Not all Black women who sustain pro-active positions and commitments to social change consider themselves womanists. However, Black women activists and womanists alike rely on their personal relationship with God for guidance and determination. Like Ella Baker, they pray their feet be guided by God so their work will not be in vain. This faith informs and sustains their visions of social change.

Our praxis in the past has been to do anti-racist work with Black men, to do women's work with Black women within the Black community, and sometimes to do work on women's issues in coalition with white women and other women of color. The womanist praxis in Central Brooklyn has shown that when Black women develop their own power, consciousness, and skills, this resonates with Black people's overall survival, development, and peace. Andree McLaughlin challenges us to understand that our praxis must attempt to be nationalist, feminist, and socialist all at the same time, in opposition to the "multiple jeopardy which undermine the standard to all people's existence." (McLaughlin, 54)

Ella Baker believed, like many others, that a baton is passed from one generation to another to keep the struggle for social change alive. As the tireless "fundi" (a Swahili term for "the person in a community who passes on the crafts from one generation to another"), Ella Baker passed on her baton to me, a direct descendant of her praxis and her work. But I had to shape and redefine the baton to fit the requirements of my own time, and needs. The power of her baton has grown to be shared with other women.

Our womanist praxis has to been birthed, extended, and embraced by multiple circles of sisters, sometimes led by the "woman in front" and other times led by the "sister within the circle." While other children can afford the racial or gender privilege of ignoring or dropping the baton she offered them, Black womanists can never forget that Ella Baker was our mother, and that, as her daughters, we owe it to her to continue to struggle in her name.

12

BLACK CODES AND RACIAL DRAMAS

THE CENTRAL PARK JOGGER CASE

ULTIMATELY, CRIMINALITY of the Black male regardless of its nature, truth or reality, resides in any act or attitude on the part of Black males which appears to white Americans to defy white American authority, control, or dominance. It is white America which defines criminality and writes the criminal justice codes. It writes these codes not in the interest of justice as defined by its own moral code, but in the interest of maintaining, justifying and enforcing its continued dominance of the African American. (Wilson, 9–10)

Black Codes were instituted to govern the lives of African Americans in the aftermath of Reconstruction and the Civil War. These laws passed by southern legislatures at the end of the Civil War were both reminiscent of the slave codes and precursor of segregation or Jim Crow laws.

> ... the Black Codes were deliberately designed to take advantage of every misfortune of the Negro [sic]. Negroes were liable to a slave trade under the guise of vagrancy and apprenticeship laws; to make the best labor contracts, Negroes must leave the old plantations and seek better

terms; but if caught wandering in search of work, and thus unemployed and without a home, this was vagrancy, and the victim could be whipped and sold into slavery. (Du Bois, 167)

In fact, Black Codes have become any set of race specific laws, policies, or customs aimed at containing or controlling the lives of Black people.

Since the Brown vs. Board of Education Supreme Court decision outlawing racially segregated schools, state and federal laws referring to race have quickly disappeared. Desegregation of the public sectors of American life has become common place. There is an African American presence in the country's major institutions: media, education, law, medicine, and military.

Yet we continue to see, understand, and know the world through a relentless, color struck prism. American life remains racially stratified and divided: things are either Black or white. Moreover, in every measurement used to gauge American life, Black men, women, and children live shorter, sicker, poorer, and more violent lives than white men, women, and children.

For some, today's racism is simply a continuation of the segregation era (1896–1954), and the changes brought on by the Civil Rights Movement mean little. Others have declared the end of racism, viewing individual moral fortitude as the only obstacle to Black advancement. Neither of these perspectives engage the current "desegregation" and "resegregation" era's specific set of racial dynamics.

This essay uses the Central Park Jogger rape case to demonstrate the continuation of "Black Codes" in spite of the end of race specific statutes. The Central Park Jogger (CPJ) case as a sensational "race" crime with a great deal of media coverage became a public theater where racial stereotypes, roles, and scripts were "acted out" within the context of prosecuting the crime. As a source of racial representation and symbolism, the CPJ case compels us to review the interfacing of race and gender with a feminist and nationalist analysis of injustice. Furthermore, the case allows us to explore the multiple representations of the race/gender system underlying white supremacy.

Race is this country's central mythological paradigm. Whether American identity is symbolized in the "taming of the west," "immigrant hordes at the Statute of Liberty," or "protecting and defending democracy in the world," racial assumptions and constructions shape and guide the content. Joseph Campbell says all societies invoke mythic symbols: agrarian societies constructed their myths around the magical power of seeds and hunting societies invoked mythic symbols of warriors. Colonial and slave owning Western societies such as the United States have based their myths and symbols on skin color and the dyad of Black vs. white skin. The mythic power of skin color or race determines evil and good; guilt and innocence; and ignorance and knowledge in the real and symbolic lives of Black and white people. Concepts such as "people of color" attempt to more accurately and objectively describe the cultural and ethnic reality of the American population. However, these terms often miss the irrational, more powerful reality that in this country, all those who are not white are Black and those who are not Black, are white. This same reality forces African Americans to mute and mask their African, African American, and African Caribbean ethnic and cultural identities. African ethnicities have become synonymous with Blackness. For people of African descent, ethnicity is equated with "race."

Racial mythology is not, however, an explanation, but the beginning of an examination of the social order which exposes its class, gender, and other constructions. I argue that race is the *primary* factor explaining stratification, domination, and inequality in American culture and society. Irrespective of theories that assert the primacy of gender, class and other constructs, the day-to-day lives of theorists and intellectuals as well as everyone else are determined by race. *The* factor which decides who we sleep, eat, work, learn, and play with is *race.* Everyone in our society *believes* that race matters most, in all social interactions. Although I know that a race-gender system operates daily, it is race which permeates and dominates our society.

The actual privileges which white people have in relation to Blacks are indications of white supremacy. White people have more real wealth and resources; more opportunity and access to employment, and a cultural and social apparatus which affirms and recognizes their supremacy in every field and endeavor.

The ideas and social mores critical to white supremacy are a Protestant work ethic in which original sin could only be absolved or eased with work and accumulation of wealth; a pornographic view of sexuality as evil and fascinating; and an irrational fear and belief in Blackness as embodying both sexuality and evil. White supremacy has been held in place by ruthless violence and militarism:

> ... crimes committed in the service of white American domination—
> the rape and robbery of nations, the murder and exploitation of native

peoples and their lands, the denial of the humanity of non-European peoples, the enslavement, lynching, racial discrimination and disenfranchisement of African Americans infinitely outweigh the alleged crimes of African American men. (Wilson, 10)

Post-industrial American society has rid itself of historic systems of Black containment. The present "structure of racial oppression" is organized around two inter-related processes: the criminalization of Black men and the mammification of Black women, both maintained by public policy, discriminatory public institutions and cultural "Black Codes."

Stephan Chorover, after studying what he refers to as the "false assumption that incarceration is a valid index of criminality," concluded that:

> . . . criminal acts are far more equitably distributed across society than are the acts of punishment. Of the crimes punishable by imprisonment, 98.5 percent go unpunished. The 1.5 percent who are prisoners should not be confused with the total population of criminal offenders. (as quoted in Wilson, 19)

> . . . in 1986 Blacks accounted for 46.5 percent of all arrests for violent crimes even though Blacks comprised 12 percent of the US population. Blacks accounted for 48 percent of the persons arrested for murder, 46.6 percent of all arrests for rape, and 39.8 percent for assault. . . . Over 40 percent of all jail inmates throughout the nation are Black—and the percentage is rapidly rising." (Wilson, xi)

More than 50 percent of all Black males under the age of 21 are unemployed, and most live in families with incomes less than $10,000. The fact that only 58 percent of all Black young adult males, 34 percent of all black males aged eighteen to nineteen, and 16 percent of those aged sixteen to seventeen were employed in 1984 reveals a problem of joblessness for young black men that has reached catastrophic proportions. (Wilson, 43)

As Black male crime, incarceration, and unemployment rates soar, high profile "race" cases involving them and white assailants and/or victims usually generate protests from activists in the African American community. The trials of the white murderers of Black men such as Yusuf Hawkins and Michael Griffith have been used by Black protesters to expose racial injustice and put white racist community values as well as white assailants on trial. Although the race and gender of the assailants and victims were different in the CPJ case from cases where Black men were the victims of white violence, it was nevertheless viewed by many

African Americans as another case of criminalizing Black men. Black men and women at the trial and at demonstrations were there to bear witness and to protect through protest young Black men from being the crushed by the white supremacy in the criminal justice system.

On April 19, 1989, a young white female jogger was brutally assaulted in New York's Central Park. Both the African American and the Euro-American communities initially reacted with shock and horror when a group of young Black men were charged with the rape. Mayor Koch spoke of "a whole city filled with distress and pain at the plight of this young girl." (Powell and Ladd, 24)

On April 26, 1989 unity rallies and vigils were held to "heal the racial wounds" and pray for the comatose woman's recovery. Appalled Black community leaders such as the Revered Herbert Daughtry joined the vigil demonstrating compassion and concern. Echoing the feelings of many, a member of the Harlem's Boy Choir attending the vigil said he was there "to show that Black and teenage youth are not animals." (Powell and Ladd, 24)

Outraged Black women pointed out that rapes perpetuated against them no matter how brutal were never afforded such attention in either the Black or white community or media.

On May 11, 1989, a community March and Vigil against Violence was held in Brooklyn, because eight days earlier a Black woman was raped, beaten, and thrown off a roof. The vigil was sponsored by more than fifteen Black Brooklyn based organizations.

Prompted by the Central Park Jogger case, on May 18, 1989, the Medgar Evers College (MEC) Center for Women's Development held a press conference announcing an "Offensive" regarding Violence Against Black Women. Conference participants included Rev. Herbert Daughtry and Assemblyman Roger Green and other Black male activists in anti-racist and community politics. They joined Black women activists such as Daphne Busby of the Sisterhood of Black Single Mothers, Carletta Walker of the Black Woman's Health Project/NYC, Esmeralda Simmons of the MEC Center for Law and Social Justice, and others to call for an end to Black male chauvinism and rape. They spoke of a new political agenda to stop all forms of violence within the Black community. Neither white or Black media, both invited, covered the press conference.

The vigil and press conference were part of a continuing effort by Black women's organizations opposing violence. On July 6, 1989, twenty Black women at a roundtable discussion on violence founded Women Against Violence Everywhere (WAVE), "a sisterhood of conscious, self-loving women committed to a violence free world." In August, they sponsored a day-long session to discuss the violence in their lives.

Rather than using the CPJ case to condemn sexism, violence, and rape against all women in all New York City communities (as the efforts of Black women in Brooklyn suggested), the media turned a polarized racial lens on the crime. The research and expertise of Black women attorneys, social scientists, and activists regarding violence and sexism were ignored. The brazen indifference of the media and authorities to other brutal rapes added to a lynch mob atmosphere and cast an ugly racist pall over the CPJ case. Lisa Kennedy pondered, "If I accept the premise of the coverage, that this rape is more heartbreaking than all the rapes that happen to women of color, then what happens to the value of my body? What happens to the quality of my blackness?" (Kennedy, 36) The CPJ case was not simply a horrible case of gang rape (which unfortunately frequently occurs)—this case was constructed out of the America's racial past where race is always more important than rape, especially when it is the rape of a white woman by "wild Black men."

The alleged assailants were described as "animals" and "their actions in the park a form of wilding." These words were a code to "broad stroke young Afro/American males as subhumans who rape, pillage, and throw themselves into a urban bacchanalia." (Cooper, 28) "Wilding" implied that the dark of night and uncontrollable Blacks had turned Central Park into a "jungle," an idea strengthened by the charges that the same assailants also mugged and threatened other white people in the park the same night of the rape. Other female joggers came forth to talk about being previously assaulted or threatened in the park by other Black men.

The victim who came to be known as the Central Park Jogger was an intelligent, ambitious executive who had graduated from an ivy league school, worked as an investment banker, and lived alone. Her only vice seemed to be that she dared to jog during odd hours. Her attack was portrayed as much a crime against upward mobility as a crime against women. She became a white yuppie heroine whose name was too precious to be mentioned and her sex life too pure to be questioned. Although many feminists have advocated that the secrecy and shame of rape should be removed by identifying rape victims and allowing their voices to be heard in the courts and their names to be used in the media, only the *Amsterdam News,* a Black-owned newspaper, printed the jogger's name.

The jogger's inability to speak because of the beating and the silence regarding her identity made her a traditional white female victimized by Black men: so silent, delicate, and pure that only her men—white men with racial power, could protect her and speak on her behalf.

By presenting complex details about her medical condition, and trivial aspects about her personal life, the media obsessed over every detail of the crime. Comments from medical and legal spokesmen were reminiscent of all of America's racial history, in which the rape of a white woman by a Black man is viewed as a crime against civilization and humanity, demanding collective retribution and public murder.

Becoming as watchful as a lynch mob, the major newspapers and television news programs repeatedly published the names and faces of the young Black male assailants. Designed to drive home the reality that these Black boys were not merely suspected of the crime, this coverage attempted to show them as vicious, violent, and guilty brutes. Because DNA evidence linking the semen of the young Black men with the woman was inconclusive, Attorney Colin Moore suggested that the jogger's boyfriend and other male associates should also be considered suspects. But Moore himself was considered an insensitive brute for even raising the issue of other suspects.

After the heady days of the comatose victim's fight for her life, the attention of many African Americans shifted to the racist treatment of the now indicted male suspects. For one thing, the suspects were all boys under eighteen years old; three of them were fourteen years old. In the eyes of many in the community, these were no common crackheads and thugs, these were *our good boys.* They did not come from the "underclass," but from good families whose single, surrogate, or coupled parents worked hard and were good citizens. They did not live in a tenement or welfare hotel, but in the Schomburg, a housing development. The boys attended school and church. They worked and participated in community activities. Many in the Black community felt that although the young boys might have "run as a posse" or stuck together, it was racist to consider them guilty of the crime without more conclusive evidence.

Many Black community members thought the videotaped "confessions" of the young suspects indicated naiveté and youthfulness. One of the boys didn't seem to even know the mechanics of rape. They didn't appear vicious and indifferent as the media suggested but as isolated and genuinely confused Black boys.

The police and the district attorney's office appeared overzealous and anxious to answer the media's call for blood, especially, I would add, Black male blood. The prosecutor did not proceed with the careful and prudent investigation this complex case deserved. One defense lawyer raised these seldom considered questions: "When did the police charge these suspects and when did they inform them of their rights . . . whether (the) suspects were questioned for 12 and 14 hours without being charged or allowed to stop and consult with a lawyer." (Cooper, 34)

"In pretrial hearings . . . a parade of police officers admitted that they failed to promptly inform at least three defendants of their" constitutional rights; that "all parents were separated from their children . . . and that at least two of the teenage suspects were later taken to the crime scene without the presence of their lawyers or parents" in violation of their constitutional rights. (Hornung, 32)

Sexist attitudes encouraged many to wonder why the jogger went running at night in the Central Park in the first place. Among Black people there grew a gnawing reminder of innocent Black men swinging from trees simply because white men *thought* they had raped a white woman. The familiar and historic treatment of the young Black male rape suspects began to overshadow African American horror of the rape and assault.

A Black male suspect's guilt or innocence of raping a white woman can not be accurately adjudicated in a society which believes in racial mythology and thirsts for hanging Black flesh. If Black men are innocent of raping a white woman, they still remain guilty of the crime of being Black and male which takes precedence over legal innocence. If they are guilty of raping a white woman, who can separate the guilt associated with their race and gender from their guilt for the crime? Which crime are they being tried for? Black men can *always* be found guilty of raping white women irrespective of the actual circumstances of the crime. And white women can always accuse them of the rape regardless of the man's guilt or innocence. I am suggesting not that Black men can not rape nor be found legitimately guilty of rape, but that their race and gender are never separated from their guilt and innocence.

Just as I believe that no matter what the actual facts were in the Tawana Brawley case (that of a young Black girl who accused white men of abducting and raping her), in a society which believes a Black woman can not be raped because of her "nature," it is impossible to sort out the truth or the lie of her story. Initially with similar physical evidence to that of the CPJ—a bruised body and inconclusive DNA—Brawley's rape was believed to be a hoax. However, in the CPJ case, although the woman has no recollection of the crime and could not identify the man or men who assaulted her, the young Black men were assumed guilty. The confused "confessions" offered by the young men were believed to be "true." Assumptions of guilt bound up with race and myth point to the lack of objective and legal criteria for judging the guilt and innocence of Black victims and suspects within a white racist belief system.

The complex terrain of race and sexuality complicates feminist analysis of rape. If the suspects are found to be innocent of this particular crime, then their arrest and treatment in the media and the court would become symbolic of the criminalization of the Black man. It then seems that feminists who hold universalist notions of rape and male domination would have to reassess their analysis to include the ways the racial patriarchy uses the charge of rape to dominate and punish *men* of color solely because of *their* race and gender. African American womanists such as Angela Davis have challenged white women to include unjust charges of rape against Black men within their anti-rape theories and campaigns. These anti-rape concerns should also include support for Black women rape victims, whether their assailants are white or Black.

Status differences between Black males and white males point out the weakness of universal notions of male domination and suggest factors more salient than gender in highly stratified social systems. Perhaps the young white men who murdered Yusuf Hawkins and the Black men of the CPJ case share similar vision quests of working class male aggression. However, Keith Mondello was given a 5–10 year sentence for the "Bensonhurst" *murder,* and Kharey Wise of the CPJ case received 8–26 years for sexual abuse, assault, and riot! What structural rationale other than racism can be offered for such sentencing differentials, between Black and white men of the same class? Because of the racial positions they occupy, white working class men such as Keith Mondello are able to move with impunity against Black men, overriding any similarities in their gender experiences.

It's the peculiar experiences of Black men which complicate feminist analysis and challenge the Black community's allegiances. If indeed these suspects are guilty—legally or actually—they and other Black rapists pose powerful dilemmas and issues about male chauvinism and rape for the Black community. Because if these boys are our "good" boys, then what does this signify about Black people's ability to "see" Black male sexist behavior as "bad"? "Good" boys can and do commit rape because it is a common male ritual in nearly all communities, including the African American community.

The Black male rapist is part of a broader Black male practice of violence against Black women and children and each other. Our "best" boys and men can be part of a "posse" which frightens, robs, hurts, and yes, rapes. When the victim of rape is Black, the Black perpetrator is usually not even arrested or charged. Because this time the victim was white and not Black, the "alleged rapists" have been swiftly and severely punished.

Perhaps recalling their own youth, several politically progressive Black men felt the young suspects in the CPJ case could be guilty because most teenage boys "hang together," fighting and "messing" with girls. This and similar confessions of Black male sexism are too problematic for Black families and communities *to admit on any public level.* Black male sexist crimes are seemingly denied to protect Black men from white vengeance. Many families fear any accusations of crime, especially from Black victims, will only make Black men more vulnerable. This protection, designed to save the life of the accused Black man who is innocent, also winds up protecting the Black criminal. The more the media portrayed the CPJ accused as "wild animals," the more the Black community's protests and demands were necessary to demand if not insure a just trial and sentence. Race became a more central issue than rape and more important than addressing the issue of sexism in the Black community.

Black women who work on exposing and eradicating sexism and the Black on Black crimes of rape and abuse are stymied by the Black public's desire to remain silent about crimes committed by Black men against Black women. Curtailed in their attempts to bring their work to the attention of Black community leaders, advocates for Black rape and incest survivors remain marginalized and the survivors remain hidden. The Black community's unwillingness to publicly discuss issues of sexism and male chauvinism exists because of fears that this discussion might compromise the (symbolic and actual) strong Black men needed for fighting white supremacy. Black women are perceived as breaking ranks with their people if they accuse Black men of a crime and place him at "the mercy of the white man's unjust system."

The young men in the CPJ case remind Black women of our "innocent" sons, victimized by the white man's racism. Although they sometimes rape our daughters and sisters we forgive Black men because they often also protect and help their mothers and sisters. bell hooks suggests that too many Black males' discussions of their social reality are "narratives of victimization," preventing any meaningful discussions of gender and sexism. Black male "narratives of victimization" provoke sympathy and maternalism from Black women because our men lack social standing and power. These representations also indict the Black father who has failed to protect and care for either his woman or his children. To Black men, I believe the convicted Black youth represent the public humiliation of their sons, their failures as patriarchs, and their own precarious manhood.

The CPJ case occurred during a social science blitz about "endangered" Black males being poor, jailed, uneducated, and despised. The Black man then became a heroic and besieged "victim" of white racism whose "endangered status" is used to rationalize and justify his violence. The pain of Black women and children who are "endangered" by these same Black men is ignored. Sexism and male chauvinism, persisting in spite of—not because of—Black men's own oppression by white supremacy, are not examined. Black male responsibility for violence *within* the Black community continues to be ignored.

Although the young Black men of the CPJ case are from a community with little economic, political, or social power, and have been found guilty of raping a white woman from a *race* and community with all such power, they are also from a *gender* which can rape and abuse women of their race with the same impunity white men use in murdering or judging Black men. What construct other than sexism can be offered to explain Black resistance to condemning all forms of rape irrespective of the victim's color? What other than rejection of the value of the Black female body can explain the Black community's protests and furor about the guilt or innocence of the CPJ boys who allegedly raped a white woman, and its lack of concern about the boys who harass and rape Black women every day!

The Central Park Jogger case's multiple racial and gender meanings challenge both nationalist and feminist theorists. Nationalist and feminist thought both have serious weaknesses which prevent them from effectively explaining phenomena riddled and intertwined with both race and gender.

Although feminist analysis of gender, sexism, and male chauvinism enable us to theorize about the subordination and domination of women, it too often ignores gender relationships between and among oppressed peoples and elite groups. Feminists tend to marginalize the solidarity required of ethnic men and women for their survival. They also ignore their allegiances to their own class and ethnic group, which transcend the female solidarity they often promote. In spite of separate gender domains and sexism, men and women within each class live together connected by religious, cultural, and historical ties.

Nevertheless, white feminists persist in theoretically extrapolating and generalizing about women's experiences in order to "fit" them into a notion of worldwide female oppression. They downplay the significance of race as the central organizing principle in Western society and American life. Consequently feminists have been unable to intellectually address the issues of race and racism in their analyses. The explosive issues of the CPJ case and other high profile racial/gender incidents are ignored by white feminists in spite of the role they play in feminists' concerns for access and safety in public spaces. Racism continues, in part, because white people, including white feminists, engage in a widely understood but unspoken bargain of silence about the persistence of skin color mystification and distortion.

On the other hand, African American nationalists view racial oppression solely in masculine terms. For them the nation's—community or people's—power is equated with a powerful manhood that can subdue and dominate its women. Since nationalism is ultimately concerned with a group's existence, nationalists tend to focus on protecting boundaries from outside attack. However, by asserting that all major problems in the Black community result from either white racism or the absence of Black consciousness, nationalists dismiss the approaches and programs necessary to address the problems caused by Black people acting against themselves. Black male chauvinism has been able to hide behind the mask of white male blaming and bashing. Because the external enemy is seen as some kind of powerful superhero and not as a complex system, many nationalists focus too much attention on fruitless sparring and ineffective protests.

Masculinized nationalism because it often admires and venerates white men for their power and violence, replicates domination over the "weak." In fact, many regard their right to oppress women—"keep them in their place"—as the right of manhood restored by the nation. By constantly viewing any discussion of sexism as a white female invasion of Black life or as a frivolous aside by some misguided and disloyal Black "bitches," masculinized nationalists deny women any authentic place in the nation or community.

However, women's participation in nation building is fraught with tensions between their subjugation and their contributions to the nation's (or male's) liberation. Yet it is precisely because women are also nationalists and have many beliefs and desires in common with their men that they are willing to tolerate their own subjugation.

All women, even white feminists, exist in nations and groups which require their subordination and silence for membership. Masculinized nationalists and their women who refuse to seriously consider a gender perspective or feminist analysis are like white feminists who are ignorant of their own racial and nationalist history. Too bad, because there can be no analysis of race without an analysis of gender and there is no understanding of gender without an understanding of race.

While class arrangements structure and engulf gender and race, usually within national boundaries, they are also, paradoxically, rendered impotent by the pervasiveness of racial and gender biases and myths. Otherwise, class-conscious organizing would have been able to transcend or at least effectively compete with racial and gender allegiances.

No matter how popular and powerful feminists and nationalists are within their own circles, neither can claim an effective social practice which radically influences public policy. While nationalists mount mechanical protests against racial injustice and violence, and feminists celebrate their integration into male bastions of power, many in both camps pursue essentialist analysis of either melanin or female moral superiority. Most feminist and nationalist theorists have confined their activities to the rarefied atmosphere of the academy, away from the courtrooms and daily lives of everyday men and women. Both exist within a conservative social order and a stratified economic system which they are unable to fundamentally transform.

Only African American feminists or womanists situated at the cross section of race, gender, and class, can inform and combine feminist and nationalist theories and practices while exposing the actual operations of class stratification at the same time. I urge a systematic examination of the race/gender system which operates within and along with white supremacy because I am convinced the key to social transformation lies in interfacing theories and constructs of feminism with those of nationalism.

High profile racial crimes are morality plays which sell newspapers and occupy television spots but they also represent significant arenas where race and gender dynamics are played out. Addressing issues of justice often pits feminists and Black protesters against each other as they separately engage in redefining the public discourse around race and gender.

The multiple symbols and representations of the Central Park Jogger case defy any singular or simplistic analysis. The rights of the state, the rights of the victim, the rights of the accused are juxtaposed both against the civil and human rights violations against all African Americans and those against all women. All these rights compete within a legal culture so imbued with stratification and racial mysticism that it is difficult to determine whose rights have precedent and whose representations are accurate and can stand up in court.

The CPJ case demonstrated how strong nationalism and color truly are, because it pushed Black women and white feminists to stand silently by their color and their men. Other than the efforts at Medgar Evers College and the words of Black women reporters such as Lisa Kennedy, there was little done to address the race/gender issues of the CPJ case at the time. For, once again, race became more important than rape.

The use of the courtroom to expose racism and segregation was a part of the legacy of pioneering African American jurist Charles Hamilton Houston. He believed that "the primary social justification for a black lawyer in the United States was the social service he [sic] could render the race as an interpreter and proponent of its rights and aspiration." (McNeil, 218)

Practical cooperation and interventions by feminists, womanists, and nationalists could have redefined the public discourse and the legal culture around the Central Park Jogger case. They could have simultaneously examined the violence and rape experienced by all women, the unjust treatment of Black men in the criminal "justice" system, and the city's racial-gender-ethnic polarity. At the very least, authentic public discussions could have exposed the links between the continuation of black codes and violence in the lives of all women.

Houston predicted "that the first reaction of the powers that be is going to be silence and oppression, censorship, and other things. They are going to try to cut off the intellectuals from the masses. So that in this day, while there is still little time, the primary task is to probe, to struggle . . . to teach the masses to think for themselves . . . to know their place and to recognize their power and to apply it intelligently." (McNeil, 208)

The divisions between feminists, nationalists, and womanists restrict everyone to racial and ethnic communities which contain and rationalize violence against women. The multiple knowledges and perspectives learned at the crossroads of race and gender break down boundaries and offer the possibilities of transforming communities into nonviolent and nonsexist cultures.

13

BLACK MEN, BLACK WOMEN, AND TAWANA BRAWLEY

THE SHARED CONDITION

IN LATE NOVEMBER 1987, a fifteen-year-old Black girl named Tawana Brawley was discovered in an upstate New York community smeared with excrement and racial slurs. She claimed that she was raped by a group of six white men, one of whom she believed to be a police officer.[1] The immediate reaction of many Blacks was to demand justice and retribution. Others merely waited for public revelations and specific details about the case, but Tawana Brawley remained silent.

At the request of the Brawley family, in the early part of 1988, attorneys Alton Maddox and C. Vernon Mason agreed to handle the case. Maddox and Mason are two lawyers known for their militant and victorious legal strategies in cases of racial violence and racial bias. Reverend Al Sharpton, a controversial Brooklyn-based political activist and minister, joined Maddox and Mason as Tawana Brawley's spokesperson and adviser.

Throughout the early part of 1988, while Tawana Brawley's lawyers and adviser sparred with the white legal power structure in New York State,[2] a growing number of Black attorneys, political activists, and feminists privately questioned the wisdom of Tawana Brawley's silence and non-compliance. On Thursday, September 29, 1988, nearly a year after the rape,[3] Tawana Brawley spoke publicly for the first time—a short statement which gave thanks to her supporters, but no explanation.[4]

SILENCE AND THE RAPE OF BLACK WOMEN

The lack of explanation surrounding Tawana Brawley's rape concerned many Black women. Just the mention of her name by trade unionist Lillian Roberts, at a March 1988 meeting of the Coalition of Black Trade Union Women, caused the 500 women present to gasp and sigh.[5] We embraced Tawana Brawley as daughter and sister, a Black woman whose condition we share. But even as we gasped and cried over Brawley's pain, something felt very wrong with the case. Black women wondered aloud: Why not bring her forth, let her tell us what happened? Was justice truly served by keeping silent about the details of her rape?

Yet it is the very silence around the specifics of Tawana Brawley's rape that links her to the historical conspiracy of silence surrounding all Black women's lives. Tawana Brawley's silence stands as an evocative symbol of Black womanhood: damned and raped, without voice or power to defend, describe, or define her own experiences.

The first layer of the silencing of Black women began during slavery. Black women's slavery in the United States, like all women's enslavement throughout history, was interwoven with rape and sexual abuse. Rape was an integral part of the master's right to use the slave woman's body. Silence surrounded these acts of violence, for a Black woman was powerless to charge her white master with rape. To do so would have been a radical political act; an act met with suspicion, denial, and physical harm or death.

In 1861 Harriet Jacobs wrote one of the most vivid accounts of the sexual abuse of a Black woman during slavery. In *Incidents in the Life of a Slave Girl*, she described how her white master's constant sexual attacks forced her to hide for seven years in a small storage room and eventually to escape to the North.[6] Her story of private and personal anguish contrasts with the public speeches of women such as Harriet Tubman and Sojourner Truth, who spoke out against slavery but did not specifically raise the issue of rape. How then did Sojourner Truth get thirteen children? She was raped by her master, John Dumont, who later forced her to marry an older slave by whom she had five children.[7]

During Reconstruction, few ex-slave women (or men) told their children and relatives details of their "concentration camp" experiences. Since many children were the product of the rape of a Black woman slave by a white male master, silence protected the children from shame and stigma, enabling the newly freed women to forget the painful aspect of their enslavement and to lessen feelings of rage in their Black spouses and children. Silence muted the sharp edges of slavery's legacy and enabled Black men and women to get on with their lives.

But even after emancipation, the rape of Black women by white men persisted, enveloping Black women in a second layer of silence. One of the few public descriptions of a Black woman's rape by a white man was given during this period in testimony before the Joint Committee of the Mississippi Legislature called to investigate the Meridian riot of March 21, 1871. Ellen Parton reported her experience:

> [H]e then took me in the dining room, and told me I had to do just what he said; I told him I could do nothing of that sort; that was not my way, and he replied, "by God you have got to," and then threw me down. . . . I yielded to him because he had a pistol drawn; when he took me down he hurt me of course; I yielded to him on that account; he . . . hurt me with his pistol.[8]

A third layer of silence grew around Black women during the early and mid-twentieth century as the rape of Black women by white men continued. These rapes were not widely publicized, especially when compared with the public discourse, debate, and protest against lynching. The Black community always pointed to lynching as the most blatant and vicious aspect of white males' attacks on the Black community, but no such discourse and protest surrounded the rape of Black women by white men. Yet, rape was frequently part of white males' attacks on the Black community.

> The systematic terrorization of black communities by the Ku Klux Klan frequently included the rape of Black women. A common practice of the Klan during an attack on a black community was to rape the women and burn peoples' homes and churches. Rape served to terrorize the entire community in the same way as lynchings.[9]

By not making these rapes a central part of Black political protest, the Black community reinforced Black women's silence.

In addition to blatant "systematic terrorization" of communities through rape, the rape of Black women by white men during the twentieth century took more invisible forms. Black women domestic servants in every region of the country have complained of the sexual "harassment" that went along with domestic work, especially as a "sleep-in maid." One maid explained: "I believe nearly all white men take and expect to take undue liberties with their colored female servants, not only the fathers, but in many cases the sons also."[10] To prevent their female children from coming into close contact with white males, many families encouraged their daughters to obtain an education and become school teachers within the Black community.

A fourth layer of silence surrounds Black women today. Few Black men acknowledge the rape of Black women by Black men. During the early twentieth century, Black social scientists, such as E. Franklin Frazier and W. E. B. Du Bois, condemned white men for sexually abusing Black women.[11] But, few Black men have understood that rape is also a sexist crime, and they are especially silent about the frequent rape of Black women by Black men.

For many Black women who have been raped by Black men, only other Black women have heard their sisters' pain. The fear of being abandoned by Black male lovers and spouses, of being condemned by Black fathers and community leaders, and of being considered a traitor to that race if they report the rape to the police (also knowing that the police would not take the rape seriously anyway), often stopped Black women from attempting to have the Black men who raped them punished. Black women could only turn to other Black women, and those stories have remained our shared secrets.

Black women rape victims have wiped that semen off, cried themselves to sleep, lied to doctors and lovers, gotten up and gone to work, keeping the secret within themselves. Their secret became fibroid tumors, bleeding ulcers, rage, sorrow, and heartache—a no-smiling-evil-bitch who directed her rage against everyone, especially white women and Black women who seemed happy and privileged. More than anything else, their secret became a constant pain which they endured in silence.[12]

These four layers of silence obstruct the ability to examine the rape of Tawana Brawley. The initial silencing of Black women by white men during slavery, the continued rape of Black women by white men during Reconstruction, the little-publicized and invisible rape of Black women by white men during segregation and of domestic servants throughout the twentieth century, and the silence within the Black community about Black women's rape by Black men combine to mute Black women's voices and experiences. These historical mutings, when combined with contemporary lies and distortions about Black women by the academy and the media, as well as with the refusal of police or judicial officers to take the rape of a Black woman seriously, silence us today and make it impossible for Tawana Brawley to get a fair and just hearing.

Tawana Brawley's rape, like the rape of all Black women, is surrounded by suspicion and doubt. The notion of a Black woman being raped has always been considered patently absurd by white society. To be a Black woman has meant to be sexually "loose" and "available." But many of the suspicions surrounding Tawana Brawley's rape are also common to all rape cases:

- what did she do to invite it?
- did she lie?
- could she have constructed her own rape; in other words, could she have raped herself?
- can she feel pain if she is raped?
- could she feign rape and pain?
- does she deserve to have her body kept hidden? (At least one news program in New York City showed a picture of Tawana Brawley's nude body without her consent.)
- is she deranged?

The special New York State grand jury that reviewed the Brawley case concluded that: "Tawana Brawley was not the victim of a forcible sexual assault. . . . There is no evidence that the sexual assault occurred."[13] The grand jury also concluded that there was a possibility that Tawana Brawley "self-inflicted" the "condition" in which she was found.[14] However, because the grand jury did not have adequate knowledge about rape victims and because they lacked an understanding of the history and psychology of Black women, they could not know what a Black female victim of rape is supposed to look like or supposed to do.

FEMINISTS: A LACK OF RESPONSE

Feminism is an ideology which views the world from a perspective of women's experiences and seeks to transform social, political, and economic institutions in order to liberate women. Black and white feminists have long acknowledged the silencing of women's voices. Yet, there has been virtually no feminist outcry about Tawana Brawley's rape. Feminists' failure to defend Tawana Brawley publicly has further muted her voice. This lack of a consistent response represents a serious inability of feminist rhetoric, thought, and vision to become applicable to political practice.

Black and white feminists have neglected to address the significance of Tawana Brawley's rape in different ways. White feminists, like much of the white left, have become paralyzed over how to treat issues of race and racism. During the early 1970s, white feminists callously ignored Black women and other women of color. Now they cling to them, anxious to discuss and analyze the connections between race and gender. But the need to publicly *respond* to racism and racial violence has not been seen by white feminists as a feminist issue.

After fighting anti-abortionists and suffering through internal strife about pornography, white feminists have seemingly retreated from organizing against institutionalized sexism. They have grown to exchange political activism for intellectual and cultural activity, and they have substituted research and writing about women for organizing women to fight their oppression. In contrast to the feminist organizing campaign waged around *Roe v. Wade*,[15] few white feminists have even written or commented on Tawana Brawley's rape.

Black feminists have made a few attempts to address the Brawley case. For example, the New York State Women of Color, an *ad hoc* group, called a press conference in support of the Brawley family on June 21, 1988 at Bethany Baptist Church in Brooklyn. The church provided sanctuary for Tawana Brawley's mother, Glenda Brawley, after she refused to cooperate with the grand jury investigating her daughter's rape. Presidential candidate Dr. Lenora Fulani, Dr. Andree Nicola McLaughlin from Medgar Evers College, and other Black feminist activists spoke publicly on the case. Dr. McLaughlin expressed her views:

> We, Women of Color, have a right and a duty to demand equal protection under the law for our children, our future. Governor Cuomo has declared a New York State Decade of the Child, and ain't Tawana a child? We must stop racists and sexist violence, stop the victimizing of the victims, and stop attacks on defenders of justice. If the Governor and elected officials cannot provide the kind of leadership necessary to protect *all* children, we—ordinary citizens—must assume the baton. For Tawana is everybody's child.[16]

The few public statements made by Black feminists do not fully reflect the widespread concern Black women hold for Tawana Brawley. Black feminists often submerge their feminism to join other Black women and Black men in fighting racial violence. They are frequently unable or unwilling to raise feminist issues within nationalist struggles. National solidarity has been used by Black men to block any feminist critical analysis of their private and public practices.

Under these circumstances, Black feminists have failed to stand up for Tawana, independently or with Black men. Her rape has become the symbol of Black nationalist oppression, not women's resistance to oppression. One reason for this might be that Black feminists are also Black women and, unlike many Black male nationalists, Black women have no wives to give them financial and moral support for their activist efforts. Black feminists are constantly stymied by a lack of time and resources, resources which might have allowed one of their own to become a full-time Brawley adviser.

Too bad, because Black feminists remain at the intellectual cutting edge of political and societal transformation. Many have participated actively in nationalist organizations, the civil rights movement, and Black community struggles. In addition, there are many Black feminists who advocate improved health care, education, and employment opportunities for Black women. They also aid in organizing Black women in unions, churches, and communities, and raise Black women's consciousness about sexism and racism.

A Black feminist movement would have made this case pivotal to a political strategy capable of exposing the crime of rape against Black women, whether perpetrated by white or Black men, and could thereby have broken the historic silence surrounding Black women's rape. A Black feminist activist political strategy could have, first of all, shown the motivations underlying rape, such as racism or male dominance through violence, and challenged the negative views of rape victims; second, it could have presented a more sympathetic understanding of Tawana Brawley and her family to the Black community; and third, it could have organized and rallied financial and political support of Black women for Tawana Brawley and other Black women rape victims.

Both Black and white feminists share a philosophy that is supposed to give women voice and power. We said we would take on the personal and the political; but while we are attacking the personal oppression and intellectual foundations of women's oppression, the political struggle cannot stop. Only a feminist analysis of the sexual abuse of women can prevent women's rape from being further muted. And only a Black feminist political movement can enable Black women to tell our story, in our own words, in a context that will bring about justice and public vindication.

THE LONE WARRIORS:
THE POTENTIAL AND LIMITS
OF BLACK NATIONALISM

The political movement that did emerge from the Brawley case was initiated by three Black men who share the racial condition of Tawana Brawley in ways as powerful as the sexual condition she shares with Black women.

In the past, there have been many men and women like Mason, Maddox, and Sharpton—lone warriors who have shaken their fists in the face of their oppressors. Black lone warriors of the past were vilified and ridiculed like the controversial and often strident advisers to Tawana Brawley. The lone warriors in this case follow in the tradition of Paul Robeson, who, against the advice of many of his supporters, refused to tell the House Committee on Un-American Activities whether he was a member of the Communist Party or not. They are in the tradition of Assata Shakur who was declared a public enemy after being implicated, some say falsely, in a police murder, and was mistreated in prison because of her political beliefs. The advisers are also in the tradition of Martin Luther King who, writing from a Birmingham jail, attempted to justify to supporters his refusal to cooperate with the authorities who asked him to move slowly and not use mass demonstration in his demand for integration. When everyone, Black and white, told these warriors to be reasonable and cooperate, they stood defiant.

Mason and Maddox have consistently stood defiant in the face of what they perceived as racial injustice in New York. Prior to the handling of the Brawley case, they represented three Black men who, a year before Tawana Brawley's rape, were chased by a gang of white men yelling racial epithets and brandishing bats in the Howard Beach section of Queens. One of the Black men was chased onto a highway and was struck and killed by a car while the other two were beaten.[17] Maddox and Mason advised their clients to refuse to cooperate with the Queens District Attorney, whom they believed was doing an inadequate job, until a special state prosecutor was appointed by the Governor.[18] They extended their strategy to Tawana Brawley's case. Maddox and Mason advised Brawley and her family not to cooperate with the special state prosecutor until the Governor appointed someone who would be more "sensitive" to the case.[19]

Following in the tradition of most Black civil rights lawyers, Maddox and Mason combined their legal strategies with political pressure and public demonstrations. They added Tawana Brawley's name to the litany of those Black people in New York who were killed and maimed by white

police officers and white civilians and adopted a strategy of non-coopera-
tion, a strategy they claimed was based on that used by Rosa Parks when
she refused to comply with the laws of segregation. By early spring,
demonstrations and rallies supporting Tawana Brawley grew in both
Dutchess County and New York City.

Reverend Sharpton became an adviser to the Brawley family after Mason
and Maddox accepted the case. He is known locally as an outspoken "civil
rights" leader, self-promoter and hustler[20] who has consistently managed
to be spotlighted on television. Reverend Sharpton's involvement in the
case added to the media "hype" of Tawana Brawley's rape. However, others, many of whom were supporters of the Brawley movement, considered
Reverend Sharpton to be a working class hero who wasn't afraid to speak
out against racism and political cover-ups while defending the raped
teenager. Negative public opinion about Sharpton's "antics," the militancy
of Maddox and Mason, and Tawana Brawley's silence fused, causing many
to doubt the validity of Brawley's rape allegation.

Mason, Maddox, and Sharpton have not merely defended Tawana
Brawley, they have placed Tawana Brawley's case at the center of a complex indictment against racism and Black political powerlessness in New
York. This public discussion of Tawana Brawley's rape has historic significance. It is one of the few occasions that Black men have moved the rape
of a Black woman into the *center* of Black political protest. Our lone warriors see the rape of Tawana Brawley as the last straw in a series of racist
crimes in New York where Black victims have not only been killed,[21] but
where, they and their supporters assert, there has been white male denial
and collusion among medical, judicial, and police authorities.[22]

The lone warriors lifted Tawana Brawley's case from obscurity and kept
it in the public discourse. They are, to date, Black women's most staunch
defenders in the political arena, especially against racial violence, while
white feminists have yet to address racial violence and Black feminists
remain stunned in their own resounding silence.

Nevertheless, the lone warriors also follow in the tradition of those Black
patriarchs who consider the defense of their women critical to both their
manhood and to Black nationalist politics, patriarchs who are frequently
too sexist to admit to either Black women's autonomous voice or Black
male oppression of the Black women. The words of Attorney Alton
Maddox express the Black patriarch's concern for Black women—
his women. He warned that anyone who attempted to arrest Tawana
Brawley's mother at the church where she sought asylum would "have to
come through me. . . . Please have a bullet designated for me. We will stand

tall and we will stand as men, protecting the rights of black women."[23]

Few of these Black patriarchs understand the subtle dynamics of sexism. Without this understanding, Black patriarchs such as Maddox and Mason do not recognize the implications of Tawana Brawley's rape as a sexist crime. So the lone warriors proceed to defend without understanding, and to publicly discuss the case although the victim's voice has been muted by both the crime and the lone warriors' legal activist strategies.

In addition, the lone warriors are too "lone," too disconnected from the Black community and its organizations. Although they have many supporters, the lone warriors have only a fledgling organization. They lack a broad-based inner circle of experienced Black male and female organizers. Such organizers could devise strategies and tactics for creating a political movement which links the rape of Tawana Brawley with the economic and political rape of Black people and with the historical rape of all women, including the rape of Black women by Black men.

This lack of support is unfortunate, for Maddox, Mason, and Sharpton embody the potential of Black nationalism[24] as an effective rallying point for Black rage and protest against white racism. Nationalism is necessary to build solidarity and cooperation among Black people as well as to fight against white power.

The lone warriors also embody the very limits of Black nationalism: the tendency of Black nationalist struggles to focus only on racial oppression (without texturing race with class struggle or connecting it with gender oppression); the use of aggressive rhetoric to spar publicly with the state and white men; and the inability of nationalists to work effectively in coalitions with other Black activists, such as Black feminists, because that work requires concession and fosters criticism.

It is ironic that Tawana Brawley, a Black teenager, has challenged our feminist and our nationalist politics so thoroughly. She is a muted symbol of our collective rape as women and as Black people. In order for her and ourselves to become active agents in our own liberation, feminists and nationalists must do what we have been reluctant to do: jointly challenge white male authority and the state it controls. Both nationalism and feminism must learn from each other—connecting and transcending the weaknesses and strengths of both to create a movement based on the condition Black men and Black women share with Tawana. Black women, especially feminists, have a critical and pivotal role in making the shared conditions real and powerful. For there will be other Tawanas whose stories we must hear and act upon.

14

WE SPEAK FOR
THE PLANET

AS WOMEN OF COLOR live and struggle, we increasingly realize that it's time for us to speak for earth and its future. We have heard the voices of white men who speak for earth and its future. When we look at the hunger, despair, and killings around us, we see what white men who speak for earth have done. Their weaponry and visions speak clearly of a future of more and more war.

Science fiction films record and mirror the white man's vision of future life on planet earth in which he has assigned himself centrality and placed people of color at the periphery and margins. In his future visions the lands of people of color and the ways and beliefs of their ancestors and progeny will no longer exist. Earth will be populated primarily by white men, their machines, a few white women, and even fewer people of color. These movies reflect a future in which the planet (earth) will either be devastated by war or made irrelevant, for Western civilization will be able to continue on spaceships or satellites, as Huns become Klingons, Pygmies become Ewoks, Egyptian rites become Vulcan mysticism, and our ancient First World wisdom becomes the property of an eight-hundred-year-old, nonhuman named Yoda. In this future world people of color will have been divested of their cultures and disconnected from their communities. Women of color will be like Lieutenant Uhura, communications specialist of the *Starship Enterprise* under Captain James Kirk, functioning within the culture and machines of Western man.

The messages of enlightened Western scientists present us with another vision of the future. Futurists such as Fritjof Capra and Alvin Toffler tell us that Western civilization, using a combination of advanced technology and nuclear physics and matching Western scientific advancement with Eastern mysticism, will enable Western civilization to survive and advance. Although these scientists warn of the limitations and dangers of Western domination and violence and recognize the virtues of non-Western culture, they still envision a world based on Western assumptions of progress and technology. They don't include people of color as creators and participants in the creation of new dimensions to the human experience in the future.

Peace activists also fail to see people of color as initiators and creators and make assumptions about our limited abilities to work for peace and fundamental social change. Those opposed to nuclear weaponry and stockpiling project an equally disturbing politic and vision, which excludes people of color. The antiwar and antinuke organizers and their supporters have gathered millions to march and demonstrate against nuclear war and the existence of military conflict from the cultural and historical context that created that path in the first place.

Recent efforts by Soviet leader, Mikhail Gorbachev and President Ronald Reagan to limit nuclear testing, stockpiling, and weaponry, while still protecting their own arsenals and selling arms to countries and factions around the world, vividly demonstrate how "peace" can become an abstract concept within a culture of war. Many peace activists are similarly blind to the constant wars and threats of war being waged against people of color and the planet by those who march for "peace" and by those they march against. These pacifists, like Gorbachev and Reagan, frequently want people of color to fear what they fear and define peace as they define it. They are unmindful that our lands and peoples have already been and are being destroyed as part of the "final solution" of the "color line." It is difficult to persuade the remnants of Native American tribes, the starving of African deserts, and the victims of the Cambodian "killing fields" that nuclear war is *the* major danger to human life on the planet and that only a nuclear "winter" embodies fear and futurelessness for humanity.

The peace movement suffers greatly from its lack of a historical and holistic perspective, practice, and vision that include the voices and experiences of people of color; the movement's goals and messages have therefore been easily coopted and expropriated by world leaders who share the same culture of racial dominance and arrogance. The peace movement's racist blinders have divorced peace from freedom, from feminism, from education reform, from legal rights, from human rights, from international alliances and friendships, from national liberation, from the particular (for example, black female, Native American male) and the general (human being). Nevertheless, social movements such as the civil rights-black power movement in the United States have always demanded peace with justice, with liberation, and with social and economic reconstruction and cultural freedom at home and abroad. The integration of our past and our present holocausts and our struggle to define our own lives and have our basic needs met are at the core of the inseparable struggles for world peace and social betterment.

> The Achilles heel of the organized peace movement in this country has always been its whiteness. In this multi-racial and racist society, no all-white movement can have the strength to bring about basic changes.
>
> It is axiomatic that basic changes do not occur in any society unless the people who are oppressed move to make them occur. In our society it is people of color who are the most oppressed. Indeed our entire history teaches us that when people of color have organized and struggled—most especially, because of their particular history, Black people—have moved in a more humane direction as a society, toward a better life for all people.[1]

Western man's whiteness, imagination, enlightened science, and movements toward peace have developed from a culture and history mobilized against women of color. The political advancements of white men have grown directly from the devastation and holocaust of people of color and our lands. This technological and material progress has been in direct proportion to the undevelopment of women of color. Yet the day-to-day survival, political struggles, and rising up of women of color, especially black women in the United States, reveal both complex resistance to holocaust and undevelopment and often conflicted responses to the military and war.

THE HOLOCAUSTS

Women of color are survivors of and remain casualties of holocausts, and we are direct victims of war—that is, of open armed conflict between countries or between factions within the same country. But women of color were not soldiers, nor did we trade animal pelts or slaves to the white man for guns, nor did we sell or lease our lands to the white man for wealth. Most men and women of color resisted and fought back, were slaughtered, enslaved, and force-marched into plantation labor camps to serve the white masters of war and to build their empires and war machines.

People of color were and are victims of holocausts—that is, of great and widespread destruction, usually by fire. The world as we knew and created it was destroyed in a continual scorched earth policy of the white man. The experience of Jews and other Europeans under the Nazis can teach us the value of understanding the totality of destructive intent, the extensiveness of torture, and the demonical apparatus of war aimed at the human spirit.

A Jewish father pushed his daughter from the lines of certain death at Auschwitz and said, "You will be a remembrance—You tell the story—You survive." She lived. He died. Many have criticized the Jews for forcing non-Jews to remember the 6 million Jews who died under the Nazis and for etching the names Auschwitz and Buchenwald, Terezin and Warsaw in our minds. Yet as women of color, we, too, are "remembrances" of all the holocausts against the people of the world. We must remember the names of concentration camps such as *Jesus, Justice, Brotherhood,* and *Integrity,* ships that carried millions of African men, women, and children, chained and brutalized, across the ocean to the "New World." We must remember the Arawaks, the Taino, the Chickasaw, the Choctaw, the Narragansett, the Montauk, the Delaware, and the other Native American names of thousands of U.S. towns that stand for tribes of people who are no more. We must remember the holocausts visited against the Hawaiians, the aboriginal people of Australia, the Pacific Island peoples, and the women and children of Hiroshima and Nagasaki. We must remember the slaughter of men and women at Sharpeville, the children of Soweto, and the men of Attica. We must never, ever, forget the children disfigured, the men maimed, and the women broken in our holocausts—we must remember the names, the numbers, the faces, and the stories and teach them to our children and our children's children so the world can never forget our suffering and our courage.

Whereas the particularity of the Jewish holocaust under the Nazis is over, our holocausts continue. We are the *madres locos* (crazy mothers) in the Argentinean square silently demanding news of our missing kin from the fascists who rule. We are the children of El Salvador who see our mothers and fathers shot in front of our eyes. We are the Palestinian and Lebanese women and children overrun by Israeli, Lebanese, and U.S. soldiers. We are the women and children of the bantustans and refugee camps and the prisoners of Robbin Island. We are the starving in the Sahel, the poor in Brazil, the sterilized in Puerto Rico. We are the brothers and sisters of Grenada who carry the seeds of the New Jewel Movement in our hearts, not daring to speak of it with our lips—yet.

Our holocaust is South Africa ruled by men who loved Adolf Hitler, who have developed the Nazi techniques of terror to more sophisticated levels. Passes replace the Nazi badges and stars. Skin color is the ultimate badge of persecution. Forced removals of women, children, and the elderly—the "useless appendages of South Africa"—into barren, arid bantustans without resources for survival have replaced the need for concentration camps. Black sex-segregated barracks and cells attached to work sites achieve two objectives: The work camps destroy black family and community life, a presumed source of resistance, and attempt to create human automatons whose purpose is to serve the South African state's drive toward wealth and hegemony.

Like other fascist regimes, South Africa disallows any democratic rights to black people; they are denied the right to vote, to dissent, to peaceful assembly, to free speech, and to political representation. The regime has all the typical Nazi-like political apparatus: house arrests of dissenters such as Winnie Mandela; prison murder of protestors such as Stephen Biko; penal colonies such as Robbin Island. Black people, especially children, are routinely arrested without cause, detained without limits, and confronted with the economic and social disparities of a nation built around racial separation. Legally and economically, South African apartheid is structural and institutionalized racial war.

The Organization of African Unity's regional intergovernmental meeting in 1984 in Tanzania was called to review and appraise the achievements of the United Nations Decade for Women. The meeting considered South Africa's racist apartheid regime a peace issue. The "regime is an affront to the dignity of all Africans on the continent and a stark reminder of the absence of equality and peace, representing the worst form of institutionalized oppression and strife."

Pacifists such as Martin Luther King, Jr. and Mahatma Gandhi who have used nonviolent resistance, charged that those who use violence to obtain justice are just as evil as their oppressors. Yet all successful revolutionary movements have used organized violence. This is especially true of national liberation movements that have obtained state power and reorganized the institutions of their nations for the benefit of the people. If men and women in South Africa do not use organized violence, they could remain in the permanent violent state of the slave. Could it be that pacifism and nonviolence cannot become a way of life for the oppressed? Are they only tactics with specific and limited use for protecting people from further violence? For most people in the developing communities and the developing world, consistent nonviolence is a luxury; it presumes that those who have and use nonviolent weapons will refrain from using them long enough for nonviolent resisters to win political battles. To survive, peoples in developing countries must use a varied repertoire of issues, tactics, and approaches. Sometimes arms are needed to defeat apartheid and defend freedom in South Africa; sometimes nonviolent demonstrations for justice are the appropriate strategy for protesting the shooting of black teenagers by a white man, such as happened in New York City.

Peace is not merely an absence of conflict that enables white middle-class comfort, nor is it simply resistance to nuclear war and war machinery. The litany of "you will be blown up, too" directed by a white man to a black woman obscures the permanency and institutionalization of war, the violence and holocaust that people of color face daily. Unfortunately, the holocaust does not only refer to the mass murder of Jews, Christians, and atheists during the Nazi regime; it also refers to the permanent institutionalization of war that is part of every fascist and racist regime. The holocaust lives. It is a threat to world peace as pervasive and thorough as nuclear war.

WOMEN OF COLOR AND DEVELOPMENT

Women of color speaking from the underdeveloped countries and underdeveloped communities on the fringes of the so-called developed world are well aware that development has meant war and the violent reorganization of our cultures and our lands to produce the resources that will meet the needs, especially military, of multinational corporations and conglomerates. These include cash crops, precious ores and metals, and labor. The world economy is dominated by "11,000 transnational corporations whose production was estimated at $830 billion in 1976. Through their price manipulation they have caused the underdeveloped countries to lose between $50 and $100 billion a year."[2]

Fidel Castro describes the underdeveloped world as follows:

- More than 500 million people are hungry.
- 1.7 billion have a life expectancy of less than sixty years.
- 1.5 billion lack medical care.

- More than 1 billion live in extreme poverty.
- More than 500 million are under- and unemployed, and more than 800 million earn an annual per capita income of less than $150.
- 814 million are illiterate adults (many of them women).
- More than 200 million children do not have schools or are unable to attend schools.
- 2 billion (or about one-half the world's population) lack permanent and adequate water sources.
- More than 1.5 billion depend on firewood for their vital needs.[3]

We speak for a planet whose merchants of war spend $515 billion per year on weapons and in which military expenditures in Third World countries increased from $33 billion in 1972 to $81.3 billion in 1981. These expenditures have risen from 8 percent of the world's expenditures to 16 percent in the last ten years.[4] Women of color represent the majority of the world's people—six-sevenths of whom are people of color and the majority of whom are women and girls—and we "do two-thirds of the world's work hours, receive a tenth of the world's income, and own less than a hundredth of the world's property."[5]

Under the guise of progress, development has robbed women of color of our former status in traditional societies. In these societies we were the primary agrarian work force. Our traditional roles as mother and wife were given high status, albeit in a patriarchal and sexist manner that often rendered these roles inhumanely burdened and unjustly discriminated against. Nonetheless, our primary role in agriculture and trade blunted the full impact of sexism and enabled us to accumulate wealth. In agrarian societies when single-crop, nonedible cash crops have taken over the most fertile lands, usually financed by multinational conglomerates, women farmers, particularly in Africa, have become marginalized, although we grow most of the food for domestic consumption.

When machines are introduced into our underdeveloped communities, we become further underdeveloped because we are denied access to these machines. Money and technology for farm expansion go to men. Mechanized farming uses male wage earners as its labor supply. Women must then farm with dated technology. Money and machines overpower the work of women of color worldwide while we prepare and serve food. We take care of children, the sick, and elderly. We sew garments. We care for shelter.

Men in underdeveloped countries have developed only those sectors of the society that benefit themselves. They ride in cars while women walk or ride in lorries. They turn on water from faucets in their homes, while most women walk to public spigots and wells. They sit and meet while women work and do. They make weapons by signing papers ordering production, and white male workers in the developed sectors manufacture them. They sell the weapons to each other and those men of color who rule developing nations by diverting their countries' resources and money from food, shelter, and education into money for weapons. Their wives and lovers have labor-saving devices—washing machines, refrigerators, dishwashers, and freezers—while the majority of the women, men, and children in the world starve or are malnourished.

In developed countries, if women of color can find work at all, we work for the lowest wages, in the most labor-intensive areas of the economy. We also prepare and serve food and care for children, the sick, and the elderly. (Traditionally we worked for wages as domestics, caretakers, and lower echelon factory workers.) Women of color have been employed in public-sector jobs as buffers between the poor and powerless and the state. We work in welfare agencies, nursing homes, prisons, hospitals, and schools.

In the United States, Native American, Afro-American, Afro-Caribbean, Asian, Latin, and immigrant women from the Third World live at the bottom of all quality-of-life indicators. We recoil in horror as armies of the police occupy our neighborhoods and declare black and Hispanic men criminals to be shot on sight, with questions asked later. We watch the miseducation of our children and social workers' attempts to destroy the strengths of our families. The destruction of the black mind is an everyday occurrence. The continued existence of sweatshops and cash crops for illegal immigrants is an integral part of the U.S. economy. It is common for men to beg and for women to live out of shopping bags while young people live in abandoned buildings or on the streets. It is ordinary for there to be madness, murder, and mayhem in our daily lives. We live terrified, not only of ultimate war but of how we "gonna make it one more day, how we gonna keep on keeping on."

In an article entitled, "Peace, Disarmament and Black Liberation," Damu Imara Smith asks us to consider the following:

> As we lose in our fight for jobs with decent pay and stand in long unemployment lines, let us remember the MX missile, funded at a cost of $2.4 billion for FY 1983. As we lose our fight against dilapidated, rat infested slum housing, let us remember the 2.2 billion dollars for Phoenix and Sparrow air to air missiles. As we lose in our fight to put shoes on our children's feet and adequate clothes on their backs, let us

remember the Pershing II missile. As we lose our struggle to put enough food on the table, let us think about the Minuteman 3 missiles. As we shiver in our homes and apartments this winter because we can't pay our utility bills, let us reflect on the Polaris and Poseidon missiles. As we witness plant closings, the resulting massive layoffs in our communities and the shutting down of day care centers, let us think about the SSN-688 nuclear attack submarine build at the cost of a whopping $900 million each! As we fall further into debt, let us remember the 5 year trillion dollar defense budget and the fact that all of the Pentagon's bill are paid while ours aren't. . . . As we protest the myriad problems afflicting our communities and society, we should always link them to the military budget. We should make it clear to those who rule our society that we do understand how huge military expenditures affect our daily existence.[6]

Women of color are the present and historic victims of development and militarism. Our work has always represented the underpinnings of each society in which we reside. We make and maintain the life supports that everyone else depends upon, including the elite men who dominate the developed world, deciding when and where to militarily and socially wage war. But the work of women of color is invisible, and, when seen, it is devalued.

Our blood and our ancestor's blood have already been shed in continual war precipitated by the movement of a group of self-defined white men. They named themselves white and declared themselves superior to the darker-skinned people they encountered. They divided the world along racial lines and the biological distinctions of color. Military terrorism has become the method of world domination; capitalism, the method of social organization; and racism, the ideology and world view that holds together the rational and cohesive system of exploitation and oppression they established and that we live under. Racism is an all-encompassing, economic, social, cultural, political, and military war against a group of people whose physical characteristics have been denigrated and used to divide and isolate them from others. Women of color in the developed and the undeveloped world have come to share the same condition and position regardless of different languages, cultures, and methods of colonization or domination. We are victims of untold violence against our person, our children, and our communities. Therefore, we speak against all wars—economic, social, and political—for we and our children are often the first casualties.

A COMPLEX LEGACY:
BLACK WOMEN, THE MILITARY, AND WAR

Women of color, such as Black women in the United States, have a legacy of resistance to war and enlistment and a legacy of support for war and soldiers. We have cheered Black soldiers. We have jeered them. We have benefited from Black veterans. We have been their victims. We have become soldiers for a war machine. We have become warriors for peace. Throughout history, Black men and women have not been merely victims of wars and holocaust but have frequently supported the U.S. military and collaborated with the holocaust-makers.

Black U.S. soldiers fought against the Mexican people and helped white men extend the borders of the United States in 1848. Black Buffalo soldiers fought against the Sioux, the Comanche, and the Apache and helped "tame" the West. Black soldiers helped conquer San Juan Hill and Puerto Rico, the Philippines and Cuba for the United States. They struggled to fight in World War I—a war that furthered the consolidation of Western colonial powers—and then got lynched when they returned home. During World War II, African, Asian, and Caribbean men went willingly, although some were forcibly conscripted. They helped to defeat fascism and give support to the British, French, and U.S. neocolonial empires. Ironically, while Japanese people were in concentration camps in the United States, many Japanese-American men volunteered to fight for the United States against Japan. Afro-American soldiers integrated the U.S. Army and were then given the dubious privilege of fighting alongside white men against the Koreans. Back in the United States, they could not work next to these same white men. During the same historic periods Black people fostered and nurtured kinships with other people of color and resisted attempts by the U.S. military to enlist their support in conquering other oppressed peoples.

From the beginning of New World contact, runaway slaves joined Native American tribes and white indentured servants in the common cause for freedom. They fought with the Mexicans and the Cubans and questioned U.S. government policy toward Native Americans. They welcomed Puerto Rican freedom fighters, such Albizu Campos.

In this century, U.S. overseas empire building and European expansion were viewed by many black people as part of the same process that limited and held them inside the color line within the United States. The white man who lynched and persecuted Black people was the same white man who declared war on other people of color and denied their attempts to be free. Before many said, "No Vietnamese ever called me nigger," black people felt, "We didn't lose nothing over there, so we don't belong over there—these are white man's wars." Many stood proudly by the fight of the so-called Mau-Mau, the Kenyan Land and Freedom Army, and the Hindu-Pakistani efforts of Gandhi against the British, and raised money to support them. We volunteered and served in the Spanish Civil War against Francisco Franco and fascism. We saw ourselves as part of the world of brothers and sisters struggling for a liberation far bigger than any single national effort for freedom. This struggle, beyond the ideologies of either communism or capitalism, was for a new day for the people of the planet.

There were also daily and practical struggles for family and community survival that made the conflicting legacies of simultaneous collaboration and resistance to U.S. wars and the military even more complex and intricate. Black women, in our relationship to our men (fathers, brothers, mates) and our children, were concerned with immediate and long-range, personal and political liberation, survival, and struggle.

During all these wars, black women were happy that black men were soldiers. We lined the streets of Harlem when our men came back from overseas. We cheered and dated soldiers, "who sure looked good in those uniforms." Being in the army made black men more desirable, for black soldiers were seen as responsible, disciplined, and ready to take their rightful place in U.S. society. They had demonstrated that their manhood equaled the manhood of the white man. After all, they reasoned, military service is the right and responsibility of male citizens. If black men could be in the service, then they could become first-class citizens and their women could be supported and protected.

Black men as well as other men of color have always had difficulty earning enough money to support their families and obtaining self-respect and social status within a racist or colonial system. Economic discrimination in the form of black male unemployment and under-employment has been a form of economic war against men of color at home. It has been a useful way for the ruling elites to protect and promote the armed services as a means of employment and personal advancement. Soldiers received tangible benefits when they return home. Many black soldiers were given economic opportunities, loans, and, of course, status. They were more desirable mates, more respectful sons, more responsible church deacons, more reliable workers—at least that was the hope and the belief.

My father was a noncombatant in the Navy during World War II when the black community was still fighting for the right of black men to fight.

He used his GI Bill benefits to make a down payment on a house in Brooklyn and to gain a stable job. He was a civilian worker in the navy for twenty years. He was able to provide a stable childhood for my sister and me. Some men who came back, such as Amzie Moore and Medgar Evers, were determined to become fighters for justice for black people in this country, although most returning black soldiers hoped that they would be treated individually as citizens and men.

The Vietnam War exposed and illuminated for many of us the contradictions of people of color—the oppressed in one country living in one part of the world fighting people of color from another part of the world who were struggling for their own self-determination and freedom in their own countries. Many black men arrived in Vietnam and realized too late—in the midst of the white man's bullets at their backs and the Vietnamese in front of them—that they were the cannon fodder for the whites against the Vietnamese. Some realized that black people had no war with the Vietnamese. The pain of these contradictions drove many to drugs and madness.

My cousin John Francis died in Vietnam, but his brother survived it. He came back a killer who neither repudiated nor regretted his killing of the Vietnamese child in the tree. When he lamely told me, "It was me or him," I cringed because he was a gentle, country boy cousin from North Carolina. He is now a cop in Norfolk, part of the American dream, married, divorced, children here and there. Can the murders he committed in Vietnam leave his memory or his life? Does my cousin beat his wife? Does he terrorize his children? Are the prisoners he arrests in Norfolk only a reliving of his treatment of the "VC"? My cousin is just one of many men of color whose material successes seemingly prove that the military is a road to "upward mobility of our people"—although at the price of the blood of Vietnamese women and children.

But the Vietnamese were not the only victims of U.S. soldiers. By 1974, Max Cleland, the head of the Veterans Administration, reported that "an estimate 125,000 Vietnamese vets were serving time in America for crimes committed since their discharge from service . . . [and] around one in five Vietnam-era veterans has some kind of problem that he hasn't been able to deal with, that has kept him from entering the mainstream of society. It can be lack of education, unemployment, drugs or alcohol or a personal problem."[7] The highest percentages of unemployed veterans are black and Latino men. Far too many vets continue perpetrating the horrors of their war experience on our communities and on our bodies.

Women have had to care for Vietnam vets unable to cope with civilian life. Some of these women have been shot, beaten, and maimed because the vets thought they were the VC. Their position was very similar to that of the women and children of Vietnam. Both occupied the same position and condition in relation to those who dominated and those who committed violence. Unless former Vietnam veterans recognize and repudiate their heinous crimes against Vietnamese women and children, they can never learn to love and respect women of color, although they might give them marital support. Men of color who as soldiers in Vietnam committed acts of atrocity, ignorance, and oppression cannot use fighting a war in someone else's country as an excuse or rationale for their actions.

Economic possibilities and patriotism offer only partial explanations for the participation of men of color in the war. The U.S. myth of a rugged frontiersman, detective, or police officer fighting against nature and the savages to gain a golden treasure, to rescue the troubled maiden, or to reach glory for the fatherland has captured the minds and hearts of many men and women of color. Male chauvinism and the relationship between manhood and the military have blinded men and women of color to our backward roles in Vietnam and other wars.

Many women of color hope that the army will make men out of their men but fail to realize that "the purpose of basic training is to dehumanize a male to the point where he will kill on command and obey his superiors automatically."[8] The obedient participation of black soldiers from the United States and other Caribbean islands in the invasion of Grenada has sadly proven that black soldiers will fight other black people in their own country. Military operations in Central America have been no lesson to Chicano and Puerto Rican soldiers to resist participating in denying the people of these Central American countries their rights of self-determination. Men and women of color hope for manhood and the promise of better lives as a result of employment in the armed services. But a Congressional Black Caucus reports

> the total effect of a black serviceman's encounter is that when he leaves he is usually in worse condition than when he entered. He has generally received little training (especially for non-military technology or jobs) ... has been subject to harassment and discrimination at the hands of his superiors and he too often winds up with a less than honorable discharge which guarantees that his civilian life will be at least as difficult as his former life. In 1979, although Blacks were only 43% of army personnel, they comprised nearly 51% of the army prison population, and

they received 40% of all less-than-honorable discharges.[9]

Nevertheless, black women are being encouraged to join the military for better economic opportunities. The June 1984 issue of *Essence* magazine, along with an article on black women millionaires, featured an article, "Careers in the Military for Black Women." According to the article, the 2 million people who work in military operations and the $231 billion military budget constitute the largest government operation. The article continues: "Although the military is a good place to develop job skills, think long and hard before you enlist. The military helps to develop career direction and personal discipline, but you will be expected to adhere to military regulations and codes of conduct. . . . Also the job you perform and skills you acquire are determined primarily by military rules."[10] But one navy lieutenant, a former research biologist states, "The advantage of a military career has given me the opportunity to get my master's degree without a financial strain and to switch careers."[11] Nevertheless, only 2 percent of military personnel and 1 percent of military officers are black women.

The careerism implicit in this black woman's assessment of her naval career is the message of the ad campaigns for the "new armed services." The ads avoid the issue of war and avoid the dangers of enlistment in a "peacetime" army. They aim directly at offers of training, college, and careers. But increasing numbers of U.S. service personnel are dying while patrolling the Persian Gulf, while barracked in Lebanon, while sitting in West Germany. Others have been called for military alert in Honduras and Panama. Regardless, the finality of death and "peacetime" wars, the development of a fascist personhood, and the misdirection of our human resources should be sufficient reason for women and men of color to resist enlistment, the draft, and draft registration.

Nonetheless, every day black women encourage our men, especially our sons, to enlist as an alternative to unemployment and street crime. Black mothers know that the system offers little possibility for our manchildren. Young black men who are not in college or employed will increasingly become prey to a negative life of petty crime and drugs. Without economic self-sufficiency these men will have to be housed, fed, and taken care of by their lovers, mothers, or wives, which creates a tense and painful predicament of dependency for both.

Few black women can live outside the dilemmas posed by this predicament. Which war zone does she protect her son from: the military or the street? Either can render him an addict to drugs and violence. Will the military prepare him for a better job or leave him a personal wreck? Either choice confronts her and her son with systemic and systematic limitations beyond their control. They are surrounded by the walls of an economic and political system that simply has no place, no room for him, an ordinary black man, other than jail or the army. Black motherhood is stretched to become continuous care of her sons through adulthood. What are the limits of her resources and her ability to care?

Lovers and wives of black men wonder how will we live with our men. Both the military and the street cripple and confuse. Will the military ultimately keep them from the street? Will it exacerbate or diminish their personal and economic problems?

All women wonder, if there is a war—will he be drafted? Will it be like Vietnam? Will he be killed or maimed? Who are we fighting anyway? What are our choices anyway? In answering these questions, black women have had to make agonizing decisions, frequently separate from the powerful legacies of resistance and collective political struggles.

BLACK MALE WARRIORS AND THE ANTIWAR MOVEMENT

Cleveland Sellers, an organizer with the Student Nonviolent Coordinating Committee (SNCC), explained his refusal to be drafted in the Vietnam War this way:

> The central question for us is not whether we allow ourselves to be drafted, for we have resolved that this shall not happen by any means. But rather the central question for us is how do we stop the exploitation of our brother's territories and goods by a wealthy hungry nation such as this. . . . I shall not serve in this army or any others that seek by force to use the resources of my Black brothers here at the expense of my brothers in Asia, Africa and Latin America.[12]

Sellers connected his resistance to a worldwide brotherhood fighting exploitation. He was, in turn, connected to the movement for justice and equality being shaped and waged by both black men and black women in the South.

The first civil rights movement protest of the Vietnam War was circulated in a July 1965 leaflet of the Mississippi Freedom Democratic party newsletter of McComb, Mississippi. Among the five reasons the leaflet listed for black noninvolvement in the war were:

1.   No Mississippi Negroes should be fighting in Vietnam for the White Man's Freedom, until all the Negro People are free in Mississippi.

4.   No-one has a right to ask us to risk our lives and kill other Colored People in Santo Domingo and Vietnam, so that the White American can get richer. We will be looked upon as traitors by all the Colored People of the world if the Negro people continue to fight and die without a cause.[13]

In January 1966, SNCC issued the following statement expressing its disagreement with U.S. foreign policy and affirming its involvement in the black people's struggle for liberation and self-determination in this country: "Our work, particularly in the south, taught us that the U.S. government has never guaranteed the freedom of oppressed citizens and is not yet truly determined to end the rule of terror and oppression within its own border. . . . Where is the draft for the Freedom fight in the United States?"[14]

SNCC's statement expressed what may men and women of color felt. Because Julian Bond endorsed it, he was refused his seat in the Georgia House of Representatives. Because Muhammed Ali refused to fight, he risked his heavyweight boxing title. Thousands of black men and other men of color refused to go and went AWOL in the United States and in Vietnam.

SNCC's position was part of a national response by black people to the war. This response included Malcolm X's growing internationalism and his attempts to raise the question of black human rights within the United States at the United Nations. He tried to develop independent political alliances between black people and progressive Third World governments. Martin Luther King issued public denunciations of the war and demands for a cease-fire, as well as a radical demand that ministers give up their ministerial exemptions to protest the war by becoming conscientious objectors: "These are the times for real choices and not false ones. We are at the moment when our lives must be placed on the line if our nation is to survive its own folly. Every man [*sic*] of humane convictions must decide on the protest that best suits his convictions, but we must all protest."[15]

That movement was strong and far reaching because it was, as the leaflet in McComb suggested, part of a national movement to fundamentally change this country, particularly regarding the treatment of its "black citizens." The civil rights-black power movement (1955–1972) which at times involved seventy thousand to one hundred thousand actively organized black people yearly in sit-ins, boycotts, demonstrations, jailings, was not simply to end segregation but to challenge and transform the system. Those who made the challenge discovered, often with their lives, the interlocking infrastructure of repression and duplicity in this country.

This organic and holistic movement originated in the black communities of the deep South and in the black communities of the North. The southern communities amassed hundreds of thousands to resist the tyranny of local government power in the hands of racists. The northern movement mobilized hundreds of thousands to resist segregated school housing; to demand jobs; and to build independent black institutions, such as the Nation of Islam and black schools.

The free speech movement of white college students began as an effort to support the Freedom School Movement in Mississippi. It grew from the questions white and black college and high school students were raising about the relationship between the university and high school and their responsibility to end injustice and inequality. These students challenged the neutral, "objective" centers of so-called learning. The people's law movement grew from the twenty-five-year-old legal challenges of black lawyers to segregation. The free clinic-people's health movement came from clinics organized during many demonstrations and campaigns in the South. Federally funded day care and the Head Start concept developed from efforts begun in Mississippi during the civil rights movement. Second-wave feminism was developed, inspired, and initiated by white women working and learning from powerful black women and men. And yes, white men such as Tom Hayden and Staughton Lynd were also inspired and taught how to organize by black organizers in the southern movement. They then returned North to become leaders of the anti-Vietnam War and the peace movements, which in turn were given impetus and power by the leading national spokesperson for peace in the post-World War II era—Martin Luther King.

After learning from and following black leadership, many white peace activists began to dominate the issue, neither remembering nor articulating their black connections. Some would ignorantly ask, "Where are the black people? Why aren't they interested in 'peace' issues?"

Black people originated the modern peace movement from an organic and holistic movement for social change that we developed and led. The obliteration of the true history of our movement has enabled whites to ruthlessly ignore what black people have done to solve some of the problems of war and peace. This ignorance has reinforced white chauvinism and blinded the white activist to his/her accurate history and historical role in movements for social change.

WOMEN WARRIORS

Black and brown men said, "Hell no, we won't go!" White men joined them, white women were discovering their own power, and black and brown women warriors said, "Continue to struggle to free us all—to break our chains." Every demonstration, organizing effort, or act of defiance was surrounded by women who encouraged, urged, demanded *freedom*, with peace and love.

Rosa Parks refused to move and was jailed. Fannie Lou Hamer and Annelle Ponder were beaten in jail for daring to be citizens. Septima Clarke lost her job because she was a member of the National Association for the Advancement of Colored People. Teenage girls were hosed. Annie Pearl Avery snatched the menacing billy club from the hands of a southern sheriff. Old women were handcuffed and still they wouldn't stop.

The actions of these warriors were reflected in the refusal of Chicano women in lettuce fields to work, in the demands of Puerto Rican women in New York and San Juan for liberation, in the marches of Asian women, and in the protest by Native American women at Wounded Knee. And still they wouldn't stop. Everywhere there was space to say, "No!"—women of color hollered it, chanted it, and, if silenced, glared out our protest against all the evils and demons that limited and tied us down.

Our strength to "keep on keeping on" comes not from weapons but from the power of our prayers and visions—of peace, love, and freedom. Often we don't join *the* organization or the movement of men or of white women because our time, our moves, our ways are creatively complicated and cumbersome, woven ways of holding everything together around us. For underneath the conflicts between resistance and collaboration, the wholeness and connectedness of all things are understood by women warriors—for only if we survive, by any/all means available, can we resist. Women of color warriors are constant warriors who dig in bare earth to feed the hungry child, who pray for health at the bedside of the sick when there is no medicine, who fashion a toy to make a poor child smile, who take to the streets demanding freedom, freedom, freedom against armed police. Every act of survival by a woman of color is an act of resistance to the holocaust and the war. No soldier fights harder than a woman warrior for she fights for total change, for a new order in a world in which she can finally rest and love.

Everywhere women of color gather we realize a common concern, a common agenda for the planet, and a common practice to achieve the reality of liberation. We are sisters; at last we have found each other. For many women of color who have traveled and spoken with other women of color, sisterhood is a living reality.

> In Israel, the Palestinian woman eloquently pointed at the same brown-
> ness of our skin.
> In China, women treated me like their daughter.
> In Jamaica, poor women gave my children sugar water.
> An Indian woman shared her poetry and stories of womanhood with
> me.
> When Puerto Rican women speak Spanish I find myself listening with
> my heart.
> A Sioux Medicine woman gave the ring from her finger and the earrings
> her mother made for her.
> They all said to me,
>
> We are your sisters, at last we have found each other.[16]

We will meet again and again—to fulfill a remembrance, to become stronger warriors, to "organize, before it's too late." We will speak as best we can, as truthfully as we must, for the billions of women and children and their men throughout the world who can not yet come forward to say:

> I am the woman who holds up the sky.
> The rainbow runs through my eyes.
> The sun makes a path to my womb.
> My thoughts are in the shape of clouds.
> But my words are yet to come.[17]

We reach out knowingly, for we are your sisters; at last we have found each other. Our visions and our warriorship speak for and claim this planet, earth, for we have a precious covenant with our ancestors, our brothers, our sisters, and our progeny to "lay down the swords and shields" of the "masters of war," so we can "study war no more."

15

LAMENTATIONS

Oh that my head were waters, and mine eyes a fountain of tears, that I might weep day and night for the slain of the daughter of my people.

Jeremiah 9:1

I LEFT AMU, EPHAN AND SANGEYA standing at Bard's campus lit by the spring greenery. They were the campus Black activists, and like thousands of Black students across the country, they were teasing out ways to bring a Black presence to the colonial academy.

Today my eight year old son Krishna had a city wide reading and math exam. Neither he nor his classmates were aware of the maelstrom of public school debates circling around them. Those debates, more about power than education, both do and do not concern them. Meanwhile, Ms. Guss, white and female, patiently provides pencils and encouragement for her thirty third graders, gifted Black boys and girls.

Last weekend, I left my daughter's Boston apartment feeling relief and anxiety as she tried to plot out a meaningful life for herself. All her friends and sisters have become mothers or man addicts. She is seeking another path. Yet jobs are difficult to find, community college is boring, and pursuing men relentless. As young, Black women, both she and her sisters have already been overworked, and exploited as workers—same story, different era. Having received his college degree, my son is trying to sustain himself as a free lance illustrator and artist and be about the business of surviving as a Black man in America. But jobs are hard to come by and the streets are dangerous.

Ladeeta, a Black high school student here in Brooklyn, was featured in the New York Times, "Children of the Shadows" series about teenagers. (Lee, A1) Her story was poignant because she and her sisters have been orphaned by her parents who died, killed by drugs and AIDS. Even as her life demonstrates courage and strength, she says she has two strikes against her because she is Black and female. All around me the young, gifted and Black are struggling, killing, or being killed because families, communities and societies have failed them.

My closest friends and I work at the City University, teaching, counseling and trying to create some space for our people, Black men and women and other working people, who want an education. We struggle to acquire knowledge and intellectual rigor for ourselves and them. We try to communicate pride, vigilance, and hope but have our own myriad of personal and political difficulties.

We are weary at the Black politicians who have never delivered on anything meaningful for our children, and at the causes we fought and worked for. (No, I don't count summer jobs as meaningful.) We're in a stupor at the failure of our best ideals about social change to be realized. I long, like a lot of people, for a powerful social movement to lift us up toward the 21st century, bringing peace, equity and prosperity. I want to give that movement as a legacy to my children, and to all our children.

We are less than a decade away from the end of the 20th century, which began with the prediction by W. E. B. Du Bois that it would be a century of the "color line." Both color and gender lines have been profoundly drawn in this century. The gender line has informed powerful forms of feminist and womanist expressions long dormant in the world's women. A class line was drawn by the Soviet Union, born in 1917 as a hopeful alternative to unbridled capitalism, yet by the 1990s it has fragmented and declined.

During the 20th century we have witnessed consciousness about human and civil rights struggling to rise in the face of world wars, the underdevelopment of human resources and the overdevelopment of natural ones. Ecological damage alone would single this century out as one of the most destructive in human history. Great technological expansion brought forth holocausts and nuclear bombs. Unparalleled social and cultural displacement has occurred. Because their speakers are endangered and dying, nearly all of the six thousand languages known at the beginning of European expansion five hundred years ago are nearly extinct. Only about two hundred, the languages of sovereign states, are secure. (Diamond: 81)

These monumental changes will probably be examined and re-examined as we approach the end of the century. But I suspect few will turn their analysis of the century to the worldwide condition of women, and their children, and teenagers.

Jeremiah's five mourning poems make up the book of Lamentations in the Old Testament. Between 626 and 587 B.C. Jeremiah prophesied and witnessed the conquest and exile of his people (of the kingdom of Judah) by the Babylonian Empire. Jeremiah prophesied that their defeat was a direct result of God's judgment against their sinful practices, and not of His weakness. This lament was both sorrow for his people's suffering and a condemnation of those who continued to disobey God. His expressions of sadness about his people's condition informs my own grieving for the victims of the unabated, daily wars waged against women and children in nearly every country. My prayers are also for the perpetuators of violence, young armed men who are themselves victims of state violence and fratricide. I also recognize the dilemma and pain of poor men caught between upholding an empty patriarchy and creating a new manhood. I am pained at the reign of terror being mounted against gay men and lesbians, just as many in society are prepared to address homophobia.

I am angered by the weakness of the "radical intelligentsia": socialists, feminists, progressive political activists, and revolutionary nationalists, who are the product of past political struggles against racism, colonialism, and capitalism. It angers me that we in the radical intelligentsia as a whole have failed to investigate, frame, and contribute to a praxis or ideology of resistance and struggle. We have failed to stand with the "winter soldiers" of the world, those less privileged, mainly women of color fighting oppression and struggling to better their material conditions. Given our background the radical intelligentsia's weak response to the latest machinations of white and male power and supremacy is astounding .

Progressives and radicals have become paralyzed and defensive by the way conservatives view history. Fukuyama, for example, sees the end of the Cold War as "the end of history as such: that is, the end point of mankind's ideological evolution and the universalization of Western liberal democracy as the final form of human government." (Fukuyama, 4) However, the violence and destruction we are facing at the end of this century makes such notions of finality and universality simplistic.

The enormity of ethnic and racial violence has challenged the ideals and promise of nationalism, feminism, socialism as well as conservatism. Our approaching century's end also feels like the end of progressive political thought and praxis. Hope for progress and peace rests in pockets of winter soldiers of various political perspectives and experiences, as they continue to develop new ideologies and strategies for social change.

AFROCENTRICITY AND AFRICA

There is a debate going on about Afrocentricity in Africana or Black or African American studies, especially the central role of Africa in the history of the West. Afrocentricity has become less a study of historical location and beginnings—a starting place for identity for Africans in diaspora —than the center of ideologies and beliefs organized around ancient Egyptology and the cult of melanism.

From a privileged place within the American academy, aging African American professors with money and resources regularly visit Africa, along with equally privileged African American professionals who wear and read African garb and texts, while pontificating about the imperial glory of ancient peoples in the motherland. Afrocentrists ignore an authentic relationship between African American intellectuals and Egyptian or other African societies.

Although visiting African American, Afrocentrist tourists enjoy the secular Egyptian state's protection, its struggles against Islamic theocratic takeover are rarely mentioned. Certainly, African American intellectuals who themselves benefit from being part of the West and its most prestigious institutions—the secular state and academy—should be concerned about the relationships between those institutions and the state in Egypt and the rest of Africa. Throughout the Motherland, the secular state and the concept of revolutionary nationalism so central to anti-colonial struggles is being undermined. African human and natural resources are being decimated and devastated, defeating the noblest intentions of Africa's best thinkers.

By the end of the century, twenty million Africans will become infected with the AIDS virus. Already because of AIDS there are between 1.5 and two million children in Africa without fathers or mothers. (Lorch, A1) The disruption of food production by African farmers, many of them women, and resulting civilian deaths are widely known. In Africa both disease and famine are accelerated by continual civil wars between combatants previously armed and supported by the former Soviet Union and the United States.

> The Soviet Union and the United States waged the cold war in large part through surrogates in the third world, supporting local leaders who would offer their loyalty to one side or the other. Many of them

used the aid they got to build their own tyrannical power. And some remain to plague their unfortunate people. (Lewis, A17)

Jeremy Harding, author of *Trial by Fire,* describes how superpower domination of Africa has curtailed the "unfinished business of national liberation in African conflicts in Angola, Namibia, Western Sahara, South Africa, Mozambique, and Eritrea, the shortest of which has been going on for two decades." (Packer, 8)

Civil war and ethnic conflicts continue even in the "stable" states of Africa. While the Gulf War occurred in Iraq, the Liberian state fell, and its capital, Monrovia, was destroyed, a result of a bloody struggle for power between "guerrilla leaders" from the Gio, Mano, and Krahn peoples. "At least twenty thousand Liberians have been killed and hundreds of thousands have been uprooted . . . Fifty thousand people have been uprooted and one thousand have been killed in Kenya during 1991–1992 as a result of ethnic conflicts allegedly fomented by President Daniel arap Moi." (Binder and Crossette, 14)

In early 1993, "after a long buildup to a supposed democratic transition" (Noble, 3) Nigerians elected Moshood Abiola, a civilian President. However, he has yet to take office because a former President, General Ibrahim Babangida canceled the results of the June 12 elections. A strike, threatened economic instability, and dissension within the military forced Babangida to begrudgingly concede civilian rule, although he clings to power by hiding behind his own weak presidential choice. New York Times columnist Kenneth Noble writes that "if democracy fails here, in the [continent's] richest and most populous nation, the chances that it will bloom elsewhere on the continent are that much dimmer." (Noble, 3)

Taking advantage of the crisis of the nation state in Africa are Western powers and pundits who feel some African countries should be "re-colonized" because "they are unfit to govern themselves." (Johnson, 22) The United States' and United Nations' policies in Somalia signal the beginning of the "re-invasion" of Africa under the guise of bringing social order. Ostensibly on a mission to aid food distribution to starving Somalian victims of civil war in which three hundred thousand died and a million were made homeless, an American led military force has found itself mired down by armed attacks from Somalian leaders, and increasingly forced to use its military power to establish "governmental rule." Cold war superpowers fostered and armed rivalrous local chieftains who are now regarded as lawless "war lords." Supposedly peacekeeping forces have been shot at, and shoot back at Somalian civilians.

Because of the legacies of colonialism, and the complexity of neo-colonialism and cold war politics, indigenous African leaders like the Somalian chiefs have had to focus on holding power by military might. Those leaders who willingly cooperate with Western and Japanese multinational companies, in turn, gain weapons and support which enable them to stay in power. Islamic superpower expansion has also increased civil and ethnic wars in many African states.

Internal wars have left civilian sectors impoverished and dislocated in a stasis between tradition and modernity. In spite of efforts to build strong nation states, African populations have fallen back on tribal derived ethnic identities. Many, not all, African leaders, foment ethnic and religious divisions, because they realize that ethnic blaming can divert civilians from holding their government responsible for their destitution. Rather than attempting to mediate these divisions, leaders often characterize rivals and opposition forces in ethnic rather than political terms. Those oppositional forces refusing to retreat into ethnic "warmongering" and remaining supportive of nationalism, are frequently jailed, murdered, and exiled.

In spite of ethnic warfare, most states recognize the rights and changed roles of urban, elite, and educated women. However, traditional gender divisions and views of women as the appendages of male authority remain widespread. In 1990, Ugandan president Yoweri Museveni's government had a woman Minister of Agriculture, but women were still portrayed in local newspaper cartoons as beasts of burden driven by husbands. (Perlez, A4) Although they have been recognized for their leadership role in the anti-apartheid struggle for decades, women are protesting their exclusion from the discourses which will shape the politics of post-apartheid South Africa.

Lack of effective democratic development strategies for civilian populations has left women in Africa disproportionately burdened with responsibility for food production and family care. Left behind when their men go to fight or search for work, women must eke out an existence for their families with neither the safeguards of tradition nor the tools of modernity. "Affirming life and working for change, from a woman's point of view, is a logical move. But it is a radical position because, generally, the business of government, of economic system's and of war is men's business." (Bandele, 11)

Dahabo Isse is a Somalian director of one hundred and forty kitchens for the International Committee of the Red Cross, which in 1992 fed more than two hundred thousand people a day and employed three thousand other Somali women. Isse says, "The women are stronger than the men. Now the women finally understand the weakness of men: they always depend on clans; we are neutral and that is why we are strong." (Lorch, A1) Zahra Mohammed Nur, another director of a relief organization in Somalia, proposes a solution to their devastation, "To succeed, we need relief and rehabilitation. We are doing the majority of the work, and we should get our share in politics." (Lorch, A14) Yet most women in Somalia remain oppressed under the customs and practices of the very "warlords" the US led-military forces are dealing with, and now Somali men and women are further silenced and repressed under the invading forces. Support is needed for the "winter soldiering" of sisters like Zahra and Dahoba to change the condition of women while their society tries to rebuild itself.

Fighting two colonialisms is an old and familiar theme for women in Africa and other formerly colonialized societies. Ethnic violence and civil war exacerbates the violence against women and prevents stable governance where women and men can address the inequities women experience.

In 1990, Sarah Bahalaaliwo, the chairwoman of the Uganda Association of Women Lawyers, spoke to a group of women in Buwunga about inheritance rights, property rights, and divorce laws. (Perlez, A4) By 1993, the AIDS epidemic had become a major concern of Ugandan men and women. AIDS, a natural and manmade plague, has destroyed nine percent of Uganda's population—on top of a twenty year civil war which killed half a million people. (Lorch, A1, A10) AIDS has spread rapidly in the heterosexual populations because of a combination of malnutrition, sexually transmitted diseases, other infectious diseases, and an underdeveloped healthcare system. Soldiers and migrant workers spread the disease by having unprotected sex with multiple partners in many different locations. Fatalistically accepting AIDS as a consequence of having sexual relations with their men, many of the Buwunga women felt powerless to demand that their men at least wear condoms.

"Gender inequities still prevent women from gaining access to education, capital inputs, technology, and training. This is one of the major reasons why too little progress has been made in the fight against societal problems such as poor health, excessive workloads, illiteracy, and widespread inequality between the sexes." (Benson, 28) Too many African American women tourists coming back from the Motherland laden with nostalgia and souvenirs from the market places rarely talk about the conditions of African women. Middle class African Americans promote African-inspired rites of passage, to assure their children's "passage" into manhood and womanhood. Yet the role of female mutilation in traditional rites of passage is rarely discussed in connection with our contemporary efforts.

American Afrocentrists continue to sanitize and romanticize the African experience by concentrating on pre-colonial and ancient African empires, while ignoring their own needed role in assisting contemporary African societies. We have an obligation not simply to view Africa as a place to experience our own catharsis of identity, but to pursue relentless organizing drives challenging American and Western foreign policy to address the most dire needs of the people of our Motherland while respecting their autonomy and sovereignty.

African and African American women can bring their combined resources to bear on US and United Nations policies, seeking to make aid to African countries, contingent upon the state's treatment of its women citizens and its ability to end ethnic violence. By not viewing women as the property of male dominated cultures and states, but as oppressed citizens who should participate in every level of social reconstruction, US and UN policies could accelerate the development of new African societies.

While African Americans have concentrated, as we should, on supporting the end of apartheid in South Africa, a considerably more important and crucial role awaits African American intellectuals and professionals in at least framing the terms of the political debate and struggle around a US policy for all of Africa. We have the resources to do our own research among and with those "winter soldiers" trying to make progressive social changes in Africa. Black Studies scholars and departments should at the very least organize fact finding tours of the African continent in order to tell us about the real deal of African life without overlooking the debased state of African women and children.

Our inaction and silence has enabled more ominous voices to rise suggesting the "recolonization" of Africa. A recent *New York Times Magazine* article by Paul Johnson suggests "trusteeships" for those states in Africa (Somalia, Liberia, Zaire, Angola, and Mozambique) who "are not yet fit to govern themselves" and "whose continued existence, and the violence and human degradation they breed, is a threat to the stability of their neighbors as well as an affront to our consciences. There is a moral issue here: the civilized world has a mission to go out to these desperate places and govern." Not only does he include Europe, Japan, and Germany in the civ-ilized world, but adds China, Russia, and India to the list of "civilizing nations," in spite of their similar difficulties with governance, ethnic vio-lence, and economic stability. (Johnson, 44)

African countries need and deserve the kind of billion dollar effort and technical assistance being given to Russia to protect its sovereignty and create a viable economy. Why does the United States reward its enemies more than its allies in Africa? In order to develop the continent's produc-tive sectors and stabilize schools, hospitals, and family farms, African Americans, with their access to media and liaisons with other progres-sives, can support the efforts of indigenous Africans, including powerful women, to govern themselves without "outside" interference. Demo-cratically elected, non-military African regimes do not need foreign "trusteeships" in order to create stable and productive societies.

In both historical and political terms, the liberty and success of Africa is directly connected to African Americans. We used to say, "same struggle, same fight," but now, for the first time in our history, there is a virtual absence in discourse among the intelligentsia of critical analysis about the political state of Africa and its relationship to African Americans. While I believe that African Americans have a particular obligation to lead and frame such a discourse, other progressives such as feminists and socialists in the West are also challenged to deal with the crisis in Africa in a sup-portive and progressive manner.

GLOBAL BLOODLETTING

The point is that what is happening in Africa is not simply a Black thing, understood only by those with dark skins, but a global condition of life with dimensions almost impossible to comprehend. In every corner of the planet, small groups of armed men have turned plowshares and ide-ologies into half cocked notions of territoriality and have transformed cultural identity and ethnic pride into ideas to die and kill for. While fun-damentalist Christians warn against the dangers of one world order gov-erned by the "anti-Christ," and economic treaties try to consolidate the northern and southern hemispheres, most societies in the world seem to be breaking up into their lowest common denominators.

The millions killed by Nazi state terrorism and the bombing of Hiroshima/Nagasaki during World War II were warnings to us of the destructive capacity of violence and hatred. Many agreed with former British Prime Minister Margaret Thatcher about the civil war in the former Yugoslavia when she said, "I never thought I'd see another holocaust in my life." (Darnton, section 4, 1) Yet here we find ourselves, in addition to witnessing the torturous civil wars in Yugoslavia and Liberia, mourning wanton genocide against the Indians in Brazil's rain forests, pogroms against Muslims in Bombay, and race riots in the streets of LA.

The war against civilians in the former Yugoslavia is presented to us nightly as a symbolic funeral of this post holocaust - holocaust. "Not for a half century has the world witnessed events in Europe that have stirred such an agonizing echo of past horrors." (Darnton, section 4, 1) Past holocausts were understood in terms of the physical and mental torture of a whole people, while rape and sexual abuse against women and children were not as visible or visual. With nearly twenty thousand raped Muslim women, the Bosnian-Serbian-Croat ethnic wars have allowed us to better understand the connections between rape, civil war, and holocaust. Using the rape of women to attack and destroy the nation, to "ethnically clean it" and to lift the spirits of soldiers is not all that unique. The daily televising of European—white on white—violence, though, has enabled the world community to see what colonialized and captured women of color have already long experienced and known. Our bodies are terrains of nationality and ethnicity to be mutilated and abused by racist enemies.

While the sexual abuse of women in the ethnic wars of the former Yugoslavia has received widespread attention from Western feminists, similar practices have taken place in other parts of the world. The Japanese government, for example, has finally apologized to Filipino women captives whom it forced to become sexual slaves of its World War II armed forces, although compensation is still being debated. In Peru, policemen and soldiers attempting to put down the insurgency of the Shining Path guerrillas routinely rape rural women. "For some security personnel in remote rural areas, the violence of rape seems to be part of routine interrogation of suspected rebel guerrillas." However, "rape is not mentioned in a 1992 report of rights violations in Peru by the National Coordinate of Human Rights." (Brooke, A4)

The routine use of rape by soldiers and armed men complements other forms of sexual abuse around the world. Most of the foreign maids, the one hundred thousand domestic servants employed by Kuwaiti families, are young women from India, Sri Lanka, and the Philippines. Their unregulated wages and working conditions are often accompanied by rape and sexual abuse. The costs of breaking their contracts force many to remain with abusive employers. The practice of sexual and physical abuse is familiar to all groups of domestic servants who become contracted labor to wealthy elites, lacking rights as workers or citizens. (Hedges, A3)

In India, the publicity surrounding a 10 year old girl being sold into marriage by her poor family to a wealthy, 60 year old Saudi Arabian has highlighted the continued practice of marrying young girls to old men and children to each other, and the generally debased state of women in rural areas. (Gargan, A4) In Kenya, girls attending a private school were raped and murdered by their male schoolmates. Young girls around the world continue to be mutilated and abused by family in the name of tradition in rural areas, and by men in the name of sexual freedom and pleasure in urban areas.

Families of poor men, women, and children continue to be victims of violence by terrorists who claim, like the Serbians, ideological and ethnic rationales. In March 1993, for example, at least thirty-three Vietnamese people—fishermen and their families—were slain in Cambodia in continued mass killings by the Khmer Rouge. Similar bloodletting has occurred in Brazil, South Africa, East Timor, and Haiti.

Yet, as the Haitian refugee situation indicates, Western forces, especially the United States, are unable and unwilling to address daily wars against women and children in other countries. Their foreign policies support leaders and dictators who have no regard for civilian human rights and who persecute those who do.

THE GULF WAR

Daily wars and the lack of viable political opposition to its foreign policies have enabled the United States to slide into an international moral mishmash. Nowhere was this more evident than in the Gulf War, when US forces were marshaled to fight Iraq, on the side of Kuwaitis and Saudi Arabians who not only abuse domestic and foreign workers, but have no commitment to democracy for their citizens. Allegiance to democracy was supposed to be the prerequisite for US support to troubled nations.

The requirements of the one-billion-dollar-a-day Gulf war erased the promised peace dividend which was to result from decreased needs for weapons and armed forces to fight the Cold War. The war also had a more offensive direction: the unquestioned integration of women and people of color into an American war and its armed forces. Sixty to eighty percent of US troops sent to the Gulf were people of color and most of the rest were white working class people. Black people made up forty percent of the deployment, and women ten percent. An astounding thirty percent of all enlisted women in the war were African Americans. (Fuentes, 516)

Since 1948, the armed forces have been viewed by African American men as a source of employment and upward mobility. The Gulf War indicates that Black women also regard soldering as a means of social and economic advancement. Yet some had misgivings about being in the military when their reserve units were activated during the Gulf War. Some Black women soldiers lost apartments and jobs and jeopardized their children when they were called up to fight.

Aimee Allison, a Black working class student accepted at Stanford University, signed up to become a medic in order to receive financial help with her education. Although conflicted because she believed in peaceful negotiation and non-violence, Aimee continued in the military. However, as the Gulf War broke out, she rejected any role in the "war machine" and, with her family and friends support, filed her conscientious objector's papers. (McDaniel, 10)

According to Allison, "the (Black) community's goal was to support individuals, whether they went with their military orders or refused them, and to work for peace without condemning individual choices." (McDaniel, 11) Although many Black Americans and their leaders questioned the US position in the Gulf, Black community organizations continued to celebrate and reward General Colin Powell for his achievements, among them his leadership of the Gulf War and the war in Panama. Contradictorily, they questioned the foreign policy issues but not the participation of African Americans in implementing that policy.

In the years since Vietnam and the death of both Malcolm X and Martin Luther King, African Americans have changed. Instead of being this country's moral conscience and opposition, we, as a people are no longer exempt from responsibility for America's guilt and sins. Our uncritical participation in the armed forces and the lack of a mass oppositional movement helped the US destroy the New Jewel movement of Grenada. As members of the military, African Americans willingly facilitated the invasion of Panama. We helped to drop bombs on Iraq and tried to murder Baghdad. In Somalia, we have helped the West invade Africa. As it really turns out both to our shame and my horror, it hasn't made any difference to the dead and invaded that Black Americans have carried out these deeds wearing the uniforms and toting the guns of the US armed forces. It didn't matter that our skins and our history of resisting racism and colonialism connected us to the Panamanian, the Somalian, the Grenadian, and many Iraqis. The payment for our patriotism is our integration into the armed services, purported to be the nation's most effective institution for promoting racial integration. Unlike civilian life, the military is able to force people of different races to live and work alongside each other. It encourages merit based promotions and allows Black men to advance to the top of its ranks. Yet our government is unwilling to foster and duplicate this model among civilian populations, hence we have a racially integrated army, and a racially stratified society. Black soldiers of the past, like Medgar Evers, resisted and organized against segregated society after leaving the military. However, Black soldiers from today's military passively accept racial and gender barriers for themselves and for their community.

The invasion of Iraq also proved that the armed services could accommodate women as "equals." Women's participation in the Gulf War bolstered their demands for advancement and equality within the army, but it indicated many different points of view about women's rights. Women have the right to do whatever men do, but *should* we defend a man's or woman's right to do the wrong thing—like fight in a war, invade a country, or to take up arms at all? If we do not do these things, the argument goes, then how can we ever get gender equality?

I tremble every time I hear a woman say she should be allowed to fight in combat because women are just as good as men—or that she is determined to prove that "competence has nothing to do with gender." Our presence *should* make a major difference, not because of our biology but because of our history. When Black people and women were excluded from the major institutions of this country, we said that once inside we would transform these institutions, making them more equitable and more just.

"But those whose vision of feminism extends beyond career trajectories to the search for wholeness inextricably tied to justice need to say there is another perspective on citizenship, valor, and patriotism. A first-class female citizenship is founded on serving people, not destructive foreign policies." (Fuentes, 519) The best of past Black struggle also affirms these principles of patriotism and struggle. No Black nationalist nor feminist can honestly continue to believe the presence of women or Blacks alone can make an appreciable difference in all white or male institutions.

We are now asked to believe that when gays and lesbians are "outed" in the military, a major milestone in human justice will occur. Like Black people and women, gay men and lesbians soldiers also say they are just as good as "straight" soldiers. They want the right to express their sexuality. Being gay or lesbian is, not in and of itself, a political statement and fighting for the rights of gays and lesbians to become integrated into "straight" society is neither radical nor revolutionary. If they continue to display the same kind of blind allegiance to the flag as Blacks and women have, gay men and lesbians will become incorporated into the pseudo-equality of the military, which does not tolerate opposition or critical stances.

During the Vietnam War, a strong radical youth culture created spaces within the society for voicing opposition and for raising objections to the war and US foreign policy. Both the culture and its critiques were a result of the radicalizing impact of the Civil Rights Movement. But at the end of the century, the expanded role of white women, people of color, and gays and lesbians within the military is occurring without radical context or critical political discourse. There are no significant numbers of activists asking, what is the relationship of formerly marginalized groups in the military to their general condition in the society, and what is their relationship in the military to US policies in other countries? Our opposition and resistance to the status quo is a product of a conservatizing of the American population and an integration or neutralizing of its radical elements into the mainstream.

> Remember, O Lord, what is come upon us: consider, and behold our reproach. Our inheritance is turned to strangers, our houses to aliens. We are orphans and fatherless, our mothers are as widows. We have drunken our water for money; our wood is sold unto us. Our necks are under persecution: we labour, and have no rest.
>
> Lamentations 5: 1–5

THE WAR AGAINST OURSELVES

The current popularity of vulgar and violent rap among both Black and white young people symbolizes the decline of radical and progressive traditions. In the Vietnam war era, gifted Black youth led and inspired oppositional discourses and cultural responses. Lyrics and music performed by Black artists such as Curtis Mayfield, Marvin Gaye, and the Temptations promoted Black unity and critiqued racism and war. However, end of century, vulgar rap by Black youth debases Black women, demonizes and sexualizes violence, and obfuscates power relations.

bell hooks compares "misogynous rap to crack because it gives people a false sense of agency and a sense that they have power over their lives when they don't." (Marriott, 42) Black ministers and womanists are speaking out and demonstrating against the perniciousness of these cultural forms in the Black community. Their opposition has revealed the white financial backing for rap and the lack of consciousness and the nihilism of the rap artist who believes he is simply chronicling what exists. Vulgar rap is not some innocent industry which merely gives its performers a venue for expression and an opportunity to become wealthy. Rather, it seduces and narcotizes young, gifted, and Black artists to ignore their responsibility. Rappers won't acknowledge that behavior and consciousness are linked and that rap like all popular cultural forms attempts to reach consciousness and hence behavior through its beat and lyrics. Rap artists could be helping to end bloodshed in their surroundings by promoting critical understanding and a higher level of consciousness *among* young Black people.

However, vulgar rap has become a form of pornography passed off as Black male rage and free speech which contributes to the abusive behavior of young Black men toward young women. For Black women in America who live in the midst of a population of young men who listen to a daily diet of vulgar rap, the connection between sexualized violence portrayed in rap videos, and the sexual behavior and violence in everyday life is troubling. Selling and promoting Black women as "hos" and sexual commodities, these rappers are participants in the mainstreaming of pornography against women and are part of an industry in which many adult men from all communities participate. And pornography is an act of violence against women.

"Is there a relationship between the pornography consumed, the sexualization of the environment of torture and predation, and the sexual acts that are performed?" is a question Catharine MacKinnon raises about the links between pornography and the filming of the sexual abuses of women in the "ethnic cleansing" by Serbians. (MacKinnon, 29)

Hiding behind the curtain of their victimization by white racism, many in the Black community pretend vulgar rap is somehow disconnected from the "rape as genocide" used by Serbian males who view themselves as noble resisters to ethnic domination by Bosnians. Yet, in their roles as both victims and victimizers, vulgar rap connects Black men and women to these other forms of rape and pornography.

African American young people are not, in spite of their poverty, isolated from or immune to the abuse and exploitation of their own and other people around the world. Everyone is aware of how young drug entrepreneurs use terror to accumulate money, mimicking the same practices their oppressors use to exploit their people. But the relatively privileged positions of African American youth as consumers also connects them with forms of exploitation in other parts of the world. Nike, for example, is a 3.4 billion dollar business with a one hundred eighty million dollar advertising budget, promoted in large part by Black athletic super stars like Michael Jordan, who is reportedly paid $20 million to sell its sneakers. The Nike factory in Indonesia, however, pays its workers an average of 19 cents an hour or $1.30 for an eight- to ten-hour work day. Most of its workers are rural women who live in barracks: a hut/room without indoor plumbing or electricity, housing groups of women who sleep on the floor. Three quarters of the women are malnourished. The Nike company claims that local factory managers and the government set wages and conditions for which they are not responsible. But, what, I wonder, is Michael Jordan's responsibility to those women who make his sneakers or to the Black mothers who struggle to buy them for teenagers who regard Jordan as a hero? Black youth need to challenge Black superstar endorsements of sneaker companies which both exploit workers in other parts of the world and neglect industries which could employ Black youth in our own country.

The actions of young Black men and the safety of my daughters and sons in the streets of my own community are linked to the war and famine African women face, the exploitation of Asian women domestics, and the gynocide and rape of Muslim women in the former Yugoslavia. The guns in the hands, the sneakers on the feet, and the sexual violence in the heads of young men are products of international social conditions and corporate interests. Irrespective of history and circumstance, women are brutalized, raped, and demeaned in private and in public, by armed young men who are themselves oppressed, poor, and desperate. Because they are our sons and brothers, the insidious use and victimization of young powerless men rends our hearts. Used by politicians as well as drug, gun, sneaker, and record manufacturers, they mindlessly obey impulses rooted in pain and violence.

We need to keep the international context and connections in mind when we turn to examine the violence of young men within the United States. While Afrocentrists and others continue to assert that African American cultural and biological differences make us morally superior to white people, our young people are increasingly integrated into a national and international culture of violence that respects no one. We as African Americans cannot falsely separate ourselves from the daily wars facing everyone in our nation: the drive-by shootings, serial killings, child abuse, murders, and rapes. All of us, even the most ardent separatists, are integrated into the same social order. However, young Black men have been both "fired up" and kept ignorant by a false sense of racial identity and no discussion of their responsibility to their communities or the society.

It is folly for African Americans to keep talking as if we do not belong or have a stake in the future of this land. Like Afrocentrists, I do not want to be swallowed up in Europe's or America's whiteness. I, however, insist that we maintain a distinct and authentic African American culture without chauvinism, denial, or violence. As the sons and daughters of Africa who built, lived, loved, died, and survived in this nation, we are integral to its institutions, politics, and future. We should refuse to allow white racism to deny Black people anything, including our agency and power to transform this land.

While recognizing that institutional racism, economic disadvantage, and social dislocation among African Americans are controlled and manipulated by the decisions of white elite men, my lamentation is for the way Black people, often unwittingly, collaborate with these oppressors. Not only do our rulers need to be challenged to eradicate the violence of racism and the daily physical violence we all face, African Americans have a responsibility to ourselves to help create communities and a nation which can sustain our people's lives and future.

The African American social movement to dismantle legal segregation offered us ways to oppose injustice and inequality without reinforcing violence and inhumanity. While not without flaws, such radical movements are "borning struggles" which free up and enable small groups of people, for a limited time, to safely cross false social boundaries, strive for ideals, and raise critical questions about the status quo. These struggles are able to eradicate specific forms of racial and other inequalities. They offer the hopeful promise that men and women can come together to create and sustain loving and equal communities.

Our generation benefited from the social movement created by our African American foreparents. Their courage and unity demonstrated their love for us. We were able to use their examples and wisdom to stretch that movement forward into the Student Nonviolent Coordinating Committee, the Black Panther Party and other organizations led by Black youth. We were militant. We were brave; and young, gifted, and baaad.

But we also made mistakes. There are things we did, such as our sexism and arrogance, that shouldn't be emulated or repeated. But our courage and sense of community should be honored and replicated. We were participants and leaders of a time when revolutionary social change seemed near enough for us, a group of Black men and women, to risk our lives for it. Most of the time, we worked with and for our people. We did the best we could with what we knew of the world at that time.

THE INTELLIGENTSIA AND PUBLIC DISCOURSE

Many middle age and now middle class radicals from the social movements of the 1960s are writing memoirs and autobiographies of those powerful times. Recently, two Black feminist titans, Elaine Brown and Alice Walker, squared off at each other in the editorial pages of the *New York Times*, to debate possible homoeroticism among some male leaders of the Black Panther Party. (Brown, Walker, A23) A few weeks later, two male Black intellectuals, Cornel West and Henry Louis Gates Jr., argued, on the same op-ed pages, this time about Black-Jewish relationships. The *Times* seems to have become another forum for the endless debates among today's Black intellectuals. Yesterday it was the media blitz over the film *The Color Purple*. Today, it is the machismo of males in the Black Panthers and Black vs. Jewish sparring.

However, most former radicals and popular intellectuals fail to address the alienation and despair of our people's daily struggles to survive. Lacking praxis (concrete practical strategies or programs), these intellectuals cannot connect their analysis of the past with the current concerns of our people. The real tragedy is that Black young people can't even enter into these intellectual discussions about Black men in the Panthers because most of our youth don't even know that there ever was such an organization. In a similar way, few Blacks can systematically examine their anti-Semitism or Black-Jewish relationships because they lack basic information. Black intellectuals and spokesmen engage in fruitless debates about Black anti-Semitism and Jewish racism without addressing more fundamental problems faced by our people.

Look at every city that has a sizable Black population. The streets are mean, dirty, and crowded. More and more men have a "lean and hungry look." The women are often drugged with relentless toil as "mammies at work" and as mothers at home. They have been designated an "underclass," a term used to describe the creation of a caste system which relegates many Black people to permanent poverty and crime. Although, in fact, most Black people are the working poor, the "underclass" concept dominates analysis of Black people. Rather than examine class structures within the Black community as a whole, most commentators and scholars contrast the Black underclass with the Black elite, a privileged, wealthy, and comfortable minority.

Many of these privileged Black people, including former radicals, have gained status and wealth as a result of political struggles which opened up the racial and gender boundaries of society. Yet, once successful, they have no clear concept about what their connections or responsibilities are to those struggles. As individuals they can choose to connect and help our people or they can do nothing for or with them.

Not so long ago we believed, because we were Black, that we had a special relationship to each other which transcended class and privilege as well as political and ideological differences. Our communities seemed implicitly oppositional; because we were victims of racism, we thought ourselves innocent and that we could commit no sins. Our skin seemed to be emblematic of radicalism and resistance to oppression. Feminists made similar claims about women. Female powerlessness and marginality within patriarchal systems supposedly created a separate sphere of nonviolence, nurturance, and love which made us different from men with their aggression and weapons. We have discovered that Black people and women can be ignorant, insensitive, and bigoted. We have come to realize that the oppressed are not immune from committing horrible acts of violence and oppression against those who share the same gender or skin color.

The Black intellectuals of my generation, my sisters and brothers, have failed in their mission to, at least, accurately articulate the political terrain of our people's lives. Black intellectuals are responsible to call for, suggest, and participate in praxis, a series of acts which not only raise consciousness but also ameliorate and change the material condition of the lives of the oppressed. Having won access to the print and electronic media by political struggle, Black intellectuals should make use of them to speak to our people's dire needs. Instead we have used those spaces to display and play out the post-industrial and hip version of "coon dances" for favor with the elite.

Afrocentrist intellectuals choose to romanticize Africa, and other Black intellectuals like me reminisce about the Civil Rights Movement. Analyzing the past is useful, not merely because there is an absence of the Black voice or presence in the knowledge base or public discourse, but because Black intellectuals are supposed to analyze and study. However, we have a mission to use our knowledge to help our young people make sense of their times and situations. There will always be ideological and other differences among the Black intelligentsia but we should have a common goal—to inform our people. We have always been given a platform to debate each other, but have we demanded or been given enough space to report on the lives and the conditions of our people and to challenge the status quo?

Lamentably Black people have become altered and transformed, not in the radical way anticipated two decades ago, nor in Black success stories—the Ebony magazine version of the near rich and the pseudo famous. We are divided, sinking, and despairing with weak leaders and diffused visions. Our once noble fate transcended the white people with whom we waged continual war, and resisted the enslavement of our minds and bodies. We have become more socially and culturally integrated with whiteness in a curious brotherhood of racial bloodletting, rhetoric, and mind games.

Social theorist, Andrée McLaughlin raises the challenging question, Can the oppressed be the oppressor? In the past, she argues, most asserted that the have-nots, women and people of color, could not be the oppressor because they did not have "state power, ownership of the means of production, or control of production policies and the distribution of wealth." (McLaughlin, 5) "The new pluralism" of the present era, McLaughlin asserts, "allows people of color and women, albeit as individuals and not groups as a whole, to enjoy economic and social mobility within mainstream society and even state power as represented in the undeveloped nations of the Third World." (McLaughlin, 5)

The new pluralism has allowed those of us in the Black intelligentsia to acquire "conceptual status" where our participation with feminists and other racial ethnic groups in knowledge production enables us to achieve status and rewards for the dissemination of our ideas. Other privileged groups include professionals, elected officials, high level government appointees, military leaders, wealthy businessmen and superstars whose degree of economic prestige, social mobility, and influence places them in positions where they can either help or further oppress less privileged Black and other groups.

In the past, many Black intellectuals, as Cruise indicates in the *Crisis of the Black Intellectual,* were conflicted, coopted, and contained by their relationship to white liberals and others. Nevertheless, in the old reality, when the Black intelligentsia was less privileged and recognized, it helped shape and frame political analysis and posed sharp questions about power, equity, and justice. The work of many segregation era Black intellectuals was directly connected to praxis and activist political work within the Black community. The role and purpose of the new pluralism's Black intelligentsia is more diffuse and less clearly defined. The Black intelligentsia includes womanists, nationalists, Afrocentrists, gays and lesbians, conservatives, and liberals; however, womanists or Black feminists/ nationalists purport to speak directly to a Black woman's standpoint and experience, and to the needs of the Black community.

> Mine eye affecteth mine heart because of all the daughters of my city.
> —Lamentations 3:51

Patricia Hill Collins suggests that "one key role for Black women intellectuals is to ask the right questions and investigate all dimensions of a Black women's standpoint with, and for African American women. Black women intellectuals thus stand in a special relationship to the community of African American women of which we are part, and this special relationship frames the contours of Black feminist thought." (Collins, 30) However, this special relationship cannot be assumed to be progressive or liberatory. Some connections between Black women intellectuals and communities of African American women are exploitative, oppressive, and painful.

In spite of their "special relationship," womanist or Black feminist intellectuals do not speak to the daily lives of most African American women. Through their omission, silence, or inaction, womanist intellectuals are virtually absent from framing or participating in the dominant discourses concerning Black mothers and adolescents. While creative in explicating Black women's consciousness and culture, womanist works rarely relate to a praxis for transforming their material conditions.

Although womanism emerged as a challenge to the limitations and biases of white feminist and Black male nationalist intelligentsias, it means little to the life of Geraldine Wilson, a single mother of nine who lives in Newark, or the women who must barricade themselves and their children in housing projects in Chicago. I am, of course, proud and uplifted by the literary works of Black womanists and of the achievements of successful Black women. However, my issues and concerns as a single mother of four and those of other single mothers more resemble the characters of Sethe and Celie than the achievements of their authors. A recent book about Black mothers and daughters, for example, was more focused on the veneration of the elderly or dead working class mothers who birthed contemporary Black womanists than the day-to-day struggles of Black mothers.

This struggle is made even more arduous by a public discourse which equates Black single mothering with criminal behavior and with "incubating" criminals. Womanists have not effectively challenged the distorted notion of a Black underclass and its relationship to Black women. Not only does public discourse shape public policy, but it also shapes the way Black men and women "see" their own.

Just the other day, I was told by three different people I care about that there is something wrong with my relationship with my twenty-four-year-old son who still lives at home with my eight-year-old son and twenty-two-year-old daughter. Although there is an economic depression severely limiting both employment and housing opportunities for even college educated Black youth, I have been told to push him out into the world to make him a man. This advice is based on a rather curious definition of manhood and a suspicious means for attaining it. It is interesting how Michael Jordan can say that his late father was his best friend and devoted fan, but when Black women are all these things to their sons, we are judged pathological.

Black single mothers can and do raise productive and strong Black sons and daughters. However, neither Black mothers nor Black fathers control the social institutions which also impact on the development of their sons and daughters. There is little collective support given to Black families even by our own institutions or successful individuals. There are few organized efforts to transform the institutions which emasculate the power of Black parents.

While one expects male and white intellectuals to be silent and ignore the public "dissing" of Black single mothers, it is surprising that almost no womanist of note has come forth to defend contemporary Black single mothers by highlighting their experiences, validating their standpoint, or challenging the scholarship and institutions which demean Black families.

Although Alice Walker defines a womanist to be "committed to the survival and wholeness of entire people, male and female," few womanists have addressed the issues of violence facing our "entire" people. Feminist praxis, which included women of color's contribution has exposed family violence and established social remedies such as rape crisis centers, battered women's shelters, and legal reform. This praxis is begging for expansion and support by womanists, especially those with national prominence who could mount a campaigns against Black-on-Black violence of all forms.

In the meantime, what can we as womanists say to Frances Davis, a single mother who raised her three sons into adulthood only to see them all murdered on the streets of Brooklyn? Where is our organized support for women like Mozella Womack, a fifty-year-old grandmother who must now raise her six orphaned grandchildren because her daughter Tracey was killed before her eyes? Can a womanist perspective address Daisy Hutson's dilemma and crime? Like Sethe in Toni Morrison's *Beloved*, who murdered her daughter to save her from slavery, Daisy shot her forty-eight-year-old daughter to save her from the slavery of "crack." Is there potential in a womanist analysis which could have saved both Daisy and her daughter? Where was our womanist voice when Tina Roxanne Rodriguez, a twenty-four-year-old Black mother of four was murdered in a shopping center by a seventeen-year-old white supremacist girl "as ten to twenty people looked on without helping"?

Womanism has criticized other ideologies for their lack of connection to Black women's lives, yet our praxis has not been better. The challenge of Black womanism to Black men to rid themselves of their patriarchial and violent notions about relationships with Black women, must be tempered with our silence, as womanists, about police violence, and failed high schools. The Black woman principal of Thomas Jefferson High School where two Black boys got shot needed womanists to support her and her students. We condemn Black ministers for their pettiness and hypocrisy, presenting elaborate theologies of womanism at conferences that ordinary Black women are excluded from. The celebration of sisterhood by Black womanists must be sobered when we see our own elitism, homophobia, and skin color politics.

Without a national voice and social movement, Black women will continue to fight noble but disconnected fights. These missing links explain how Anita Hill's powerful statements about sexual harassment in high places could become confused and fizzle out when it reached Black students, mothers, and office workers. Without an effective political praxis of Black women, President Clinton and conservative power brokers were able to prevent Black activist and civil rights attorney Lani Guinier from becoming the government's leading spokesperson for civil rights. Although Joycelynn Elders is Surgeon General, she needs a constituency of Black women to support her pioneering work in addressing issues of

adolescent health and sexuality. Without such support, she is characterized as a flamboyant speaker. There are so many brilliant and important
Black women rising up through the ranks of their professions who need a
powerful and organized constituency to give them support and direction
in order for their work to truly help Black women and men.

One writer viewing the lives of families in a Chicago housing project
wrote, "It is impossible to see this . . . without outrage—at blacks and liberals who refuse to face the reality of the self-destructive black violence,
who will neither inquire into its sources nor act to protect its victims, who
are afraid even to acknowledge its existence." (Walinsky) Witnessing both
the destitution and the potential of my people in the United States, and in
Africa, after the promise and hope of our noble efforts against segregation
and colonialism, is equally lamentable.

Jeremiah sorrowed and despaired at the self-destruction of his people
as he implored them to trust God and rid themselves of their sins. I
implore us as Black womanists to get rid of our sin of self-congratulation
and self-delusion about our successes and accomplishments. We must *act*
to address the real needs of Black women and men in this country. We
cannot continue to hold everyone else up to close scrutiny for their treatment of Black women without examining our own personal choices as
Black women intellectuals. Our inaction and lack of praxis condones and
fosters the violence on our streets and in our homes. After all, the same
men commit both acts. Our domestic violence is, however, connected to
the violence committed against us by social neglect and inequity. As womanists it is our mission to make the connections and stand in the gap for
those who cannot speak or stand for themselves.

Local work by Black women across the country gives us hopeful models
of womanist praxis. In the New York City area, I have been a participant-
observer with some of these women. Gail Garfield is struggling to establish an institute on violence against Black women to document and
address this national crisis. Her work is now on hiatus for lack of funding.
Safiya Bandele, the director of the Medgar Evers College Center for
Women's Development has created a model center for Black women students and community members. Daphne Busby, the founding director of
the Sisterhood of Black Single Mothers has created both a model for helping adult Black single mothers and a residence for assisting teen mothers.
Freddie Hamilton has used her son's murder to organize other mothers of
murdered children. Throughout the country, many organizations and
groups are working to solve the problems Black women face.

The missing group of Black women in this work are the intellectuals and the successful Black women who could help to fund and disseminate information about these solutions. Womanists in the intelligentsia need to see themselves as activists in the material world as well as in the world of ideas. Recognition of our multiple jeopardy, our African and slave past, our immigrant status, or our female consciousness does not exempt us from anything. It only offers us stronger reasons and greater resources for envisioning and creating policies,

The work of Andree McLaughlin's Cross Cultural Black Women's Institute offers womanists a forum for similar action on a global basis. Since 1987, the Institute has organized six summer conferences in five continents for Black women from countries around the world to meet and discuss their concerns and to build mutual support. Women delegates from over thirty nationalities of origin have been brought together to foster international cross-cultural cooperation, peace, and development, and to empower women in various struggles for self-determination and autonomy. In 1989, the Institute addressed the role of African women in food production in the conference in Zimbabwe. In 1991, a delegation visited New Zealand to discuss Human Rights and Indigenous Peoples in the Information Age. Later in 1991, in the midst of rising neo-Nazi racial violence, the conference was held in Berlin. In 1993, the conference was held in Venezuela to highlight the theme: Five Centuries of Resistance and Cultural Affirmation in the Americas.

Andree McLaughlin's Institutes remind me of W. E. B. Du Bois's efforts to organize Pan African Congresses throughout the 20th century to help those suffering under European colonialism lay out a direction for liberation and to find ways to give each other mutual support. McLaughlin has this message to womanists and other intellectuals:

> Women's multiple jeopardy requires work and cooperation at multidimensional levels and in a variety of arenas. We must continue to have international forums such as this one so we can educate each other on what are the real issues and facts of our struggles, sharpen the theoretical bases of our analyses, and formalize the alliances, networks and bodies that are key to our freedom. (McLaughlin, 56)

For women of my generation, being young, gifted, and Black meant being handed a baton to run faster and better then the women before me. It meant to stand on the shoulders of Fannie Lou Hamer, a poorly educated Black woman sharecropper who sang and prayed a political message so strong that they had to interrupt the 1964 Democratic Party Presidential Convention to drown it out. Yet my sisters and I can only mount a whispering challenge. We stand on shoulders and were taught how to sing, but today, we have as Michele Wallace says, "visibility but no voice." For example, the only tangible results of the nearly two thousand Black women academicians who met at the January 1994 conference at the Massachusetts Institute of Technology are a book contract and a petition to President Clinton.

Today being young, gifted, and Black means ducking bullets from other Black people in order to attend school. It means pushing away intrusive male hands in order to learn and to think. Your family structure is routinely condemned, your mother dissed at every turn. To be poor is to be thrown below the society. And more than anything else, to be without a social movement is to be without the means to make sense of it all. Without a social movement there are few sheroes and heroes of courage who can give you hope and significance. All our successes and analysis as womanists must be measured against the reality that we have failed to give our young people support, hope, vision, and daring.

We must raise our voices and hand our batons to the young—my children, the Bard students, the violent Black boys on our streets, and the Black girls trying to weave their way with them. We must speak to the young by our courageous acts and "living not for the end of the song,/ Living in the along."

Speak to the Young: Speech to the Progress-Toward

Say to them,
Say to the down-keepers,
the sun slappers
the self soilers,
the harmonyhushers,
"Even if you are ready for day
it cannot always be night."
you will be right
For that is the hard home-run.
Live not for the battles won,
Live not for the end of the song,
Live in the along

Gwendolyn Brooks

NOTES

NOTES TO CHAPTER ONE

1. Joseph Conrad, *Heart of Darkness* (New York: Dell, 1960).

2 See Susan Brownmiller, *Against our Will* (New York: Simon and Schuster, 19750.

3. T. Obinkaram Echewa, "African Sexual Attitudes," *Essence* 2, no. 9 (January 1981): 56.

4. Sarah La Forey, "Female Circumcision," unpublished ms.

5. Winthrop Jordan, *White over Black* (Chapel Hill: University of North Carolina Press, 1968), pp. 3–43.

6. Richard C. Hofstadter, *America at 1750: A Social Portrait* (New York: Vintage Books, 1973), p. 108.

7. Conrad, *Heart of Darkness*, p. 116.

8. Angela Davis, "Reflections on the Black Woman's Role in the Community of Slaves," *Black Scholar* 3, no. 4 (December 1971): 7.

9. Barbara Chase-Riboud, *Sallly Hemings* (New York: Viking Press, 1979), p. 284.

10. Jordan, *White over Black,* pp. 3–43.

11. Ibid., p. 148.

12. Gary Nash, *Red, White, and Black: The Peoples of Early America,* 2d ed. (Englewood Cliffs, NJ: Prentice-Hall, 1982), pp. 115–126.

13. A. Leon Higginbotham, Jr., *In the Matter of Color: Race and the American Legal Process—The Colonial Period* (Oxford: Oxford University Press, 1978), pp. 43–47.

14. Jordan, *White over Black*, pp. 138–39.

15. Ibid.,

16. Cited in Carl Degler, *Out of Our Past: Forces That Shaped Modern America* (New York: Harper and Row, 1959), p. 32.

17. Ibid., p. 83.

18. Hofstadter, *America at 1750*, p. 11.

19. Ibid., p. 115.

20. Ibid., p. 116.

21. Degler, *Our of Our Past*, p. 163.

22. ———, *Autobiographical Accounts of Negro Ex-Slaves* (Nashville: Fisk University Press, 1968). p. 2.

23. Herbert Gutman, *The Black Family in Slavery and Freedom, 1750–1925* (New York: Pantheon Books, 1976), pp. 138, 76.

24. *Autobiographical Accounts*, p. 1.

25. Degler, *Out of Our Past*, p. 34.

26. Davis, "Black Woman's Role," passim.

27. E. Franklin Frazier, *The Negro Family in the United States*, rev. ed. (Chicago: University of Chicago Press, 1948), p. 53.

28. Gerda Lerner, ed., *Black Women in White America* (New York: Vintage Books, 1973), p. 156.

29. Ibid., p. 154.

30. John Dollard, *Caste and Class in a Southern Town*, rev. ed. (Garden City, N.Y.: Doubleday/Anchor, 1949), p. 139.

31. Jacqueline Jones, "My Mother Was Much of a Woman: Black Women, Work, and the Family Under Slavery," unpublished ms., 1980.

32. Quoted in John Blassingame, ed., *Slave Testimony: Two Centuries of Letters, Speeches, Interviews, and Autobiographies* (Baton Rouge: Louisiana State University Press, 1977), p. 221.

33. Chase-Riboud, *Sally Hemings*, p. 284.

34. *Autobiographical Accounts*, pp. 1–2.

35. Quoted in Anne Firor Scott, *Southern Lady: From Pedestal to Politics, 1830–1930* (Chicago: University of Chicago Press, 1970), p. 50.

36. Ibid., pp. 34–36.

37. Ibid., p. 37.

38. Ibid., p. 52.

39. Jordan, *White over Black*, p. 148.

40. Scott, *Southern Lady*, p. 52.

41. *Autobiographical Accounts*, p. 1.

42. Jones, "My Mother Was Much of a Woman," pp. 41–42.

43. David Katzman, "Domestic Service: Women's Work, " in *Women Working: Theories and Facts in Perspective,* ed. Ann Stromberg and Shirley Harkness (Calif.: Mayfield Publishing Company, 1978), pp. 381–83.

44. *Autobiographical Accounts,* p. 1.

45. Frazier, *Negro Family,* p. 47.

46. Chase-Riboud, *Sally Hemings,* p. 40.

47. Frazier, *Negro Family,* p. 47.

48. Scott, *Southern Lady,* p. 53.

49. Barbara Omolade, "African and Slave Motherhood," Masters Thesis, Goddard College, 1979.

50. Jones, "My Mother Was Much of a Woman," p. 36.

51. Results of Oral History Class Projects—Black Women's History Courses 1978–1982—comp. and ed. Barbara Omolade.

52. Frazier, *Negro Family,* pp. 73–124.

53. Joanne Grant, *Black Protest: History Documents and Analysis from 1619 to the Present* (New York: Fawcett World Library, 1968), p. 33.

54. Blassingame, *Slave Testimony,* passim.

55. W. E. B. Du Bois, *Darkwater* (New York: Schocken Books, 1925), p. 172.

56. Gutman, *Black Family,* p. 17.

57. Lerner, *Black Women in White America,* p. 291.

58. David Katzman, *Seven Days a Week: Women and Domestic Service in Industrializing America* (New York: Oxford University Press, 1978), pp. 85–90.

59. Barbara Smith, "Toward a Black Feminist Criticism," *Conditions: Two* 1, no. 2 (October 1977): 25–52.

60. Lerner, *Black Women in White America,* pp. 79, 220.

61. See, for example, Franklin Frazier, *Black Bourgeoisie* (Glencoe, Ill.: Free Press, 1957), pp. 71–78.

62. Frazier, *Negro Family,* passim; oral history survey, sited in n. 51.

63. Gutman, *Black Family,* p. 85.

64. Lawrence Levine, *Black Culture and Black Consciousness* (Oxford: Oxford University Press, 1977), p. 275.

65. Ida Cox, "Wild Women Don't Have the Blues" (Northern Music Co., 1924).

66. Lerner, *Black Women in White America,* p. xxv.

67. Ntozake Shange, quoted in Carol P. Christ, *Diving Deep and Surfacing: Women Writers on Spiritual Quest* (Boston: Beacon Press, 1980), p. 117.

68. Blassingame, *Slave Testimony,* p. 256.

NOTES TO CHAPTER TWO

This essay was first published in *Wisconsin Women's Law Journal*, Volume 3, 1987, University of Wisconsin Law School, Madison, Wisconsin. It was then edited and reprinted in *At The Boundaries of Law: Feminism and Legal Theory*, Martha Fineman and Nancy Thomadsen, London and New York: Routledge, 1991.

Berman, Marshall, *All That Is Solid Melts Into Air: The Experience of Modernity*, New York: Simon and Schuster, 1982.

Blassingame, John W., *Slave Testimony: Two Centuries of Letters, Speeches, Interviews, and Autobiographies*, Baton Route: Louisiana State University Press, 1977.

Commager, Henry, *Documents of American History*, New York: Appleton-Century-Crafts, 1973.

Davis, Angela, *"Reflections on the Black Woman's Role in the Community of Slaves,"* *The Black Scholar*, Volume 3, Number 4, December 1971. Reprinted, Vol. 12, No. 6, November/December 1981: 4–15.

Evans, Sara, *Personal Politics: The Roots of Women's Liberation in the Civil Rights Movement and the New Left*, New York: Vintage Books, 1979.

Frazier, E. Franklin, *The Negro Family in America*, Chicago: University of Chicago Press, 1966, original edition published in 1939.

Gutman, Herbert G., *The Black Family in Slavery and Freedom, 1750–1925*. New York: Pantheon Books, 1976.

Higginbotham, Jr., A. Leon, *In the Matter of Color: Race and The American Legal Process*, Oxford: Oxford University Press, 1978.

Hofstadter, Richard, *America at 1750: A Social Portrait*, New York: Vintage Books, 1973.

Murray, Charles, *Losing Ground: American Social Policy, 1950–1980*, New York: Basic Books, Inc., 1984.

Nash, Gary G., *Red, White And Black: The Peoples of Early America*, Englewood Cliffs: Prentice-Hall, Inc.

Patterson, Orlando, *Slavery and Social Death: A Comparative Study*, Cambridge: Harvard University Press, 1982.

NOTES TO CHAPTER THREE

Amott, Teresa and Matthaei, Julie, *Race, Gender, and Work*, Boston: South End Press, 1991.

Barnes, Robin D. "Black Women Law Professors and Critical Self-Consciousness: A Tribute to Professor Denise Carty-Bennia," *Berkeley Women's Law Journal*, Volume 6: 1990–1991: 57–73.

Collins, Patricia Hill. *Black Feminist Thought*, Boston: Unwin Hyman. 1990.

Dumas, Rhetaugh Graves. "Dilemmas of Black Females in Leadership," La Frances Rodgers-Rose, ed., *The Black Woman*, Beverly Hills, California: Sage, 1980: 203–15.

Du Bois, W. E. B., *Philadelphia Negro*, New York: Schocken Books, 1967; orig. pub. 1899.

Foner, Philip S. *Organized Labor and the Black Worker 1619–1973*, New York: International Publishers, 1978.

Franklin, John Hope, *From Slavery to Freedom, A History of Negro Americans*, New York: Alfred A. Knopf, 1967.

Hamburger, Robert, *A Stranger in the House*, New York: Macmillan 1978, (xii).

Henri, Florette, *Black Migration North, 1900–1920*, New York: Anchor Press, 1975.

hooks, bell and Cornel West, *Breaking Bread, Insurgent Black Intellectual Life*, Boston: South End Press, 1991.

Jones, Jacqueline, *Labor of Love, Labor of Sorrow: Black Women, Work, and the Family from Slavery to the Present* New York: Vintage Books, 1985.

Katzman, David, *Seven Days a Week: Women and Domestic Service in Industrializing America*, New York: Oxford University Press, 1978.

Katzman, David. "Domestic Service: Women's Work," in Stromberg, Ann H. and Harkness, Shirley, eds., *Women Working: Theories and Facts in Perspective*, California: Mayfield Publishing Company, 1978: 382.

Lerner, Gerda, *Black Women in White America: A Documentary History*, New York: Vintage Books, 1973.

McClain, Leanita, *A Foot In Each World*, Evanston, IL: Northwestern University Press, 1987.

McFadden, Robert D. "More a Builder of Bridges than a Typical Scholar," *New York Times*, May 25, 1993, B2.

Mitchell, Alison, "Posing as Welfare Recipient, Agency Head Finds Indignity," *New York Times*, Feb. 5, 1993, A1, B2.

Nelson, Jill, *Involuntary Servitude: My Authentic Negro Experience*, Chicago: Noble press, 1993.

Pleck, Elizabeth. "A Mother's Wage: Income Earning Among Married Italian and Black Wives 1896–1911," in Michael Gordon, ed., *The American Family in Social-Historical Perspective*, Second Edition. New York: St. Martins Press, 1978: 490–510.

Russell, Kathy, Wilson, Midge and Hall, Ronald, *The Color Complex: The Politics of Skin Color Among African Americans*, New York: Harcourt, Brace, Jovanovich Publishers, 1992.

Scott, Kesha, *The Habit of Surviving*, New York: Ballantine Books, 1991.

Scully, Judy. "Not Always," *Berkeley Women's Law Journal*, Volume 6, 1991: 58.

Stafford, Walter, "Up or Down the Ladder?" *Journal of Current Social Issues*, 39–43.

Sokoloff, Natalie, *Black Women and White Women in the Professions*, New York: Routledge, 1992.

United States Department of Commerce, Bureau of the Census, *The Social and Economic Status of the Black Population in the United States: An Historical View, 1790–1978*. Current Population Reports: Special Studies Series P-23, no. 80.

White, Walter, "Work or Fight in the South, 1919," *Voices of Black America, Major Speeches by Negroes in the United States*, Philip Foner, ed., New York: Simon and Schuster, 1972: 725–729.

Williams, Patricia, *The Alchemy of Race and Rights*, Cambridge, MA: Harvard University Press, 1991.

NOTES TO CHAPTER FIVE

hooks, bell and West, Cornell, *Breaking Bread: Insurgent Black Intellectual Life*, Boston: South End Press, 1991.

Harley, Sharon, "For the Good of Family and Race: Gender, Work, and Domestic Roles in the Black Community, 1880–1930," Malson, M., Mudimbe-Boyi, E., O'Barr, J., and Wyer, M., editors, *Black Women in America: Social Science Perspectives*, Chicago and London: University of Chicago Press, 1988: 159–172.

Mann, Susan A., "Slavery, Sharecropping and Sexual Inequality," Malson, M., Mudimbe-Boyi, E., O'Barr, J., and Wyer, M., editors, *Black Women in America: Social Science Perspectives*, Chicago and London: University of Chicago Press, 1988: 133–157.

Strickland, William, "The Road Since Brown: The Americanization of the Race," *The Black Scholar: Journal of Black Studies and Research*, September–October 1979:2–8.

Williams, Sherley Anne, "Two Words on Music: Black Community," Dent, Gina, editor *Black Popular Culture*, Seattle: Bay Press, 1992: 164–172.

NOTES TO CHAPTER SIX

1. Paula Giddings, *When and Where I Enter: The Impact of Black Women on Race and Sex in America* (New York: William Morrow and Company, Inc., 1984), pp. 5–6.

2. A bibliography of key historical works on Black women: Angela Davis, *Women. Race And Class* (New York: Random House, 1981); Gerda Lerner, *Black Women in White America: A Documentary History* (New York: Pantheon, 1972); Bert James Lowenberg and Ruth Bogin, eds., *Black Women*

in 19th Century American Life (State College: Pennsylvania State University Press, 1976); Jeanne L. Noble, *Beautiful, Also, Are the Souls of My Black Sisters: A History of the Black Women in America* (Englewood Cliffs, N.J.: Prentice Hall, Inc., 1978).

3.   Since this essay was written there has been considerable movement of Black women in the academy which merits mention. Works pertaining to the special song of Black women include those by Terborg-Penn, Harley, and Rushing; Jones; Steady; and White. In addition, there is an Africana Women Studies Series at Atlanta University, founded by Shelby Lewis. Many fine monographs and bibliographies chronicling the experiences of women of color have been published by the Center for Research on Women (Memphis State University). Among the most significant writers and researchers are Bonnie Thorton Hill, Patricia Hill Collins, Elizabeth Higginbotham, and Maxine Baca Zinn.

NOTES TO CHAPTER SEVEN

Hurston, Zora Neale, *Sanctified Church*, Toni Cade Bambara, "Some Forward Remarks," Berkeley: Turtle Island, 1981: 8.

Collins, Patricia Hill, "The Social Construction of Black Feminist Thought," Malson, Micheline, et al., eds. *Black Women In America: Social Science Perspectives*, Chicago: University of Chicago Press, 1988: 297–325.

Collins, Patricia Hill, *Black Feminist Thought*, Boston: Unwin Hyman, 1990: 11.

Davis, Angela, "Reflections on the Black Woman's Role in the Community of Slaves," *Black Scholar*, December 1971, Vol. 3, No. 4.

Franco, Jean, "Beyond Ethnocentrism: Gender, Power, and the Third-world Intelligentsia," (503–515).

Herndon, Calvin C., *The Sexual Mountain and Black Women Writers*, New York: Anchor Books, 1987: 38–39.

hooks, bell and West, Cornel, *Breaking Bread: Insurgent Black Intellectual Life*, Boston: South End Press, 1991.

Sudakarsa, Niara, "The Status of Women in Indigenous Africa," in Terborg-Penn, Rosalyn, editor, *Women in Africa and the African Diaspora*, Washington, DC: Howard University Press, 1989: 25–41.

NOTES TO CHAPTER NINE

Billingsley, Andrew, *Black Families in White America*, Englewood Cliffs: Prentice Hall, Inc., 1968.

"The Classroom Climate: A Chilly One for Women?" *Project on the Status and Education of Women*, of *The Association of American Colleges*, Washington, D.C.: Fund for the Improvement of Post Secondary Education, United States Department of Education: Grant # G008005198, February, 1982: 12.

Di Leonardo, Micaela, "The Female World of Cards and Holidays: Women, Families and The Work of Kinship," *Signs* 1987:442–443.

Fuller, Sophronia, "DeSegregation: The Movement—1960's," unpublished paper, 1988: 1.*

Gumbs, Ida, "Segregation," unpublished, 1988: 3.*

Hale, Janice, *Black Children: Their Roots, Culture and Learning Styles*, Brigham Young University Press, 1982: 66, 170–171:

Holmes, Barbara, "Why Black Teachers are Essential," *Black Issues in Higher Education*, Vol. 5, No. 11, August 15, 1988: 19.

Hughes, Langston, "Cowards from the Colleges," Berry, Faith, ed., *Good Morning Revolution and Beyond, Uncollected Writings of Social Protest*, 1973: 55–63.

Kunjufu, Jawanza, *Countering the Conspiracy to Destroy Black Boys*, Chicago: Afro-American Publishing Co., 1984: 6 (quotes from Morgan, Harry, "How Schools Fail Black Children," *Social Policy*, January-February, 1988: 49–54.

Kuppersmith, Judith, "The Double Bind of Personal Striving: Ethnic Working Class in Psychotherapy," *Journal of Contemporary Psychotherapy*, Vol. 17, No. c, Fall 1987.

Lee, Patrick and Voivodas, Gita Kedar, "Sex Roles and Pupil Role in Early Childhood Education," publication and date unknown: 111.

Lightfoot, Sara, "Socialization and Education of Young Black Girls," National Institute of Education, *Conference on the Educational and Occupational Needs of Black Women*, Volume 2: Research Papers: December 16–17, 1975.

Malveaux, Julianne, "Comparable Worth and Its Impact On Black Women," *Slipping Through The Cracks: Status of Black Women*, Review of Black Political Economy, Vol. 14, Nos. 2–3, Fall 1985.

O'Brian, Eileen M., "Young Women Ignored, Mistreated in Urban Schools, Report Finds," *Black Issues in Higher Education*, Vol. 5, No. 14, Sept. 29, 1985.

Okazawa-Rey, Margo, Robinson, Tracy, Ward, Janie Victoria, "Black Women and the Politics of Skin Color and Hair," *Women Studies Quarterly*, XIIV:1 and 2, Spring/Summer, 1986.

Reid, Pamela T. "Socialization of Black Female Children," in Berman, Phyllis and Ramey, Estelle, *Women: A Developmental Perspective*, National Institutes of Health, 82–2298, April 1982: 144.

Rist, Ray, "Student Social Class and Teacher Expectations: Self-Fulfilling Prophecy in Ghetto Education," *Harvard Educational Review*, 40: 3, August, 1970, 411–440.

Robinson, Josephine, Director of High School for Pregnant Girls, Brooklyn, New York, Conversation, 1981.

Russell, Kathy, Wilson, Midge, and Hall, Ronald, *The Color Complex: The Politics of Skin Color Among African Americans,* New York: Harcourt, Brace, Jovanovich, 1992.

Wedderburn, Hazel, "*Untitled*," unpublished paper, April 28, 1988: 6–7.*

*These are papers from Black women students at the Center for Worker Education in African American History course taught by the author during Spring, 1988.

There has been no research report on the City College Center for Worker Education. Most of the information in this paper is based on my personal experiences as instructor, policy maker, counselor and administrator from 1981 to 1993.

NOTES TO CHAPTER ELEVEN

Braxton, Gwen, *New York City Black Women's Health Project, Suggested 12 Step Program,* flyer.

Canterow, Ellen, with Susan Gushee O'Malley and Sharon Hartman Strom, "Moving The Mountain," *Women Working for Social Change,* Old Westbury, New York: Feminist Press, 1980: 52–93.

Jackson, Dr. Phyllis, *The International Cross Cultural Black Women Studies Seminar Institute Report (1987–1990).*

McLaughlin, Andree Nicola, "The International Nature of The Southern African Women's Struggle," *Network: A Pan African Women's Forum,* Harare, Zimbabwe, Vol. 1, No. 1, Winter, 1988: 49–56.

The Uhuru Sasa School Program, *Outline for New African Educational Institute,* Brooklyn, NY: Black Nation Education Series #7, 1971.

Ya Salaam, Kalamu, *Our Women Keep Our Skies From Falling,* New Orleans: Nkombo, 1980.

NOTES TO CHAPTER TWELVE

Cooper, Barry Michael, "Cruel and the Gang," New York: *Village Voice,* May 9, 1989: 27–28, 30, 32.

Du Bois, W. E. B., *Black Reconstruction,* New York: Atheneum, 1975.

Hornung, Rick, "The Case Against the Prosecution," New York: *Village Voice,* February 29, 1990: 31–39.

Kennedy, Lisa, "Body Double," New York: *Village Voice,* May 9, 1989: 35–36.

McNeil, Genna Rae. *Groundwork: Charles Hamilton Houston and the Struggle for Civil Rights,* Philadelphia: University of Pennsylvania Press, 1983.

Powell, Michael, and Ladd, Scott, "Vigils Held to Heal Wounds," *New York Newsday,* April 27, 1989: 4, 24.

Wilson, Amos, *Black on Black Violence,* New York: Afrikan World Infosystems, 1990.

Wilson, William Julius, *The Truly Disadvantaged: The Inner City, the Underclass, and Public Policy,* Chicago and London: The University of Chicago Press, 1987.

NOTES TO CHAPTER THIRTEEN

(Reprinted from Harvard Women's Law Journal C Volume 12/Spring 1989)

1. N.Y. Times, Feb. 9, 1988, at B4, col. 5; N.Y. Times, Dec. 14, 1987, at B2, col. 5. *Cf.* The City Sun (New York City), June 29, 1988, at 6.

2. Maddox and Mason alleged that the special state prosecutor assigned to the Brawley case by the Governor of New York was covering up information, and consequently they refused to cooperate with the investigation. *See* N.Y. Times, Feb. 21, 1988, at A37, col. 4.

3. I believe that Tawana Brawley was raped, and I will refer to the incident as the "rape" rather than the "alleged rape."

4. *See, e.g.,* N.Y. Times, Sept. 29, 1988, at B4, col. 1. Tawana Brawley, addressing the Attorney General, stated: ". . . you know it's true and I know it's true. Why don't you just step aside and let me speak to people who I know can help me?" *Id.*

5. Speech given by Lillian Roberts on March 12, 1988 at a meeting of the Coalition of Black Trade Union Women, held at District Council 37, New York City.

6. H. Jacobs, Incidents in the Life of a Slave Girl: Written by Herself (1861).

7. G. Lerner, Black Women in White America: A Documentary History 371 (1973).

8. *Id. at 186.*

9. Friedman, *Rape, Racism and Reality*, 5 QUEST 42 (Summer 1979).

10. Lerner, *supra* note 7, at 156.

11. E. Frazier, Negro Family in the U.S. 3–85 (1939) (chapter entitled "In the House of the Master"); W. E. B. Du Bois, Darkwater: Voices from Within the Veil, 163–86 (1920) (chapter entitled "The Damnation of Women").

12. Members of the National Black Women's Health Coalition in Atlanta, Georgia and of the Medgar Evers College Center for Women's Development, Brooklyn, N.Y. have advanced the "conspiracy of silence" theory to explain this process of internalized oppression.

13. Report of the Grand Jury, *supra* note 1, at 88. *See also* N.Y. Times, Oct. 7, 1988, at B4, col. 1.

14. Report of the Grand Jury, *supra* note 1, at 88,

15. 410 U.S. 113 (1973).

16. Statement by Dr. Andree McLaughlin at the New York State Women of Color press conference, Bethany Baptist Church, Brooklyn, N.Y. (June 21, 1988) (on filed at the *Harvard Women's Law Journal*).

17. N.Y. Times, Dec. 21, 1986, at A1, col. 3.

18. N.Y. Times, June 9, 1987, at A1, col. 2. Mason and Maddox were successful. The Governor appointed a special state prosecutor as they requested. *See id.*

19. N.Y. Times, Feb. 9, 1988, at B4, col. 5.

20. *See* P. Benjamin, *Jive at Five*, N.Y. Village Voice, July 19, 1988, at 25. *See also* N.Y. Times, Feb. 24, 1988, at B1, col. 2.

21. Maddox, Mason, and their supporters frequently cite the recent killings of Eleanor Bumpers, Michael Stewart, and Yvonne Smallwood. N.Y. Times, June 9, 1988, at A1, col. 2. *See also* Benjamin, *supra* note 20, at 25.

22. In the case of Michael Stewart, for example, allegations surfaced that prosecutors, police officers, and hospital personnel mishandled and frustrated the investigation of the incident. Benjamin, *supra* note 20 at 29–30. in the Tawana Brawley case, Maddox and Mason charged that political and judicial authorities engaged in a cover-up. N.Y. Times, June 9, 1988, at A1, col. 2. At least one new source raised questions as to collusion between medical and law enforcement authorities. *See* The City Sun (New York City), June 29, 1988 at 6.

23. N.Y. Times, June 8, 1988, at A1, col. 1–B6, col. 1. To date, in spite of contempt of court charges levied against Tawana Brawley and her mother Glenda Brawley, and a grand jury report charging a hoax, neither Tawana nor her mother has been arrested.

24. Black nationalism is a dominant theme in Black political history which asserts the primacy of Black people in determining and pursuing their own political, social, and economic destiny without necessarily building coalitions, receiving support, or consulting with other ethnic groups.

NOTES TO CHAPTER FOURTEEN

Reprinted from *Rocking the Ship of State: Toward a Feminist Peace Politics,* edited by Adrienne Harris, Ynestra King, Westview Press, Boulder, San Francisco & London, 1989.

1. Ann Braden, "A Call to Action," *Southern Exposure* (Waging Peace Issue) 10, no. 6 (November-December 1982), p. 3.

2. Fidel Castro, *The World Economic and Social Crisis* (report to the Seventh Summit Conference of Non-Aligned Countries, Council of State, Havana, 19830, p. 142.

3. Ibid., p. 196.

4. Ibid., pp. 203–204.

5. United Nations Decade on Women Report.

6. Damu Imara Smith, "Peace, Disarmament and Black Liberation," *Southern Exposure* 10, no. 6 (November–December 1982), p. 16.

7. L. C. Dorsey, "Broken Promises, Shattered Dreams," *Southern Exposure* 10, no. 6 (November-December 1982), p. 14.

8. Victor de Mattei quoted in Helen Michalowski, "The Army Will Make a Man Out of You," *Southern Exposure* 10, no. 6 (November–December 1982), p. 18.

9. Dorsey, "Broken Promises, Shattered Dreams," p. 14.

10. Dari Giles, "Careers in the Military for Black Women," *Essence* (June 1984), p. 26.

11. Ibid., p. 26.

12. Cleveland Sellers, "Hell No," *Southern Exposure* 10, no. 6 (November-December 1982), p. 55.

13. "The War in Vietnam: A McComb, Mississippi, Protest," in Joanne Grant, ed., *Black Protest* (New York: Ballantine Books, 1968), p. 415.

14. SNCC, "Statement on Vietnam, January 6, 1966," in Grant, ed., *Black Protest*, p. 417.

15. Martin Luther King, "Beyond Vietnam," in Grant, ed., *Black Protest*, p. 425.

16. Barbara Omolade, untitled (unpublished).

17. Nancy Wood, ed., *War Cry on a Prayer and Feather: Prose and Poetry of the Ute Indian* (New York: Doubleday, 1979), p. 89.

NOTES TO CHAPTER FIFTEEN

Bandele, Safiya, "For Women, The Struggle is Twofold," *City Sun,* February 28–March 6, 1990, II.

Benson, Nancy, "African Women Cooperate to Create Development Alternatives," *Listen Real Loud,* Nationwide Women's Program, American Friends Service Committee, Vol. 12, No. 1: 26–28.

Binder, David and Crossette, Barbara, "As Ethnic Wars Multiply, US Strives for a Policy," *New York Times,* February 7, 1993: A1.

Brown, Elaine, "Fight Racism, Not Black Men," *New York Times,* May 5, 1993: A23.

Brooke, James, "Rapists in Uniform: Peru Looks The Other Way," *New York Times,* April 29, 1993: A4.

Brooks, Gwendolyn, "Speech to the Young: Speech to the Progress-Toward," *Blacks,* Chicago: The David Company, 1987: 497.

Collins, Patricia Hill, *Black Feminist Thought,* Boston: Unwin Hyman, 1990: 30.

Cross Cultural Black Women's Studies Summer Institute: A History 1987–1990. Medgar Evers College's International Cross-Cultural Black Woman's Studies Summer Institute, 1991.

Darnton, John, "Does The World Still Recognize a Holocaust?" *New York Times,* April 25, 1993: Section 4, pg. 1.

Diamond, Jared, "Speaking with a Single Tongue," *Discover,* February 1993: 78–85.

Fuentes, Annette, "Equality, Yes—Militarism, No," *The Nation,* October, 28, 1991: 516–519.

Fukuyama, Frances, "The End of History?" *The National Interest,* No. 16, Summer, 1989: 1–35.

Gargan, Edward, "Tearful Bride, Just 10, Touches India's Conscience," *New York Times,* October 21, 1991: A4.

Harding, Jeremy, *The Fate of Africa,* New York: Simon and Schuster, 1993.

Hedges, Chris, "Foreign Maids in Kuwait Fleeing by the Hundreds," *New York Times,* February 24, 1993: A3.

Johnson, Paul, "Colonialism's Back—and Not a Moment Too Soon," *New York Times,* April 18, 1993: 22, 43.

Lee, Felicia, "With No Parents, Ladeeta 18, Presses On," Children of the Shadows series, *New York Times,* April 6, 1993: A1.

Lewis, Anthony, "Cold War Wreckage, " *New York Times,* November 16, 1992: A17.

Lorch, Donatella, "Uganda, Scarred by AIDS, Turns to Its Youth," *New York Times,* February 23, 1993: A1.

Lorch, Donatella, "Somali Women Stride Ahead Despite the Scars of Tradition," *New York Times,* December 20, 1992: A1.

MacKinnon, Catharine, "Turning Rape Into Pornography: Postmodern Genocide," *Ms. Magazine,* July/August, 1993: 24–30.

Marriott, Michael, "Harsh Rap Lyrics Provoke Black Backlash," *New York Times,* August 15, 1993: A1.

McDaniel, Judith, "Three Women Who Refused to Fight," American Friends Service Committee, *Listen Real Loud* : Vol. II, No. 2, 10–11.

McLaughlin, Andree Nicola, "The International Nature of the Southern African Women's Struggle," *Network: A Pan African Women's Forum,* Harare, Zimbabwe, Vol. 1, No. 1, Winter, 1988: 49–56.

McLaughlin, Andree Nicola, "Can The Oppressed Be the Oppressor?" *Upfront,* Summer, 1984 (Vol. 1, No. 3), Washington, D.C.

Noble, Kenneth, "In Nigerian Mess, A Frustration for All of Africa," *New York Times,* August 22, 1993.

Packer, George, "The Land of Endless War," *New York Times,* August 15, 1993: A8.

Perlez, Jane, "For the Oppressed Sex, Brave Words to Live By," *New York Times,* June 6, 1990: A4.

Walinsky, Adam, "To Be in Hell," *New York Times,* December 4, 1987: A39.

Walker, Alice, "They Ran on Empty," *New York Times,* May 5, 1993: A23.

INDEX

Africa: African American responsibility to, 230–231; Afrocentricity in US and, 226; AIDS in, 226, 229; cultural retentions in US, 12, 14; ethnic warfare in, 227–229, 233; women in 3, 25, 228–230, 233; *see specific countries*

African American Community, 29–30; as "Beloved community," 84, 89, 99, 95; civil rights movement and, 82, 241; desegregation in, 82–85; faith in God and, 98, 117; gender roles in, 15–16; "Imperfect, but prevailing unity" in, 81, 120; and protests against apartheid in South Africa, 168, 230; urban experience, 15, 34; women's roles in, 15, 41, 46–48, 81, 86, 120, 122, 144; *see also* Black Women; Civil Rights Movement; Rape; Segregation

African American Family, 22, 69, 79, 139–140; and education, 35–36, 40; kin, 14, 43, 144; migration of, 32, 34–35; and Reconstruction, 31–34; and slavery, 27–30; *see also* African American Community; African American Men; Black Single Mothers

African Americans and the Gulf War, 223–234

African American Men: abuses against, 81; criminalization of, 182–184, 187; employment, 77; relationships with Black women, 13–14, 86, 89–90, 91, 93–94, 143; *see also* African American Community; African American Family; Black Women

African American Women: *see* Black Feminist Thought; Black Women

African American Youth: and Black intelligentsia, 95, 97; and Central Park Jogger case, 184–185; as consumers, 238; educational experiences,